Analysing Everyday Explanation

Analysing Everyday Explanation

A Casebook of Methods

Edited by Charles Antaki

SAGE Publications
London • Newbury Park • Beverly Hills • New Delhi

First published 1988

SAGE Publications Ltd
28 Banner Street
London EC1Y 8QE

SAGE Publications India Pvt Ltd
C-236 Defence Colony
New Delhi 110 024

SAGE Publications Inc
2111 West Hillcrest Street
Newbury Park, California 91320

SAGE Publications Inc
275 South Beverly Drive
Beverly Hills, California 90212

British Library Cataloguing in Publication Data
Analysing everyday explanation: a casebook of
   methods.
1. Explanation. Sociological perspectives
I. Antaki, Charles
302.2

ISBN 0-8039-8139-2
ISBN 0-8039-8140-6 Pbk

Library of Congress catalog card number 88-060348

Printed in Great Britain by Billing and Sons Ltd, Worcester

Contents

List of Contributors

Gina Agostinelli, Department of Psychology, Spence Laboratories of Psychology, University of Iowa, Iowa City, Iowa, USA

Charles Antaki, Department of Psychology, Fylde College, University of Lancaster, England

Michael Billig, Department of Social Sciences, University of Technology, Loughborough, England

Michael J. Cody, Communication Arts and Sciences, University of Southern California, Grace Salvatori Hall, Los Angeles, California, USA

Stephen W. Draper, Department of Psychology, University of Glasgow, Glasgow, Scotland

Mary M. Gergen, Department of Psychology, Pennsylvania State University, Media, Pennsylvania, USA

Rom Harré, Sub-Faculty of Philosophy, University of Oxford, Oxford, England

John H. Harvey, Department of Psychology, Spence Laboratories of Psychology, University of Iowa, Iowa City, Iowa, USA

John Heritage, Department of Sociology, Warwick University, Coventry, England

Ivan Leudar, Department of Psychology, University of Manchester, Manchester, England

Margaret L. McLaughlin, Communication Arts and Sciences, University of Southern California, Grace Salvatori Hall, Los Angeles, California, USA

Ian Parker, Department of Psychology and Speech Pathology, Manchester Polytechnic, Manchester, England

Jonathan Potter, Department of Social Sciences, University of Technology, Loughborough, England

Peter Suedfeld, Department of Psychology, University of British Columbia, Vancouver, British Columbia, Canada

Philip E. Tetlock, Department of Psychology, University of California, Berkeley, California, USA

Dawn C. Turnquist, Department of Psychology, Spence Laboratories of Psychology, University of Iowa, Iowa City, Iowa, USA

James F. Voss, Learning Research and Development Center, University of Pittsburgh, Pittsburgh, Pennsylvania, USA

Margaret Wetherell, Department of Psychology, The Open University, Milton Keynes, England

Preface

This book is about how social scientists – broadly defined – deal with ordinary explanations – again, broadly defined. The contributions describe ways of dealing with the explanations that we give and receive in everyday talk. The range of methods is from the technicality of content analysis to the interpretative rhetoric of scholarly exegesis. The methods vary with the authors' intellectual background and particular interests.

Some contributors are concerned with explanation as an index of a person's mental dispositions (of, say, an individual's proneness to blame her or himself for failure, her or his disposition to see both sides of an argument). Others are interested in explanations for what they tell us about the conventions of ordinary reasoning and the use of explanation in its social context. Still others are concerned with the way in which social categories and processes (like, say, gender and power) are manifested in people's and groups' explanations.

These three families of interests are represented in separate parts of the book. In the introductory part, Steve Draper and I try to give some background. Part II, 'Structure and content', deals with the identification and measurement of explanation and its relation to personal variables. Part III, 'Accounts in context', deals with the analysis of explanations in their interactive domain. Part IV, 'Rhetoric and ideology', deals with the analysis of explanations in the realm of ideological reasoning and the social structures implicit in language.

After the two introductory essays, each chapter follows the same structure. Firstly, the authors describe their general area of work (ethnomethodology, say, or attribution theory), then talk a little about their particular corner of the field. The middle of the chapter is then devoted to a close look at a specific set of data which the authors use to illustrate what they say. Finally, the chapter is rounded off by a candid assessment of the advantages and disadvantages of the method described.

Naturally, the chapters are much more than mere recipes. I hope that the uniform structure will help the reader to compare not only the methods on offer, but also the intellectual traditions from which they spring.

Charles Antaki
Lancaster

PART I

EXPLANATIONS

1

Explanations, communication and social cognition

Charles Antaki

'Explanation' can mean many things, and ordinary explanations can be sought and interpreted in many ways. Different researchers will have different ways of netting explanations and different ways of making sense of their catch. The differences among researchers are not just in what they think about explanations, but also in what they think about people and how they ought to be studied.

In this chapter I want to make some remarks about how ordinary social explanation is studied by different people. I shall use two observations about explanations – that they have the power to challenge social realities, and that they seem to be implicated in changes in people's behaviour – to make a distinction between two approaches to their investigation. After seeing what differences there are between the two approaches, I shall argue that, if one had to choose between them, one would choose the tradition that was more able to cope with the unspoken metacognitive background of explanations as they are exchanged in ordinary talk.

Explanations in the public domain

The features that make something count as an explanation are far from simple or uniform, as Draper shows in chapter 2. There is certainly no mechanical way of searching through a transcript of talk and spotting everything that could count as an explanation. On the other hand, our intuitions about what does or does not have the general feel of an explanation are reasonably sharp.

We can make a start by looking at explanations in the public domain, where the conventions of explanation exchange are familiar enough. The following examples will help us see what attractions the study of explanations might have for social scientists:

(1) The initial success of the out of town centre appears a paradox in a region with the highest unemployment in mainland Britain. Mr Hall ... explains: 'We haven't got 18% unemployment, we've got 82% in work'. (*The Guardian*, London, 26 August 1985)

(2) Other people, including several other women, were kicked and knocked about. One old man who was standing inside a doorway was told to shut the door and keep out of it and when he protested that this was not the law he was told by the police 'We are the Law'. (*Jobs not Jail*, Bulletin of the South Yorkshire Defence Campaign, February 1985).

We can choose to look into the explanations in these examples in many ways, of course: we could ask questions about the social information processing going on in the explainer's or the audience's heads; we could ask questions about the linguistic and rhetorical form of the utterances reported; we could ask what symbolic significance the explanation episode had for the participants; and so on. Let us start with one of the more obvious and powerful features, which will loom large in many of the later chapters in this book.

What is immediately noticeable about both explanations is the power they potentially have to overturn definitions of reality and to impose the speaker's preferred interpretation of events. Explanations, unlike mere assertions in a stream of discourse, reveal or claim to reveal what is 'really' the case. The speaker might have been asked to make the revelation (as he presumably was by the reporter in the first extract) or may choose to unveil it unilaterally (as the policeman is reported to have done in the second). In either case, the explanatory context offers information about the episode which, unlike information exchanged in other, more neutral contexts, promises to reorient the framing of the event and the participants' place within it.

In the first example, the speaker neatly inverts the emphasis of the unemployment figures to give the situation a new and more encouraging aspect. In the second, the speaker has sufficient legitimate power to warrant his explanation of his behaviour as being self-legitimating. In both cases the explanation has the power to redefine what is going on; and, of course, the new definition suits the speaker rather better than the original.

We can pursue this feature into explicitly propagandistic literature to see how the revelatory power of explanations is exploited. It is common to see articles headed by questions (for example, 'Why world food glut amidst hunger and starvation?' *The Plain Truth*, July/August 1987) which promise to explain a very serious and multifaceted human problem. The answers to such questions in propagandistic material are often of little surprise to the reader.

The explanation is often a reprise of the general message of the publication (in this case, human failings consequent on loss of Christian direction). Reading this kind of publication one gets the strong feeling that the normal process of explanation has been turned on its head. Normally, the explanation giver describes something that is known to be a problem to both explainer and audience, and then proceeds to reveal something novel which explains it. In the closed world of explicitly ideological discourse, however, it is the explanation (it may be human sinfulness, the class struggle, or bad diet) which is well known and agreed by explainer and audience, and what is new is the particular problem that the writer has managed to use it to explain.

Seeing the partisan flavour of explanations in literature which is easily identified as ideologically committed helps us to see the same thing in ostensibly more neutral writing. The mainstream press is aware of the attraction that revelation has for readers, and subeditors are quick to exploit it in headlines and leading paragraphs. In the paper I have open in front of me, I can see two examples which might perhaps border on pseudo-explanation. 'Why Errol swapped easy sex for love' and 'Why has Britain deserted the Americans in the Gulf?' (both from *The Sun*, London, 3 August 1987). Unlike more blatantly propagandistic publications, the explanations given in answer to these questions are not completely predictable in detail. However, their general gist can be foreseen. In a popular tabloid like *The Sun*, the explanation of a pop star's new-found monogamy ('I decided I wanted love as well') is consistent with a policy of the sentimentalization of human relationships, and the identification of civil service mandarins as the cause of British faintheartedness ('There is a telltale mark on the whole shameful affair: the dead hand of the Foreign Office') is consistent with its anti-intellectual, robust policy of Proud Britannia.

In certain extreme cases, there is no need for subtle analysis, as this example about the Libyan embassy shootings of April 1984 shows:

(3) What happened at the Libyan Embassy yesterday was bloody and barbaric because the people involved are bloody and barbaric. (Editorial, *The Daily Mirror*, London, 18 April 1984).

A speaker (or in this case, a leader writer) has used the definitional opportunities of the explanatory form to prejudice the reader into accepting a certain form of explanation. Once you have described an event as 'bloody and barbaric' then you have made it easy for your audience to accept that the explanation is the bloodiness and barbarism of your chosen target.

The revelatory power of explanations is something that has made explanations and accounts of great interest to sociologically minded researchers since C. Wright Mills. Explanations in this sense appeal to a very broad range of people interested in the ways in which social upsets and faults are repaired and glossed over. This aspect of explanation is perhaps clearest in ordinary discourses of excuse and justification, where 'revealing what's really the case' has a specific, usually material, motivation. Courtroom discourse routinely involves excuses as to why defendants drove too fast, assaulted people, and so on (see Cody and McLaughlin's account in chapter 8). In the press, the sports pages routinely feature the accounts of hapless sportspersons and managers explaining away failures and disasters. Here are two examples, again from the newspaper in front of me (*The Sun*, 3 August 1987). Tennis: 'Boris killed off by battler Brad: ... "I had problems with my arms, elbows and legs. Every day this week something has been hurting."' Athletics: 'What a disaster: ... He confessed: "I'm mystified. The training has been going OK but there was no fizz when I needed it today."'

Explanations privately held

So far we have treated explanations as being offered by someone to someone else or to the world at large. Seeing explanations as things which achieve ends has oriented us to think about explanations which are essentially to do with communication (for example, their power to define realities and to reveal 'the truth'). But there is another side to the coin.

Explanations can be objects of interest in their private as well as their public sense. The account a person privately holds about an event will colour his or her attitude towards it and can, under certain circumstances, have an effect on their behaviour. If I think that the reason why my car is making a funny noise is that I am driving over a funny road surface, I will carry blithely on without stopping. If you think that the reason that you feel queasy after eating seafood is that you are allergic to it, you will stop ordering it in restaurants. And so on. If our mental apperception of the world includes personal accounts of why things happened, then our feelings and behaviour are going to be at least partly contingent on our ordinary theories. Once one has allowed that, then it becomes interesting and important to examine the cognitive machinery responsible for the explanation's processing and storage.

It is difficult to flesh out this observation with examples, since if one pushes a private explanation on to the public stage it will acquire certain features (of accountability, say) which it might not have had when held silently in the individual's mind. This is not quite the case with the people's lay or expert understanding of physical, as opposed to social, behaviour – for example, the behaviour of systems and machines. Normally such explanations would be unlikely to be transformed by being driven into the social arena. They will be given in a context of accountability only in special circumstances – when things go wrong, for example (see Reason, 1987 on the failures of expert explanations in the Chernobyl nuclear disaster). However, although there are clear overlaps of interest with explanations of physical phenomena, I shall be staying within the realm of explanations of social behaviour.

Suppose you were counselling a client who had just lost his job. After a time, you were fairly confident that you had an accurate picture of his private, internal account of himself: that it was his fault, that he was no good at his work, and that he was generally incompetent. You might well predict that he would be at some risk of depression. You would be in agreement with theorists in the cognitive tradition in psychotherapy, who make just this kind of claim – that the explanations people have affect their liability to suffer emotional and mental disturbance (see, for example, Beck's 1967 rational-emotive therapy and Abramson, Seligman and Teasdale's 1978 helplessness theory). The emphasis here is on the effect on people of the account or explanation that they hold in their minds.

The same emphasis is current in more laboratory-based cognitive theories which, although they do not set out to correlate explanations with emotional distress, nevertheless aim to find how they are processed and how they affect behaviour and judgement. As we shall see in more detail later, the dominant way of thinking in this area is called *social cognition*, and the jewel in its crown is *attribution theory*. This is a loose federation of principles which revolve around the notion that people seek explanations of the world around them, and that they arrive at these explanations by a process of quasi-rational information processing.

Traditions of research

The discussion so far has been based on observations on the one hand about the definitional properties of explanations, and on the other about their mental effects. The two features suggest that there are two traditions of work on explanations. In one, the emphasis is on explanations as they appear in communication. In

Table 1.1 *Features of research on social explanation in two traditions*

	Research on explanations held mentally	Research on explanations exchanged publicly
Types of explanation	Causality emphasized	Definition emphasized
Questions addressed	Accuracy and bias Information processing Effects on behaviour	Intention Mutual knowledge Social regulation Rhetoric
Types of theory	Social cognitive (e.g. attribution theory, schema theory)	Pragmatics Ethnomethodology Discourse analysis Symbolic interaction
Methods used	Laboratory studies Rating scales Questionnaires	Interviews Documents Linguistic corpora
Data	Individuals' responses on controlled dimensions	Discourse

the other, the emphasis is on their mental representation and how it affects individuals' feelings and behaviour. Table 1.1 sketches some of the differences.

On the one hand the theorist sees the explanation as a representation of what the individual thinks, or, if no commitment is made to the thought being an articulate one, to what is stored in the individual's cognitive warehouse. On the other hand the theorist sees the explanation existing in the space between the explainer and the audience. On this latter interpretation the question of whether the explanation corresponds to some fixed explanation in the speaker's head is not a straightforward one. We shall see the debate more clearly as we expand a little on each of the sections mentioned in the table.

Types of explanation
As mentioned earlier, identifying what it is that makes something count as an explanation is far from easy. Draper in chapter 2 shows persuasively that, in the appropriate context, any utterance (or even none) could be an explanation in some sense. If there is a feature that all explanations reliably possess, it is that they should reveal something of the explainer's mind to the

enquirer. This non-specificity seems to make sense if we are to cope with the infinite variety of surface forms a legitimate explanation might take.

Within the experimental social psychology tradition, a line quite different from this freewheeling relativity has been taken. Here explanations have been very specifically understood to be one thing: causal reports. The influential writings of Kelley and of Jones and Davis (and, to a lesser extent, of their mentor Fritz Heider) have concentrated on the individual's solution of 'why' problems. Jane chooses to go to Harvard rather than Yale: why? Monica laughs at the policeman: why? Attribution theory describes the mental processes through which an individual must go in order for the answer to emerge.

The best-known model in attribution theory is Kelley's *covariance analysis* model, in which the explainer computes the historical association between the effect and its various causal candidates. The candidate which enjoys the most reliable association with the effect is taken to be the cause. So if Monica laughs at all policemen, has always laughed at this policeman, and no one else laughs at this policeman, then the policeman is excused, and the likeliest cause of the laughter is something to do with Monica.

The shortcomings of such a view of explanation are legion and are well documented elsewhere. For our purposes, we need only note that the explanation in attribution theory is the attribution of a given event to one of a number of (usually) given causes. It is a very closed picture of causal explanation, let alone of explanation in general. It is closed in the sense that the event for which the explanation is being sought is preset by the enquirer (usually, an experimenter who poses particular and non-negotiable questions to her or his respondents), allowing none of the definitional work that is so powerful a feature of most normal explanation. If asked, 'Why did Monica laugh at the policeman?', I might, in normal conversation, ask if the questioner was sure that Monica was actually 'laughing at' the policeman, and not perhaps 'giggling nervously', or even 'laughing with' him; and so on. The closed boundary around forms of expression is perhaps a consequence of the kinds of research techniques that attribution theorists use; these are, in their turn, a consequence of the cognitivist tradition in which attribution theorists find themselves. In this tradition, the important thing about social beliefs is not their content or their communication but the way in which they are mediated by cognitive faculties.

It is probably no accident that the picture of explanation in attribution theory is a close mirror of the form of explanation that attributionists, as experimental psychologists, themselves favour.

The classic covariance model is no more than a self-conscious prose version of the statistical model that Kelley and thousands of other experimentalists use to analyse their own experimental data. Perhaps attribution theorists have ascribed to other people the kind of analysis that they use themselves to understand the world; though regrettable, the practice is at least understandable. What is less understandable is why they have been so reluctant to test out their theories of what explanations are like in ordinary talk by looking at actual examples of verbatim discourse. Had they done so at an earlier stage, the communicative features of explanation would surely have found their way into the attributional picture.

For the other tradition, the communicative features have always been much more salient. Explanations are recognized as statements and texts which offer some description of events that meet the enquirer's request – or need – for material with which to get a purchase on the event at hand. It is a commonplace of certain kinds of social analysis – anthropological, ethnological, ethnomethodological, and so on – that explanations are things which reveal categories. To force the attributional example into this kind of mould, you could say that 'Monica laughed at the policeman' separates out, for the enquiring observer, categories of gender, power and resistance. A less contrived example would be something like 'It's only a game', which serves as an explanation on many levels – it makes enigmatic behaviour intelligible and makes apparently improper behaviour legitimate, for example – without any implication of causation in the attributional sense. To a complete stranger to rugby football, 'It's part of the game' distinguishes a ruck from merely violent behaviour. The explanation is parading a category in front of not only the enquirer but also the inquisitive social scientist who wants to know how this culture categorizes the world.

Questions addressed

The cognitivist programme features questions about the mental mechanisms responsible for the selection, storage and integration of social information relevant to the judgement of causality. Graduating from the experimental social psychological tradition of person perception and impression formation, attribution theory has maintained the emphasis on cognitive process. The two best-known models of attribution are deliberately and explicitly descriptions of the steps that must logically be gone through before a judgement of causality is made. These models have been taken as a working hypothesis about the ways in which information is selected, stored and integrated, with researchers tending to assume the basic ideas they embody and concentrating on filling out particular gaps in the overall structure. This has led to a huge volume of attribution work which has multiplied findings at the expense of theoretical coherence.

Within the other tradition, there exists nothing like the umbrella of theory and practice under which attribution researchers can so neatly shelter. There is no single paradigm, and so neither an articulated set of questions to be asked nor a common way of asking them. Linguists will address questions in the pragmatics of explanation, ethnomethodologists will address questions in ordinary reasoning, and so on. Attribution theory has shortcomings in its limited view of explanations, but there is no doubting the productivity of the paradigm it offers its adherents.

The rivalry outside social cognition produces enthusiastic and radical claims of a kind alien to experimental social psychologists. Two of the most potentially far-reaching proposals at the moment are that rhetoric is an appropriate method of argument for psychologists (Billig, 1987a) and that discourse analysis can take us 'beyond attitudes and behaviour' (Potter and Wetherell, 1987). Both of these, which I pick for their very clear exposition and their determined targeting of social psychologists, are represented in later chapters of this book.

Types of theory
Social cognition theories share a general family feature: the belief in a stimulus-organism-behaviour view of persons. Psychological questions are posed at the level of the individual, and more specifically at the level of the individual's mental apparatus. Social cognition theories involving explanation, reasoning and judgement have an extra feature. They have a belief in the individual's fundamental rationality, although they allow, or claim, that it is flawed. In attribution theory, the original picture was of the individual as a 'naive scientist', not quite rational enough to pass muster as a qualified scientist. Although the picture is changing to some degree, the habit of treating people as poorer versions of oneself is dying hard in social cognition. The type of theory it generates naturally emphasizes the differences between the ordinary reasoner and the experimenter: hence the ubiquity of such concepts as the 'fundamental attribution error', the 'false consensus bias' and so on (for a full source of such theories see Nisbett and Ross, 1980).

Critics have tried to point out this lack of reflexivity, although Harré's proposal to Kelley to treat his 'subjects' more like himself (Harré, 1981: 141) probably sounds merely tasteless to social cognitivists. To others, more in tune with reflexive notions and less perturbed by the thought of finding themselves sharing their respondents' worlds, it is no more than a moderate and helpful suggestion. Linguistic analyses of explanation would fail if the investigators did not believe that they shared the respondent's linguistic resources. The investigator is able to articulate them more clearly, to be sure, but they are necessarily the same resources, and any deviation from a common linguistic background between investigator and respondent makes interpretation more and more difficult. Ethnomethodology makes a point of displaying the researcher's thorough familiarity with the respondent's culture by deliberately finding ways of upsetting it or, if that is not possible, of setting it in a context where the normality of the encounter becomes strange and alien; then its structure and its dynamics can be seen more easily. Theories in this tradition of work on explanations are explicitly aware of the roles that explanations play not only between explanation giver and audience in the usual run of ordinary conversation, but also between explanation-giving informant and investigative researcher, a combination of roles not often imagined by social cognitivists.

Methods used
Laboratory manipulations and fixed-format response sheets are the tools of the experimental social psychologist. This has led to a reliance on – perhaps a fixation with – explanations that can be presented or captured on paper briefly enough for respondents whose time may be limited and whose attentiveness cannot be guaranteed. Explanations are either independent variables (that is to say, they are presented, suitably treated, to the respondent by the experimenter, who hopes that different versions will elicit different behaviours) or dependent measures (that is to say, collected from the respondent after she or he has undergone some experimental manipulation). In either case the standard procedure in attribution theory is to strip the content of the explanation down to its causal kernel.

In attribution process experiments, respondents are presented with information which they have then to combine to form an attribution. (For example, the information might be about the relationship between various actors and a given behaviour. The respondents might be informed about the number of people who purchase Zad rather than Sno-Wite washing powder; they then have to say why John bought Sno-Wite rather than Zad.) In attribution studies which treat the explanation as an independent variable, the respondents might be given a training regime under which they have to learn a certain attribution (for example, 'I am good at maths, but I have to try harder') and are then followed to see if it has made any difference to their behaviour. In both the dependent measure and the independent variable case, the method of presenting or recording the explanation is premised on it being non-negotiable. This has to be the case in the experimental method, because the point is to make everything constant and controlled except for the experimenter's intended manipulations. The experimental set-up is one that privileges a certain mode of thinking in respondents – rational, documentary-oriented, non-frivolous – which disallows certain kinds of linguistic behaviour, even if the recording instruments were sensitive enough to pick it up.

For all its faults, the advantage of the social cognition tradition is that it offers a coherent and powerful paradigm in which questions about certain aspects of explanation can be cast. The experiment is a legitimate tool and, when used sensitively, is persuasive. In the other tradition, there is a far greater reliance on the persuasiveness of the individual researcher's interpretations of the data. This is not to say that each researcher is speaking her or his own language, and can rely on no common ground with the reader; far from it. Researchers rely on a shared set of assumptions, a shared set of interpretative devices, and a shared set of symbols to carry the argument forward. Using these conventions and relying on persuasive skills is, of course, far from an easy option. Billig (1987a) argues that the ability to sustain arguments has become nearly a lost art, and that the modern form favoured by experimentalists is a pale version of the full-blooded rhetoric practised in antiquity. His contribution to this book (chapter 14) is an eloquent example of scholarly persuasion.

Data
In all the interpretative disciplines, language – especially naturally occurring discourse – is the essential starting point of any method. The language may be transcribed down to minute aspects of stress, intonation and paralinguistics, or may be accepted at the level of a prose approximation to the rush of words in ordinary speech. In any case, the researcher almost always makes a point of collecting the data in their natural form. This means a great reliance on unobtrusive recording, interviewing, document searching and so on, and a great deal of concern with the procedures used to distil the huge volume of language down to the categories with which the particular researcher wants to work.

The source of data in the interpretative tradition emphasizes the interest in explanations as products of communication. Data are often extracted from records of public explanations, broadcast or published. Data can also come from explanations as they occur in private exchanges in mundane conversations overheard by the researcher, or deliberately trawled by a research team logging naturally occurring conversation. Almost any forum of public exchange can be a source of explanations. They appear on every page of the newspapers, in every column of *Hansard* or the *Congressional Record*, in conversations at work or at home, in television advertisements, and so on and so forth.

The source of data for the experimentalist is less wide because she or he has to bear in mind questions of control and sampling which are less critical for the interpretative researcher. This has tended to mean, until recently, that experimentalists limited themselves to the responses made by the isolated subject in the laboratory. This is changing slowly, and a few attribution studies are appearing which use written, or even verbatim, ordinary language explanations. Nevertheless, the bulk of the data in attribution theory studies, as in other areas of social cognition, comes from the response sheet.

There are large and obvious differences between discovered, ordinary language discourse and the preformatted responses available to subjects in the laboratory. Perhaps the simplest pragmatic difference is that naturally occurring talk is much more time consuming and demanding to collect, analyse and make a case with. What social cognitivists lose on the swings of validity, they gain on the roundabouts of convenience.

Metacognitive considerations

It would be tempting to conclude by saying that each way of thinking about explanations has a job to do, and that what are shortcomings to one researcher are positive advantages to another. True as that normally would be as a general principle in the social sciences, I think it would gloss over an important consideration about work on explanations.

It is a commonplace of conversation analysis that speakers make substantial assumptions about what hearers will already know, and that much of what is said is only sensible against a background of silently agreed knowledge. That knowledge is updated and customized to the particular interaction as it develops, making the resulting talk still more opaque to an observer. A sentence ripped out of a transcript is all but impossible to make sense of, and even a reasonably long extract is thought by some to be unintelligible, as Draper reminds us in chapter 2.

The perfectly understandable examples from the press that appeared at the beginning of the chapter seemed to be evidence to the contrary. But they were intelligible because they were designed to be so; not only are we aware of the conventions appropriate to reading and making sense of newspaper writing, but the journalists consciously or unconsciously understand that awareness and write accordingly. In less rigidly structured talk there is a constant stream of negotiation and trimming going on between speakers, making the overt form of any given explanation an unreliable guide to what may be going on beneath the surface.

Social cognition theories are poorly equipped to deal with elements of explanations not locatable in the workings of a single person's cognitive faculties. The strengths of the social cognition approach are the *in vitro* techniques it can bring to the analysis of an explanatory atom, or indeed any belief or attitude. On the question of the way the atom connects to other atoms, and to the surrounding tissues *in vivo*, it has less to offer. The study of social cognition understood as the examination of the single individual's mental faculties will inevitably fail to deal properly with explanations understood as joint processes.

The disenfranchisement of the ordinary speaker's right to negotiate meanings and reroute questions does make some kinds of empirical question straightforward to answer, as we mentioned above. Social cognitivists have had much to say about people's use of various kinds of information, the schemas they carry with them, and so on (see Fiske and Taylor, 1984 for a comprehensive catalogue). The location of all these features of explanation in the mental apparatus of one person does tend to skew the attention away from the dynamics of explanation in verbatim exchange.

Draper in chapter 2 will expand on the nature of everyday explanation, and he will be showing that a number of its features identify it firmly as the product of joint action based on mutual knowledge. For example, the same request for an explanation can be answered in a number of different ways, but only one will actually be chosen for a specific exchange: it will be the one appropriate to the specific need the explainer guesses the questioner has. This is true even in the limited case of questions about causation. The example Draper gives is: 'Why did the glass bounce rather than break?' The answer could be: 'Because it was tough'; 'Because I always buy unbreakable glass'; 'Because it only fell a short distance'; 'Because the floor is soft'; 'Because we are on the moon in low gravity'; and so on. All of those could be true, but the one that will be given is the one that the speaker thinks the questioner wants or needs.

If the explanatory response is sensible only against a background of the knowledge the speaker ascribes to the audience, then it is tempting to think that what attribution theorists (as the prime social cognitivists) do is to play the part of the audience themselves. So that there should be no misunderstanding, they tell the explainer what they, the requesters of the explanation, already know. This is the case with all vignette studies in social cognition, but perhaps most transparently so in the classic covariance experiments. Here a subject is asked to explain why Monica laughed at the policeman *given that* she never usually does so, but everyone who comes across this policeman bursts out laughing, and so on. The explainer is told, in this as in other studies, which element of the event the audience wants to be explained. By making themselves the enquirers, social cognition workers avoid the question of what metacognitive resources explainers need to make sense of normally more elliptical exchanges in normal discourse.

People's information processing faculties are complex and deserve the attention they are currently enjoying. But people's skills at coding and decoding the metacognitions behind mundane social explanations are equally, if not more, complex, and to make sense of them we have to look beyond orthodox social psychological methods. If this takes us into new ways of thinking about people and how they ought to be studied, so much the better.

2

What's going on in everyday explanation?

Stephen W. Draper

Although there has been considerable discussion of the nature of explanation in the philosophical literature, little if any of it (with the possible exception of Wittgenstein's *Philosophical Investigations*) seems to address the nature of everyday explanation by lay people (that is, what is ordinarily referred to by the word 'explanation'). Most deals rather with what counts as good or scientific explanation: that is, it attempts to explicate intuitions about what counts as the best quality explanation. In contrast, this chapter tries to make some points about ordinary explanation, including both private explanations and accounts offered to others, and to outline the implications for empirical work. It does so mainly by reference to common sense and to examples which, like those used by linguists, aim to elicit the same intuitions in almost all readers. It will also perhaps show the author's training in artificial intelligence in the attitudes to language and mind implicit in the arguments, though no technical appeal will be made.

The chapter makes four main points about explanation:

1 Explanation is a broad concept referring to many kinds of statement, which often have nothing to do with causality, reasons or accounts.
2 Surface cues and markers (for example, words like 'because') have no simple correlation with either the presence or type of explanation (which makes it hard to do any mechanical analysis).
3 Explanations offering reasons may concern causality or reasons for belief or reasons for a speech act.
4 Explanations occur within the complex hierarchy of goals involved in any utterance, and may be intended to satisfy any of a variety of not necessarily mutually exclusive purposes.

Finally the conclusion notes some consequences of these features of everyday explanation for the possibility of doing useful empirical work, and for studies of people's causal beliefs (cf. attribution theory) and for studies of justifying oneself (cf. giving accounts).

Explanations may contain any kind of information

The first point to recognize is that in everyday life almost anything may, in the right circumstances, count as an explanation. The *Oxford English Dictionary* tells us that 'explain' means 'make known in detail'; hence any information at all may form the content of an explanation. Thus 'explain' can be prefixed to most kinds of question, as well as to referring expressions:

Explain whom you went to see.
Explain who the queen is.
Explain when the boats leave.
Explain where you went.
Explain what a knight's move in chess is.
Explain the rules of that game.

It is not always equivalent to a tacit 'why'. For instance, while a jealous husband saying 'Explain whom you went to see' may be mainly asking for a justification or motive, a colleague asking the same question about a visit to a firm is probably asking for information about contacts, their position in the firm, and so on. Certainly 'Explain who the queen is' does not seem to reduce to a 'why' question, and is nothing to do with causality, nor necessarily with giving a socially satisfactory account of oneself.

A request for an explanation is a member of the same family that all questions come from: that is, it is a request for information, and like questions, it may refer to any kind of subject matter. As we shall see later, explanations can vary in subject in another way too: they may be not only about the aspect of the world under discussion, but also about grounds for belief or about the reason for saying something at a given point in a conversation – that is, about the conversation itself.

The inquirer does not know what's wanted
An explanation is typically informing about what kind of answer applies, as well as giving the content itself. For example: a manager returns from lunch to find the office in an uproar, and asks for an explanation ('What's going on?'). The first and major part of the information sought will be conveyed not by the detailed content, but by its type. Is the staff misbehaving? Has vital equipment broken down? Has senior management visited a crisis on this office? The feature of explanations is to convey type and structure as well as content.

Explanatory descriptions
As Appelt (1985) showed, explanatory functions may lie behind
the choice of ordinary-looking noun phrases scattered throughout
a discourse. For instance, if I say 'I'm going to the church in
Beahampton', the phrase 'in Beahampton' is necessary to specify
which church I mean. However, if I say 'I'm going to climb
Helvellyn in the Lake District', the phrase 'in the Lake District'
is unnecessary for specificity because there is only one mountain
called Helvellyn; it may have been included so that the hearer does
not have to inquire whereabouts Helvellyn is. Similarly if I ask a
visitor to pass me the corkscrew in the second drawer, I may not
be clarifying which corkscrew I mean but rather telling him where
the only corkscrew is – communicating new information. It seems
natural to say that when I added 'in the Lake District' this was
an explanation (a case of 'making known in detail'), as was 'in
the second drawer'. This is connected to the issue of explaining
what you mean when you say it, which is also discussed later in
the section on giving reasons for speech acts: creating spontaneous
explanations is a necessary part of carrying on a successful
conversation. Explanations, then, are widespread in discourse, and
in general are not marked out syntactically.

Surface cues

How are explanation requests expressed linguistically, and can a
categorization of surface cues be related to a categorization of types
of explanation content? This section proposes the answer 'no'. For
instance, there is nothing about the form of noun phrases such as
'in the second drawer' that labels their function as explanatory.

More generally, it is widely recognized that the meaning of
sentences can depend in part on the 'context' and that things may be
left unsaid if the hearer can fill them in, both syntactically (ellipsis)
and at the level of whole propositions (Gricean cooperativeness
between dialogue participants entails not wasting time by stating the
obvious: Grice, 1981). However, when one is making or replying
to explanation requests, these phenomena predominate to such an
extent that the words spoken, like the tip of an iceberg, hint at
rather than specify what is meant.

Paraphrases
Many people's first idea about analysing question types is to
characterize them by the lexical items that appear in them,
for example 'who' questions, 'why' questions, and so on. A

moment's reflection however shows that words like 'why' and 'how' can paraphrase many different questions expressed using other supposedly contrasting lexical items, as the following selection of examples from Lehnert (1978) show:

How often does the bus leave? (with what frequency)
How do you like New York? (what is your attitude)
How did you get here? (by which means)
How did you get here so fast? (what enabled you)
How did the milk get spilt? (who or what caused the spill)
How come you're angry? (what combination of factors)
How do I open this? (what method)

Just as the question word (and in fact the whole sentence) does not determine which kind of answer is wanted, so conversely in many situations question words can be interchanged without changing the meaning. For instance, walking into the kitchen and asking 'Why is the milk spilt?' and 'How did the milk get spilt?' amount to the same thing. This is not genuine linguistic paraphrase because there are situations where the questions would mean different things; but in many cases they amount to the same thing. Thus question types can clearly not be based on question words. Likewise explanations do not usually make explicit the relationship of the answer to the question: 'because' is similarly ambiguous, as we shall see in a moment.

Analysis of questions about causation
Even if we restrict ourselves to questions with 'why' in them, and even if we further restrict ourselves to those cases where the question concerns causality, a typical question is still ambiguous in (at least) two independent ways (this account follows Van Fraassen, 1980, chapter 5). The first concerns the *contrast class*, which can be thought of as an implicit 'rather than' clause. 'Why did John go shopping in Beirut?' might mean why John rather than someone else, why did he go shopping rather than do something else, or why in Beirut rather than somewhere else. The second issue is that of the implicit *relevance relation*. The basic idea here is that all events depend not on a single cause but on an indefinitely large set of enabling and contributing conditions, and 'relevance relation' refers to which subset of preconditions to the event are in question (in 'focus'). 'Why did the glass bounce rather than break?': because it was designed to be tough, because I always buy unbreakable glasses, because it fell only a short distance, because the floor is soft, because we are on the moon in low gravity.

This example illustrates firstly the multiple causal antecedents of ordinary events, any of which may be relevant, and secondly that 'because' does not specify which of these is being focused on even in a given physical situation: this depends on which aspects the discussants are attending to. Thirdly, if taken in isolation, the question is naturally interpreted as an open-ended explanation request, in which the inquirer wants to be told which antecedent to focus on – is implicitly asking which has an unexpected value (is the glass unusually tough, is the gravity unusually weak, is the floor unusually soft, and so on). However in some contexts, there may be an implicit relevance relation to constrain this, independent of the inquirer's knowledge. If a restaurant manager asks a waiter why a table is dirty, she is probably not asking which customer did it and how, but why the waiter hasn't cleaned it up. A parent asking the same question, however, probably is asking who made the mess.

These considerations show not only that a typical question leaves more unspecified than it makes explicit, but that there is little sense to the idea that there is ever one true explanation: it all depends on perspective. When the restaurant manager attends only to the waiter's negligence as a cause of the table's dirtiness, she is in one sense exhibiting an attribution bias; but it doesn't imply any kind of false theory about causation. When she goes home and asks her child about a dirty table she is likely to apply a quite different bias.

Because

As we shall see later, the subset of explanations that seems to have attracted most attention is that concerned with giving reasons. These are often marked by words like 'because' but, just as 'why' and 'how' are ambiguous, so on the one hand 'because' can mean various things and on the other it can be substituted for by a number of other words or none at all.

The previous section showed how 'because' can precede any of the multiple causal antecedents of an event without distinction. The next section shows how 'because' can occur not only in explanations that express cause but also in those that give reasons for belief ('Mansell must be going to win because that's what all the commentators say') or for a speech act ('What's the time, 'cos I've got to dash?'). Conversely, 'because' and related connectives like 'so' can be missing from utterances that are clearly (causal) explanations, for example 'Why is he limping? He tripped while staring at a passing girl', or 'Why is he off work? He swerved to avoid a child and skidded into a tree'. Causation is often implied by connectives like 'and' and 'while'.

Thus 'because' probably does always signal the presence of an explanation, but does not tell you much about what kind of explanation. Furthermore neither it nor the set of related connectives is a reliable marker: a search of a transcript for their occurrence will not pick out anything like the complete set of the explanations present.

Explanations that offer reasons

Only a subset of explanations is concerned with giving reasons for something. However, this subset is the one that most of the literature has been concerned with. As we shall see, it includes giving causes, but also other kinds of explanation.

Information about sources and about the world

In considering explanation, it is useful to distinguish between two kinds of content held in our minds: ideas about the world, and information about the grounds for those beliefs (typically the source or authority for them). This is important because so many of the ideas (provisional beliefs) on which we base our decisions are held on more or less uncertain grounds, and when a conflicting piece of putative information is encountered we can try to decide between them on the basis of their associated sources (their relative authority) if these are known. For example, suppose I believe that tomatoes are cheapest in Sainsbury and then a friend tells me they are cheaper in Tesco. If mine is a general belief about the relative prices in the two shops while his is (he says) based on a recent price comparison for tomatoes in particular, I shall change my belief to follow his; whereas if mine is based on a price comparison, I shall probably ask him when he did his.

In artificial intelligence, this idea has been explored under the name of 'truth maintenance' or 'reason maintenance' (Doyle, 1978; McDermott and Doyle, 1980). Although we do not retain the source or authority for everything we believe, it is a widespread and important kind of knowledge. In some cases an explanation may consist entirely of the citation of an authority: 'That's what the doctor said', or 'It was on the news.' This is a general phenomenon, which reflects the socially distributed nature of much knowledge, including scientific knowledge. Putnam (1975) has pointed out that concepts such as 'gold' or 'water' have meanings that are ultimately grounded in the specialist knowledge of a few, to whom the rest of us could appeal in principle. Gold for instance is defined by its chemical properties, and that is what we all mean by 'gold', even though most of us don't know what they are. Knowing what authority to appeal to for more information is itself an important kind of information stored in the mind, and sometimes conveyed in explanations.

This technique is generally needed sooner or later to 'close off' chains of explanation requests by referring to some public, authoritative information source. This matches the reality that knowledge is socially distributed, and solves the problem of infinite regressions of 'why' questions (such as children of a certain age tend to embark on).

Retaining knowledge of the source of an idea also allows rival explanations (theories) to be entertained, transmitted and discussed. Van Fraassen (1980, chapter 5) reminds us that scientists often talk of some theory explaining one observation but not another: explanations have a relationship to what they explain that does not intrinsically involve truth (although very often our interest in them ultimately does). Similarly an individual might say 'I found an explanation for that today, but I don't know if it's the right one', thus showing that constructing, like eliciting, an explanation is distinct from accepting and believing it. Explanations then may contain either an elaboration of propositions about the world or reasons for believing a proposition. An important kind of reason is an authority – who asserts the proposition.

The structure of argument
Retaining reasons for belief is what makes rational argument and persuasion possible. Toulmin (1958) has described some of the structures underlying arguments (and Voss offers empirical evidence in chapter 6 of this book). These consist of the roles that propositions play within an argument – the relationships between them, rather than their logical status. For Toulmin, a *claim* (an asserted proposition about the world) is typically supported by *data*, and the *warrant* is the general rule by virtue of which the data are a support for the claim; for example, 'Petersen is not a Roman Catholic (claim) because he is a Swede (datum) and very few Swedes are Roman Catholic (warrant).' Of Toulmin's seven roles, three commonly appear after 'because' as reasons for belief: data (as in the above example), warrants and backings. A *backing* is a reason for accepting a warrant: it may be a recursive justification (treating the original warrant as a claim to be justified), or it may be an appeal to authority or some other reason for belief. To continue the example: 'Very few Swedes are Roman Catholic, as you can see from any almanac.'

From now on I shall use 'warrant' in an extended (and more usual) sense to refer to any support for a claim – any reason for belief. Broadly speaking there are three kinds of warrant: those connected with the consistency of a claim with other accepted beliefs (this is the domain of logic in its broadest sense, and was Toulmin's main focus); those that introduce new facts about the world as support; and those that state the grounds for accepting a claim as a fact without reference to consistency, such as authority or personal experience. In artificial intelligence, 'truth maintenance' is mostly concerned with the detection of inconsistencies within a belief system, and methods of resolving these by comparing the origins of the claims (for example a default rule) for reliability. Arguments between people in addition involve determining what beliefs are held in common, and perhaps trying to introduce new facts that may have a bearing on the subject. The type of a warrant is not usually explicitly marked; for example, 'A because B' might be said when B was 'Newton said' or 'I saw it myself' or 'it is a corollary of the law of conservation of energy' or 'C caused it.'

Warrants, then, are a major type of explanation. Since they sometimes consist of an assertion of causation, they can simultaneously be a warrant and an assertion of fact about the world. Warrants (grounds for belief) and causal statements are not mutually exclusive categories; for example, 'You won't be able to use the car because it's run out of petrol'. A cause is a first-rate warrant.

An example of ambiguity

This example is adapted from an utterance reported in Antaki and Naji (1987). It illustrates the ambiguity between cause and warrant in an explanation, and shows how, in the absence of a detailed knowledge of the beliefs of the interlocutors, we cannot tell just what kind of explanation is being offered. Following the utterance, I list alternative interpretations of its meaning and status as an explanation. This will emphasize the multiplicity of interpretations of an utterance taken from a protocol in the absence of quite detailed knowledge of a particular kind of context: the beliefs of the interlocutors.

The utterance is:

> *He's a good producer because he used to run 'Open Door' for the BBC*

The alternative interpretations are as follows:

1 Causation: making 'Open Door' caused goodness by training him. (This presupposes they both know he's good, and answers 'How did he become a good producer?')
2 Warrant based on causation (from programme to producer): you can believe he is good because making 'Open Door' caused goodness by training him. (This, and the following interpretations, answer 'why should I think him a good producer?') The causal premise – the fact that such experience causes goodness in the producer – is presupposed.
3 Warrant based on personal witness (of a 'fact' about value) plus causation (from producer's goodness to choice of producer): you can believe he is good because the speaker saw 'Open Door' and saw that it was good; therefore its producer was good because goodness in a producer causes a programme to be good. Again the causal premise (though different from 2) is presupposed.
4 Warrant based on public knowledge: as 3, but using the assumption that everyone, not just the speaker, knows 'Open Door' is good. This interpretation would be more likely if 'Open Door' were a well-known and widely admired programme.
5 Warrant based on authority (about a 'fact' about value): 'Open Door' is evidence that the BBC think he's good. That is, you can believe he is good because the BBC are authorities on which producers are good, and they must think he's good because they only assign good producers to important programmes, and 'Open Door' is an important programme (presumed public knowledge).
6 You can believe he is good because 'Open Door' is a good job, but he's moved onwards and upwards, so he's even better. This is a different inference path, which presupposes that his reassignment is a promotion, but doesn't require any knowledge of his subsequent jobs or their value. It presumes that 'Open Door' was evidence of his worth in one of the above ways.
7 In addition to these ambiguities is the possibility that the speaker is deliberately exploiting them: not knowing which the hearer will accede to, he may be deliberately offering all of them. This kind of logical haziness is familiar in everyday justifications like 'Alec's a good chap because he went to Cambridge', where the speaker wants to imply that Alec must be good because Cambridge only accepts good people, and that Cambridge gives superior training and therefore makes anyone good, and even that wanting to go to Cambridge shows good values.

Most of these interpretations involve an appeal to causality (as well as to other things), but to different implied causal rules. In one his goodness caused goodness of the programme; in another the programme caused goodness in him by giving him experience; in another his goodness caused his assignment as producer to an important programme.

Note how these possible interpretations each involve several other tacit propositions, as well as having a different status in terms of the analysis developed in this chapter. If we knew which of the possible ancillary propositions were held by the interlocutors, we might be able to deduce which of the interpretations applied. For example, if we knew that both interlocutors already knew he was good, then the first interpretation (explaining an accepted fact) would apply. Or alternatively, if the speaker were well known (to the hearer at least) as a fanatical admirer of 'Open Door', then the third interpretation might be salient. If the interlocutors were television insiders who however regarded the BBC management as no judge of worth, then interpretations based on the BBC's authority would be unlikely and those based on presumed common knowledge of a programme's worth would be likely.

Thus this example illustrates both the ambiguity (to outside observers) between explanations asserting cause and those asserting reasons for belief, and how the resolution of that ambiguity depends on the knowledge of the interlocutors (which is typically not recorded in transcripts). Explanations are relative to what is known already.

Reasons for speech acts

We have explored two kinds of reason, but there are in fact three: cause (that is, another fact about the world that is a reason for the occurrence to be explained); warrant (a reason for believing a claim); and justification for a speech act (a reason for making a particular utterance). An example of the third is:

> *When are you leaving? Because I need a lift.*

Here the reason given is an explanation for the speech act – in this case asking a question. Although it is possible to argue that the need for a lift 'caused' the question, or that the explanation was given in order that the speaker not appear to be given to irrational utterances, the real issue is that without the explanation the hearer will probably not know how to respond to the question, because most responses depend on the hearer being able to recognize the speaker's intention (Grice, 1957).

The issue is not to give more detail about the world, or to give reasons for believing some assertion about the world, but to explain what is being done (or attempted) here and now in the conversation. In the example, without the explanation the hearer might answer 'When are you leaving?' by 'I don't know', or object to the abrupt change of topic, or even take it as an insulting hint that he should leave; whereas with the explanation he can understand the question as an indirect request for a lift, show (if he wishes) a willingness to negotiate the time of departure, and so on. Thus the explanation's function is to help make the conversation successfully cooperative.

A problematic example
In everyday conversation (as opposed to philosophical analysis) these three types of reason can seem to blend into each other. For instance, the utterance

> It's difficult because it's hard to do two things at once.

could be viewed as:

1 A causal statement: doing two things at once causes difficulty for me. This treats difficulty as an objective state of affairs which we all perceive directly and similarly. On this interpretation an objection would be: 'You can walk and talk, so not all pairs of activities cause difficulty.'
2 A warrant for my calling something difficult. This treats difficulty as a belief about the world which has to be supported by indirect evidence. An objection might be: 'You don't really find that difficult because you never complained before, and you were humming while you did it.'
3 A reason for calling it difficult within this conversation, that is defining how the term 'difficult' is being used here. This treats difficulty as a personal judgement whose utterance needs to be explained for the purposes of this conversation. An objection might be: 'You can't call that difficult if in the same document we tell people that typing and checking spelling simultaneously is routine.'

Such ambiguity applies to many common assertions about what is hard, attractive, nice, long, and so on. The difficulty of analysing such commonplace statements may indicate that whether an assertion is 'true' or about 'the real world' is often not of concern to interlocutors; it may often be more important to establish a way of speaking that both accept and understand for the moment. 'It's a long way to Glasgow because the journey's boring, but Majorca seems quite near'. How long is long? If this view is correct then analysis is difficult not only because surface forms do not clearly mark the type of reason being offered, but also because the type (at least with concepts like 'long') may not be distinct in the interlocutors' minds.

Conversational goals

Explanations occur within dialogues, and as such are embedded in the hierarchy of goals which underlie utterances – a view of language developed in the field of artificial intelligence by Power (1979) and Cohen and Perrault (1979) among others. On this view, I may wish to know what the time is, and to achieve this I get you to tell me, and to do that I ask a question, which in turn involves a number of decisions and actions such as beginning a conversation and seizing a suitable moment for asking. Many phenomena can be located in this hierarchy of goals, including topics, speech acts, and turn taking. Note that what can be described as a single action may serve goals at a number of levels simultaneously. For instance, in catching a stranger's eye and saying 'Do you know the time?', I simultaneously open a conversation, take a turn, announce a topic, ask a question (the direct speech act), and imply a request to be told the time (the indirect speech act).

There are (at least) three issues about the goals directly and indirectly associated with explanations. Firstly, explainers may or may not believe the content of their own explanations to be true: for instance, when scientists discuss the relative merits of alternative theories, or when someone reports an explanation asserted by a third party. Secondly, even when the explainer believes the explanation, the inquirer may or may not accept this (the explainer's) valuation of it, that is, be convinced. (This is the gap between illocutionary act and perlocutionary effect in the terms of Austin, 1962). Thirdly, the enquirer may or may not be concerned to learn more about the world (that is, intend to accept the explainer's valuation); the inquirer may just want to learn about the contents of the explainer's mind, for example when a teacher asks a pupil. Thus explaining is an illocutionary not a perlocutionary act, and a request for explanation does not in general imply a request for a perlocutionary effect.

Thus 'Explain X to me' does not necessarily mean 'Try to convince me' but may instead (for example when uttered by a teacher) mean 'What do you know about X?'. Its root meaning is something like 'Inform me what you think and believe to be true about X (perhaps including reports of possible theories and the beliefs of third parties).' In a particular case it may additionally imply a request to inform about the world by convincing the inquirer; this will probably affect the detailed content and form of a satisfactory response and so must be inferred by the explainer from the context, but it is not part of the root meaning. The same distinction applies to pedagogic and 'sincere' questions. Both teachers and students give explanations. Their overall goals are opposite (complementary), but their immediate goal (used as a means to their overall goals) is the same: to expose part of their minds to the other.

Thus even though 'Elizabeth explained calculus to him' is used to imply that Elizabeth thereby changed his beliefs and knowledge, it does not necessarily imply this. There is nothing problematic about saying 'Elizabeth explained how she got the black eye, but no one believed her.' Thus when you identify an explanation in a transcript you cannot necessarily conclude that either participant believed it or intended it to be believed.

Effects and intentions
We must look at the relationship of goals, actions, and effects. Most things we do have multiple effects, only one or a few of which were intended – that is, were the reason for our taking that action. For instance riding my bike to work gives me exercise, saves the train fare, makes me warm, and splashes mud on my clothes. Furthermore most goals can be achieved by any of a number of actions: riding a bike is not the only way to get warm, to go to work, or to get splashed with mud. The relationship of goals to actions is therefore many to many, since a given goal can be achieved by more than one alternative action, and a given action could be serving any of several goals (one for each effect).

This means that when you observe an action, you cannot reliably infer why it was done – the goal of the agent. Nevertheless such inference is both widespread and necessary in daily life. As scientific observers we must do it too, but we should be aware of the likelihood of error.

Explanations have multiple effects, and may therefore be serving any of a number of possible goals. The only essential aspect of an explanation is that it purports to expose to the hearer (H) a part of the mind of the speaker (S). That part may or may not be believed by S (it may only be a possible explanation out of a set of alternatives). Seeing it may or may not convince H of some idea about the world and thereby inform H. Thus even if H takes the explanation to be a true representation of S's mind, it may or may not be intended as or taken to be a belief of S, and (independently) a fact about the world. Further to all of this, H may draw some conclusions about S – that S is knowledgeable, rational, defensive, showing off, helpful and deserving of gratitude, and so on. In different cases, different amounts of these chains of effects will occur; even when they occur and S expected them, it still may not be the case that S intended them and spoke in order to achieve them, just as I do not ride my bike in order to get muddy even though it is an expected consequence. Thus while explaining how something works might be done to impress you (for instance in showing you round my place of work), it might be done just to help our joint activity along (for instance explaining how my bottle opener works so you can use it). Estimating what social effects are likely or intended requires knowledge of the situation and of the participants: it will probably not be flagged in the words used.

Conclusion

This chapter has surveyed from a common-sense viewpoint the topic of ordinary explanation. In general, explanations include any kind of 'making known in detail': for instance, the phrase 'Helvellyn in the Lake District' might have been chosen to explain where Helvellyn was, and 'two moves forward and one sideways' is a (poor) explanation of a knight's move in chess. Studies of explanation are typically interested in only a small subset of kinds of explanation: for instance, philosophy of science tends to concentrate on causality and the relationship of hypotheses to data. Social psychology is mainly interested in how we explain people's behaviour to ourselves and others, and in how these explanations appear in utterances. This chapter accordingly concentrated on these aspects of explanation, but it should not be forgotten that they comprise only a small part of explanation in general.

Causes of human action are only part of causality in general, causality is only one kind of reason, and reasons are only one kind of explanation, so cases where human behaviour is the explicit subject form only a subset of explanations. However, in principle we can always ask the question of why the speaker is offering an explanation. Explaining, like speaking, is a social action and reveals personal goals which are frequently social in nature: I may be explaining to gain credit, to appear rational, to convince you of something, or to change your view of my behaviour. Thus as observers we can use every explanation as the occasion for an enquiry about the social function of the explanation, but we must recognize that there may in fact be no social motive behind it – although conversely it might be socially important without this being intended by the speaker.

All studies of explanation based on records of utterances, however, face two basic problems. Firstly, the surface structure of natural language offers few cues about the presence or type of explanations. Secondly, what is stated is selected against a background of what is mutually known by the interlocutors: there is usually no point either in stating what is known or in stating something which does not attach to what is known (for example, in using terms like 'Helvellyn' without explanation). However, without knowing that unstated background we cannot understand the role and status of what is stated, as the multiplicity of possible interpretations of the 'Open Door' example illustrated. Explanations are implicitly but intrinsically interactive in character in the sense that they are constructed to build on and add to what the other already knows: thus what gets stated in an explanation is crucially dependent on what is already shared knowledge, and cannot be understood by an observer without that. The difficulties this makes for work on transcripts deserve stressing.

Problems of transcripts
Linguists who study syntax work on the basis of isolated sentences and judgements of their grammaticality. This is valid because such judgements are consistent among almost all who read the examples, and because they turn out not to depend on context; that is, a shift in context does not usually make someone change their mind about whether a sentence is or is not grammatically correct. However, this does not hold so well for judgements of meaning (for example, phrases like 'colourless green ideas' can begin to seem meaningful in the right context), and not at all for the kinds of interpretations of role inherent in looking at explanation. Consequently isolated passages taken from a transcript cannot be reliably analysed, as Goffman (1981: 32ff.) discusses and as the examples above illustrate.

This is basically because a large part of the origin of shared meaning comes from knowledge shared by the interlocutors, partly on the basis of earlier utterances (so isolated sentences do not carry all aspects of their meaning explicitly), and partly from special knowledge they may have of each other which the analyst may not share. One consequence of this is that you cannot do surface-driven counts of key words like 'because', since the function of an assertion is likely to be not marked explicitly but clear to the interlocutors on other grounds.

Another is that you cannot expect to understand in detail eavesdropped conversations where the two speakers know each other better than the experimenter does. For instance an analyst could not tell whether the phrase 'my parents' house in London' was an explanation of where the house was or a simple description clarifying which of the parents' houses was being referred to, whereas the participants would. Thus recording telephone conversations between friends will probably not be fruitful, while on the other hand conversations between strangers would put the analyst on the same footing as the participants. Getting agreement among a panel of analysts does not in any way address this problem: if the panel are all constructing an interpretation based on general knowledge of the culture but ignorance of the particular circumstances of the conversation, then they may well invent the same interpretation, but still not understand what it meant to the participants. This is like asking a panel what the most salient meaning of a word like 'round' is and then using that to analyse a transcript of a boxing commentary.

Beliefs about causality

If you are interested in people's beliefs about causality (as attribution theorists are), then a study of the subset of explanations giving reasons is relevant, although causes will be mixed with reasons for belief (for example, authority or other evidence) and reasons for speech acts ('why did the door slam? Because we're trying to hold an exam'). As the 'Open Door' example illustrated, which causal belief was implied by an utterance may only emerge from a full explication of the rationale behind a given interpretation. Thus while there seems to be a rich potential for exposing beliefs about how people's attributes and actions affect each other, these are not made explicit in ordinary speech. Although difficult, it seems conceivable that a technique might be developed to draw extended explanations from people (perhaps by asking them to explain and justify spontaneous explanations that they have given) which would expose a chunk of their causal belief structure.

Accounts

Similarly, if you are interested in the accounts people offer of themselves, then the above analysis offers various starting points. Firstly, since any explanation is a disclosure of ideas in the explainer's mind, then any explanation might serve as, and be intentionally offered as, a reason for seeing the explainer as rational, that is as holding views which are coherent even if the inquirer (or even the explainer as well) does not believe them. (Only the context can determine whether a given explanation is being offered with this as its aim.)

When the subject of the explanation is an action of the explainer, then it is the explainer's behaviour rather than rationality that is at issue. The distinction between excuses and justifications developed by Cody and McLaughlin in chapter 8 may be linked to whether the explainer is offering a reason that the explainer does not believe is necessarily valid or that will not be accepted by the inquirer, or whether the explainer does believe it and hopes to convince the inquirer that the action was in fact the correct one to take. This is parallel to the distinction between scientists discussing possible viable explanations of a phenomenon, or expounding one they are committed to.

Finally, the distinction between causes and warrants as types of reason is related to whether, in giving an account, the explainer is presented as an object being acted upon by causes ('I was forced to do it') or as making a choice for a reason ('It seemed best to do it because the baby was crying so hard').

Note

The writing of this chapter was supported by SERC fellowship B/ITF/94. The inspiration was in large part due to the two Alvey workshops on explanation held at Surrey University in March 1986 and January 1987.

PART II

STRUCTURE AND CONTENT

3

Identifying attributions in oral and written explanations

John H. Harvey, Dawn C. Turnquist and Gina Agostinelli

Attributions refer to people's understandings of themselves and their environment; more broadly, 'Attribution is part of our cognition of the environment' (Heider, 1976: 18). Someone who has just passed a driving test at the first attempt may attribute his or her success to good fortune; another might attribute it to a happy choice of driving school; a third might attribute it to their own natural driving talent; and so on. Attributions such as these are often made about matters of moment in our lives.

Most attribution research has involved the use of structured, Likert response scales designed to examine the extent to which people attribute causality, responsibility or disposition to self, other or environmental entities. Recently, however, a strand of work has begun focusing on unstructured techniques for probing individuals' attributions. Attributions identified by these methods, termed *free response* or *unstructured* attributions, presumably better reflect common-sense ways of understanding people and events because they are not influenced greatly by the format of research questions. Further, these methods allow the study of attribution in instances when traditional measures are not easily administered (for example, resistant populations, sensitive topics).

This chapter is concerned with how such attributions are investigated. Issues in the measurement of unstructured attributions will be presented, followed by examples of oral and written accounts for combat stress. Using these examples, we will describe a method for identifying and quantifying attributions, and will conclude with a discussion of the advantages and disadvantages of investigating unstructured attributions. But first, a brief review of attributional concepts is in order.

Theoretical background

Interest in attribution stems from its crucial role as a mediator of perceptions, emotions, motivations and behaviours. Indeed, how people see cause and effect has implications for or may influence their interpersonal relations (for example Fincham, 1985; Harvey et al., 1982; Yarkin, Harvey and Bloxom, 1981), their psychopathology (for example Brevin and Antaki, 1987), their response to psychotherapy (for example Antaki and Brewin, 1982; Harvey and Galvin, 1984), their decision making (for example Jones and McGillis, 1976) and their adjustment to illness (for example Janis and Rodin, 1979; Taylor, Lichtman and Wood, 1984). Further, the act of confiding, which often involves causal explanations, has been linked to physical health (Pennebaker, 1985). The confiding process allows an individual to reorganize and assimilate a traumatic experience, apparently reducing stress on physiological systems and improving health. Such a view is compatible with the presumed merit of attributional activity. Attributions may serve many other functions, including enhancement of one's perception of control, preservation of self-esteem, presentation of a particular picture of the self, and emotional release (Forsyth, 1980; Harvey and Weary, 1984).

Under what conditions do we make attributions? Spontaneous attributional activity is particularly evident after traumatic experiences and life events, presumably because one is trying to understand or to control these changes (Harvey and Weary, 1984). Other research has demonstrated that individuals make attributions in situations when their expectancies are disconfirmed (Hastie, 1984) or when an achievement outcome is attained. However, attributional activity may occur when one must understand any state or make any judgement, and thus most situations can elicit attributions.

How do we select a particular attribution? There is an infinite number of potential explanations when one is faced with an event, behaviour or internal state to explain. All of these explanations are likely to be retained as alternatives as long as they are consistent with the evidence. One may rule out many alternatives as one searches for evidence, but there may still remain more than one rival explanation. According to Kruglanski (1980), at some point an individual stops generating hypotheses and attains closure on a given belief. This 'frozen' belief is then no longer evaluated against alternatives or competing pieces of evidence, and one becomes more confident of its validity. Thus, according to this view, one may expect to hold many spontaneous attributions early in the process, but retain only one after 'freezing'.

What types of statements might we consider attributions? While some authors limit the term 'attribution' to judgements of causality, we suggest that attributions may be conceptualized as statements about such states or relations as causality, responsibility or personal dispositions. Similarly, Brewin and Antaki (1987) have classified attributions into four typologies: (1) description or labelling, (2) moral responsibility, (3) causality and (4) self-presentations.

For any type of attributional statement, several dimensions have been identified. Firstly, an attribution may be stated implicitly or explicitly. Secondly, an attribution may reflect an internal or external locus of control. Thirdly, attributions may be stable (consistent across time) or unstable. Another dimension is one of responsibility, or whether an attribution is situational or dispositional. Note that the responsibility dimension is related to both the locus of control and the stability dimensions. It is included here as a separate category because one can generate attributions which are internal, stable and situational as well as ones which are internal, stable and dispositional. Finally, attributions may be global (pervasive across many types of situations) or specific to a particular situation (see Harvey and Weary, 1984).

Unstructured attributions
The quest of our work has been to study these attributional processes and concepts by identifying, coding and analysing *naturalistic* attributions. Such attributions are not presented in isolation, but rather are contextualized and embedded within plots, stories and common-sense explanations (Antaki, 1981). Included in this domain is the study of accounts, the story-like constructions people frequently make when trying to provide meaning for confusing, significant circumstances (Harvey et al., 1986; Weber, Harvey and Stanley, in press; Weiss, 1975), as well as investigations of vivid memories for personal events (Harvey, Flanary and Morgan, 1986) and confiding after traumatic experiences (Horowitz, 1976; Pennebaker, 1985).

With some exceptions (for example Elig and Frieze, 1979; Miller, Smith and Uleman, 1981), research has established that individuals make unsolicited causal or explanatory statements and that these can be identified in oral or written free responses. Common-sense psychology (Heider, 1958) certainly suggests that attributions occur spontaneously and frequently. In general, unstructured attributional data may be obtained from (1) archival sources, (2) unstructured queries of participants in naturally occurring events, or (3) unstructured probes of subjects in experiments. However, all require consideration of methodological issues.

Archival sources
Newspapers, diaries, books, written correspondence and taped lectures or conversations are all potential archival sources for the investigation of unstructured attributions. In these instances, both the oral or written response and the event or state which elicited the response are naturally occurring. In fact, the experimenter may have no contact with the respondents except through their historical traces.

For example, Lau and Russell (1980) scored 107 newspaper articles on sporting events for outcome, expectancy of outcome, and causal ascriptions of outcome. Lau (1984) used this same procedure, but followed particular teams over time. Unlike the former study, events sampled were not independent. Schoeneman and Rubanowitz (1983) also tapped newspapers as archival data sources, identifying attributions from advice columns. The potential for sampling bias is perhaps the greatest drawback in using newspapers as a data source.

In addition to newspapers, written correspondence and diaries have been analysed for attributional content. A novel approach was taken by Bettman and Weitz (1983), who reasoned that annual corporate reports would be less subject to response withholding than public statements, and examined causal reasoning in relation to outcome and expectancy. Weiss (1975) documented the nature and poignancy of diary accounts for marital separation.

Oral archival sources are less commonly used. Nisbett, Harvey and Wilson (1979; cited in Weiner, 1985) randomly selected and surreptitiously recorded conversations. Sentences with causal content (expressing or requesting) accounted for 15 per cent of all statements. Similarly, Antaki and Naji (1987) found a high frequency of the word 'because' in unobtrusively recorded conversations. They further categorized the different types of events explained by the 'because' statements.

Naturally occurring events
Contact with the respondent allows tighter control over sampling procedures and standardizes response cues. In utilizing this source of data, events of subjects' lives are probed (in an unstructured fashion) by the experimenter. For example, Harvey, Wells and Alvarez (1978) elicited and studied verbal accounts and attributions of recently separated or divorced individuals. In another study, Carroll and Payne (1977) analysed attributions in the spontaneous verbal reports of parole officers making parole decisions.

Several issues should be taken into account when using archival sources or when probing for attributions about naturally occurring events. Most of these issues arise from the lack of experimental control over the naturalistic event. Firstly, one must consider the representativeness of the chosen event or sample when drawing conclusions. For instance, would attributions of Vietnam War veterans be generalizable to attributions of Korean War veterans? In other words, were these events sufficiently similar to generalize? Secondly, an investigator may be interested in the verity of the account (as compared with the participant's perception or recall) as well as in the convergence of the account (with or away from another individual's account). Harvey et al. (1986) argued that the accounts individuals hold for relationship dissolutions may or may not contain a high degree of accuracy, and may often express views divergent from those of their mates.

A third issue to consider is the independence of the event (see also Brewin and Antaki, 1987). Events in which outcome expectancy is dependent to some extent on a prior event often occur naturalistically, and may affect attributional activity. For example, while many repeated laboratory tasks start anew each time, one divorce may establish interpersonal behaviours which predispose an individual to a second divorce.

Finally, the amount of time which has passed since the natural event should be weighed. Memory has been considered to be a possible mediator of the relationship between attribution and some dependent variable (for example Fiske, Kenny and Taylor, 1982; Harvey et al., 1980). Further, a 'dispositional shift' in causal attributions has been identified. Subjects explained an action in which they had just engaged in terms of situational demands, but several weeks later explained the identical behaviour in terms of their own dispositional characteristics (Moore et al., 1979). Thus, restricting the event of all subjects to a particular period or merely recording and analysing the impact of time passage may be necessary.

Experiments

Most of the aforementioned measurement issues are no longer relevant when one has experimental control over both the event and the response. Several investigators of unstructured attributions have chosen this paradigm. They have asked subjects to talk aloud during task performance (for example Brunson and Matthews, 1981; Diener and Dweck, 1978) or to relay their thoughts after completion of a task (Gilovich, 1983; Harvey et al., 1980; Wong and Weiner, 1981).

Some studies involved relatively direct attribution probes such as 'Why do you think you succeeded or failed on this task?' (Elig and Frieze, 1979), whereas other studies attempted to examine attribution more indirectly. For example, Wong and Weiner (1981) asked subjects to imagine various outcomes for a questionnaire set of scenarios. Following these responses, subjects were asked 'What questions, if any, would you most likely ask yourself (given the situation imagined)?' In an even more indirect type of probe, Harvey et al. (1980) asked respondents to indicate in writing what they had seen and felt in watching short relationship vignettes on videotape. The attributional activity elicited in this fashion was labelled 'unsolicited attribution' by the investigators.

Empirical examples: accounts for combat stress

An arena in which the study of attribution using unstructured techniques is both relevant and necessary is that involving the reports of combat war veterans. The Vietnam War was traumatic for thousands of young US troops who for many months were exposed to terror, death and almost constant peril, but who survived and then returned to the United States. These veterans report considerable difficulty in understanding or making sense out of events in their lives since the war (Brende and Parson, 1985; Figley, 1984). Their accounts are filled with freely occurring, unsolicited attributions about themselves and their environment, and thus this population is particularly useful to us for studying attributional processes and adaptive functioning.

While attribution investigations are relevant to these veterans, traditional measurement with structured questionnaires is problematic. During our first contact with a sample of veterans, they told us of their strong dislike of paper-and-pencil instruments which other investigators had attempted to use previously. With consideration to participation rate, we opted to use free response techniques.

The oral account presented below is extracted from a study we are currently conducting on the effects of attributions, vivid memories and personality characteristics on the physical, occupational and social functioning of combat veterans (Harvey, Agostinelli and Claiborn, 1987). Our sample is composed of men who have seen active combat during the Vietnam War, some of whom have been physically injured. Subjects are interviewed by two Vietnam veterans who are trained in interviewing techniques, but who are blind to experimental hypotheses. The standardized interview format includes global questions regarding subjects' impressions and feelings since their return from the war and requires approximately 45 minutes for completion. Subjects' responses are recorded on audiotape, transcribed, and coded for attributional content. As our methods for this particular study do not involve written accounts, the second illustration is a reprinted example of archival data which may be analysed in the same manner as our transcribed oral accounts.

Oral account. The following narrative is a transcribed segment from a recorded interview with a former Army infantryman:

> I still can feel the sheer terror. I still have flashes of the scenes of death and dying. ... Things have a way of reminding you of a situation you encountered there ... being unable to relax. ... Sometimes I startle and want to hit the deck when I hear a car backfire. ... Sometimes I wake up in panic that I can't get my gun loaded fast enough. ... I have a great fear of the unknown.
>
> I was comfortable before I left for Nam. I had been married for two years and had many good friends. But when I returned, it was as if I had changed greatly and had no control over what I found here. My wife was waiting for me, and soon after returning our relationship started to deteriorate. ... I was in a daze. I didn't know what was going on. ...
>
> I encountered hostility when I went back to college. I had no place there. I wasn't much older but I was different ... and they made me feel that way. And the students were into various kinds of power – brown and black and so on. Before I left and in the service, I didn't encounter such groups; you just had friends regardless of colour. I was dealing with kids in college who didn't know anything about what I had experienced or what it was like over there. ... All that I could communicate with them was second level bathroom bullshit.
>
> I wanted to be off by myself and not around anyone – wife, parents, former friends, you name it. I felt then and still feel today that I can only talk about Nam with other vets who were there. ... Some of my friends were even frightened of me and didn't want anything to do with me. We were all in the same place but separated in time and by vast experience. I grew older and they had stayed the same. I not only was ostracized by them, I also was placed in a different category. ... I and vets like me were and still are somewhat totally separate from the rest of the world. ...
>
> So for years after I returned, I literally had to re-learn all about the society – the music, what had happened in this country. ... And I grew further and further from my wife until we divorced a year after I returned. ... So it was as if I no longer had a home, a wife, people who knew and loved me. Now I think that it is easier as time goes by – my understanding of that period in Nam and soon after is growing and I feel more control – I'm closing the distance between then and now.

Written account. In the following written account, a veteran writes of his experiences and their continuing effects (Brende and Parson, 1985: 46):

> My girlfriend told me she didn't know how to relate to me. ... I had expected things to be the way they were; but they weren't. She said she thought I had been killed in the war, because I stopped writing to her. Honestly, I didn't know how to relate to her now either. I dreaded going

to bed with her. ... She also said that I wasn't the loving guy she used to know and love, that something horrible must have happened to me over there to change me so completely. I told her I didn't know what she was talking about. She said the look in my eyes was the look of a deeply terrorized person, with a long-distance stare. ... She also mentioned that my frightened look and pallid complexion, my uptight way of sitting, talking, walking, you name it, my aloofness, and all that, made her too uncomfortable for us to continue our relationship. She said that besides, she had found somebody else anyway. That really hurt me. ...

When it came to my family, my mother told me that I wasn't as considerate and sweet as I used to be. My dad felt I wasn't as diligent and committed as he remembered me to be prior to Vietnam. I didn't know what any of these people were saying. I knew I was getting pissed off more and more by hearing all of this bullshit.

Techniques for analysis of unstructured attributions

As is true with all forms of data, conceptual and empirical issues are not separable. They are there whenever one decides what to count as data, interprets them, draws theoretical or practical inferences from them and frames the next research question in terms of a particular method (see Oyamai, 1985 for an enlightening discussion of this view). Consistent with the foregoing point, the procedures for analysing and interpreting free response attributional accounts data should be guided by theory. None the less, it is likely that the following steps will be pursued in transforming oral or written free response attribution raw data protocols – like those above – into quantifiable and statistically analysable data.

Identifying attributions. In the previously described work by Harvey et al. (1980) on unsolicited attribution, attributions were identified by 'phrases or clauses denoting or connoting causality or responsibility or ascribing traits'. Thus, further reduction of the process would be necessary to identify causal, responsibility or trait statements or phrases. For example, consider the veteran's recorded statements above regarding the war's effect on him and his relationships. A coder may determine the following attributions made by the veteran from the narrative: (1) a feeling of general lack of control in dealing with the environment upon return to the US; (2) deterioration in marriage upon return to the States; (3) a perception of isolation and of being an outside among peers in college; (4) a feeling of little similarity with or ability to communicate with peers or family (including wife); (5) a feeling of identification with and orientation toward Vietnam veterans upon return to the States; and (6) a feeling that it was necessary to relearn aspects of the culture and that an understanding of the period in Vietnam is growing over time.

Defining dimensions. In addition to criteria for recognizing attributions, criteria for identifying theoretically meaningful characteristics of attributions should be specified. These dimensions may be coded on a continuous or dichotomous scale. The positive–negative valence of attributions may be determined by *a priori* ideas of the experimenter, by *post hoc* content analysis and scaling within the sample, or by reference to empirical guidelines such as Anderson's (1968) likeableness ratings of trait words. The stable–unstable dimension may be judged either retrospectively (change over time is inferred from subject's report) or longitudinally (with repeated samples of a subject's attributions). Similarly, globality of an attribution may be inferred from the pervasiveness of its appearance in the subject's descriptions or it may be observed in the subject across different situations. Locus of control is generally judged by the object of explanation statements, and focus of responsibility is reflected in the dispositional or situational nature of the explanation. Finally, although there has been little work on the structure of attribution (Yarkin and Harvey, 1982), the organization of attribution should also represent an important dimension that is amenable to coding.

For instance, the explicit attribution of the first example, 'I wasn't much older but I was different … and they made me feel that way', evidences (1) negative valence, (2) instability (inferred by contrast with the last statement regarding his growing understanding), (3) globality, (4) external locus of control, and (5) situational responsibility, using dichotomous scales. Of course, with modified criteria, different conclusions may be drawn.

Coding attributions. A necessary procedure in any study of naturalistic attributions, this step usually is carried out by two or more practised coders, who are naive to the experimental hypotheses. Based on the guiding theory, a count of the total number of attributions as well as the dimensional qualities of each attribution discussed above will be of interest. Eliciting conditions of the attributional statements and subject characteristics might also be included. These data are meaningless, however, if coders are not reliable in their judgements. One would expect coefficients of agreement of at least 0.70 to argue for high reliability of judgements.

A final point is that approaches which are quite different from that outlined above may be pursued. Firstly, our approach essentially was designed to quantify all theoretically meaningful dimensions of the data so that inferential statistical tests might be applied. However, it might be as tenable to develop a descriptive analysis only.

It also may be viewed as useful and appropriate to stop at the stage of nominal-scale statistical analysis (for example, chi-square analysis of number of internal versus external control attributions).

Secondly, whether attributions are recorded or written may have to be determined by research feasibility issues. Transcription problems will be reduced when they are written, but respondents may not wish to write or fill out questionnaires as part of their participation. Writing may permit more organization and/or precision, but it may also require a degree of practice using this medium that many respondents do not possess.

Advantages and disadvantages

As has been suggested throughout this chapter, we believe that unstructured attributional methods may yield some of the richest naturalistic evidence that it is possible to collect. Also, they provide the only means of studying some populations and probing sensitive topics. Giving people the opportunity to make attributions in their own words may afford them an occasion for extended reflection and self-report that other methods constrain. Some reflection and report may be more natural and less subject to reactivity of instruments than other approaches requiring more condensed, questionnaire responses. As an illustration, people can respond to diary-type probes at times when their feelings about the topic in question are most intense and their thoughts are most penetrating (for example, awakening heavy with thought and feeling in the early morning hours).

The disadvantages of unstructured attributional methods certainly include the possible difficulty of the quantification of data. More specifically, it is usually a laborious task to train coders to make useful discriminations and thereby to secure reliable judgements. Also, as with structured methods, response bias in the form of self-presentational dynamics may be prominent. Investigators should be particularly aware of this bias during face-to-face interviews when the respondent attends to the interviewer's subtle social cues.

A further difficulty of an unstructured approach is the potential for sample bias. Overall, there are likely to be several different self-selection biases found in this type of method as compared with structured approaches. The effort and work required of respondents may be such as to reflect a self-selection bias in and of itself. Respondents who elect to participate may be people who find the task of talking or writing about their thoughts and feelings in their own words quite compelling. Archival data are also difficult to sample without introducing some degree of bias (Weiner, 1985). Therefore, it is important to test the generalizability of one's findings by comparing the descriptive characteristics of one's sample with the characteristics of the population of interest.

These possible limitations notwithstanding, we conclude by heartily recommending free response attribution methods to scholars in the field. At their best, we believe that they can be systematized so as to permit an instructive inquiry into people's continual search for meaning in critical facets of their lives.

4

Integrative complexity coding of verbal behaviour

Philip E. Tetlock and Peter Suedfeld

Theoretical background

Integrative complexity theory was originally developed to explain individual differences in the complexity of the cognitive rules people use to analyse incoming information and to make decisions (Harvey, Hunt and Schroder, 1961; Schroder, Driver and Streufert, 1967). The theory focused on two cognitive structural variables, differentiation and integration. *Differentiation* refers to the number of dimensions of a problem that are taken into account in evaluating or interpreting events. For instance, a politician might analyse policy options in an undifferentiated way by placing options into one or two value-laden categories, for example the 'good socialist policies' that promote redistribution of wealth and the 'bad capitalist policies' that preserve or exacerbate inequality. A highly differentiated approach would recognize that different policies can have many, often contradictory, effects that cannot be readily classified on a single evaluative dimension of judgement – for example, effects on the gross national product, the governmental deficit, interest rates, inflation, unemployment, the balance of trade, and a host of other economic and political variables. *Integration* refers to the development of complex connections among differentiated characteristics; differentiation is thus a prerequisite for integration. The complexity of integration depends on whether the decision maker perceives the differentiated characteristics as operating in isolation (low integration), in first-order or simple interactions (the effects of A on B depend on levels of C: moderate integration) or in multiple, contingent patterns (high integration).

Early proponents thought of this construct as a trait which they called *conceptual complexity*. Measurement of the trait relied heavily on the semiprojective Paragraph Completion Test for assessing individual differences in cognitive functioning. Subjects were presented with sentence stems (for example, 'Rules ...' 'When I am criticized ... ') and asked to complete each stem and write at least one additional sentence. Trained coders rated subjects' responses on a seven-point scale designed to measure the integrative complexity of subjects' thinking in the topic area. The higher the score, the greater the evidence of both conceptual differentiation and, above scores of 3, conceptual integration.

One change in vocabulary must be understood here, although it actually emerged after about a decade of research in this area. This is the use of the term *integrative complexity*. In contrast with conceptual complexity, which explicitly refers to stable individual dispositions, integrative complexity is defined by the level of complexity (differentiation and integration) evidenced in the verbal material or, conceivably, other behavioural aspects of the individuals or groups under study. Thus, people who are high in conceptual complexity may be defined as those who typically behave at a high level of integrative complexity; however, the latter phrase does not imply anything about dispositional characteristics. One implication of this view is that people of different levels of conceptual complexity may actually behave at the same level of integrative complexity under particular circumstances, and that an individual of any given level of conceptual complexity may show different levels of integrative complexity at different times or in different situations. Integrative complexity can, in short, be viewed as a measure of a state level of functioning – although this stance does not preclude identifying interesting patterns of cross-situational or cross-issue consistency in functioning (Tetlock, 1984, 1986).

Two points concerning the coding system deserve mention here. Firstly, with adequate training (two to three weeks), coders can rate verbal responses for integrative complexity with high levels of reliability (Pearson product-moment correlations between 0.85 and 0.95) Secondly, the complexity coding system focuses on the *structure* and not the *content* of expressed belief, and is not biased for or against any particular philosophy. One can be simple or complex in the advocacy of a wide range of political positions.

Early laboratory research using the Paragraph Completion Test supported the view that systematic individual differences exist in conceptual complexity. The test demonstrated predictive power in a variety of experimental contexts, including inter-nation simulations of crisis decision making (Driver, 1965; Schroder, Driver and Streufert, 1967; Streufert and Streufert, 1978), studies of bargaining and negotiation behaviour (Pruitt and Lewis, 1975; Streufert and Streufert, 1978) and studies of attitude change (Crano and Schroder, 1967; Streufert and Fromkin, 1972). Relative to simple subjects, subjects classified as conceptually complex utilized a broader range of information in forming impressions of others and in making decisions, were more tolerant of dissonant or incongruent information, and were more likely to be successful in achieving mutually beneficial compromise agreements in bargaining games.

Such empirical successes notwithstanding, it became clear by the late 1960s that a static trait model of conceptual complexity was inadequate. Complexity of cognitive functioning at a given time was not just a function of stable dispositional variables; several experiments indicated that situational factors also influenced behavioural complexity (Driver, 1965; Schroder, Driver and Streufert, 1967). Some environments were much more conducive to complex information processing than were others. The findings demonstrated that (1) moderate levels of threat, time pressure and information load are most likely to promote integratively complex styles of thinking; and (2) individual differences in conceptual complexity influence how people react to changing levels of these environmental variables. Schroder, Driver and Streufert (1967) and Streufert and Streufert (1978) explicitly recognized these points in their *interactionist* theories of integrative complexity, and this issue has become a major concern in the area (see Streufert and Swezey, 1986).

For some time, research on the conceptual complexity construct was primarily limited to experimental studies that examined the interactive effects of dispositional complexity (assessed by the Paragraph Completion Test) and situational variables (environmental stressors) on subjects' selection of 'low-involvement' response options (endorsing attitudes or making decisions with no important consequences for subjects' own futures or those of others). The external validity limitations of such studies are well known (see Janis and Mann, 1977; Tetlock, 1983a).

A critical development in the evolution of integrative complexity theory and research occurred in the mid 1970s. In a study of revolutionary leaders, Suedfeld and Rank (1976) used archival documents as the data base. The study showed that, unlike other measures of cognitive style that are linked to specific paper-and-pencil tests (for example, the Dogmatism or Tolerance of Ambiguity Scales, the Embedded Figures Test), the integrative complexity coding system is not tied to the coding of Paragraph Completion Test responses (Suedfeld, 1978a). The data indicated that not integrative complexity *per se*, but an appropriate shift in complexity as roles changed, was a powerful predictor of whether a particular leader was successful in retaining power after the success of the revolutionary movement.

46   Philip E. Tetlock and Peter Suedfeld

Since then, a large number of studies have used the integrative complexity coding system to analyse a broad range of archival documents and to test an even broader range of hypotheses (for example Levi and Tetlock, 1980; Porter and Suedfeld, 1981; Suedfeld, 1985a; Suedfeld and Piedrahita, 1984; Suedfeld and Tetlock, 1977; Suedfeld, Tetlock and Ramirez, 1977; Tetlock, 1979, 1981a, 1981b, 1983a, 1983b, 1984, 1985, 1986; Tetlock, Hannum and Micheletti, 1984; Tetlock, Bernzweig and Gallant, 1985). These novel methodological applications of the coding system have enormously expanded the data base of integrative complexity theory. Among other data sources, the coding system has been used to analyse diplomatic communications exchanged during major international crises, transcripts of Japanese cabinet meetings prior to the 1941 decision to attack the United States, the correspondence and speeches of eminent non-governmental figures, pre- and post-election speeches of American presidents in the twentieth century, confidential interviews with members of the British House of Commons, American and Soviet foreign policy statements in the period after World War II, and magazine editorials.

The theoretical network (Cronbach and Meehl, 1955) surrounding the integrative complexity construct has expanded to include not only individual difference predictions, but a wide array of hypotheses concerning situational determinants of complex information processing that even the later interactionist theories of integrative complexity had not anticipated (for example, hypotheses concerning the effects of role demands, societal crisis, life span, accountability, groupthink and value conflict on integrative complexity of functioning). For example, Suedfeld (Porter and Suedfeld, 1981; Suedfeld, 1985a; Suedfeld and Piedrahita, 1984) has found that complexity declines as a person's death approaches; and Tetlock (1981a, 1984, 1985) has argued that politicians strategically shift the integrative complexity of their utterances to achieve a variety of impression management objectives (for example, rallying electoral support, appearing conciliatory or tough, pre-emptive self-criticism).

An integrative theory of integrative complexity has yet to emerge. Given the wide range of apparent determinants of integrative complexity, it may not be realistic to expect the rapid emergence of such a theory. A comprehensive explanation of the findings will probably have to draw on a number of theoretical traditions, including personality theories (to explain systematic individual differences in conceptual complexity), role theories (to explain the impact of institutional and role variables), and cognitive theories of judgement and choice (to explain the impact of stress and value conflict).

Coding procedures

Whatever theoretical position one adopts on the determinants of integrative complexity, it is critical that investigators agree on the methodological procedures for assessing the construct. It is not sufficient simply to provide coders with abstract definitions of 'conceptual differentiation' and 'integration' and tell them to assess the integrative complexity of texts. Coders require much more detailed guidelines to perform their task with acceptable reliability (for such detailed guidelines, see Bluck et al., 1985; Tetlock and Hannum, 1984).

One critical distinction that coders must make is between 'scorable' and 'non-scorable' materials. Statements are treated as non-scorable if they contain purely procedural or factual statements with no causal inferences or evaluative claims. For example:

> Mr Reagan and Mr Gorbachev have agreed to meet on 11 and 12 October in Reykjavik, Iceland. The agenda will include arms control, the mutual balanced force reduction talks in Europe, human rights and Third World conflicts such as Afghanistan, Angola and Nicaragua.

To be treated as scorable, a statement must go 'beyond the information given' and either evaluate the event in question (for example, 'The unrealistically ambitious agenda ... ') or advance a causal explanation for the event (for example, 'in order to disarm domestic critics, Mr Reagan and Mr Gorbachev ... '). Among other unscorable materials are passages that consist entirely of quotations (these may be scored to measure the behavioural complexity of the source of the quotation, but not that of the quoter), clichés or proverbs, satire and sarcasm, or definitions of particular terms. A scorer may also reject paragraphs that appear incoherent or incomprehensible, or where the level of uncertainty of the scorer is so high as to be unresolvable.

Coders are instructed to assign the lowest possible score (1 on a seven-point scale) to 'conceptually undifferentiated' responses – that is, responses that could have been generated by a single, fixed rule. Coders can rely on a number of specific indicators or guidelines to determine whether a score of 1 is warranted. Firstly, does the statement place events into value-laden (good–bad) categories with a high degree of certainty? For example, 'This summit meeting is the latest sign of the spinelessness of Reagan's foreign policy. Reagan acted in a cowardly and contemptible way in the Daniloff affair; there is every reason to suppose he will continue to do so on arms control and other issues vital to the security of the free world.' Secondly, does the statement imply that absolute solutions to policy problems can be found? For example, 'We should close down our embassy in Moscow and give top priority to setting up an impenetrable space shield against Soviet ICBMs.' Thirdly, does the statement deny the existence of value trade-offs? For example, 'There is no good technological, political or economic argument for not pushing full speed ahead with the original Reagan Strategic Defense Initiative plan. This is indeed a case where all the pluses are on one side and all the minuses are on the other.' Fourthly, does the statement provide a unicausal account of events? For example, 'Soviet agriculture is a disaster because of the destruction of individual incentives to work in a totalitarian socialist system.' Finally, it should be noted that more than one perspective can be voiced; the crucial criterion then is that only one is accepted as legitimate.

Level 2 is intermediate. It is characterized by the recognition of a potential for legitimate alternatives or exceptions to the fixed rule. However, the alternatives are not explicitly delineated, and conditions under which one may be preferable can be implied. A somewhat higher level of tolerance for ambiguity than at level 1 is demonstrated.

For scores of 3, the coder must decide that the response indicates both awareness and tolerance of two different interpretations or perspectives on an issue. Statements that would receive scores of 3 typically have three features. Firstly, they recognize that reasonable people view the same problem in different ways. For example, 'The Soviet build-up of ICBMs in the 1970s looked very threatening to many American observers. The Soviets, however, may have seen themselves simply as catching up to a still strategically dominant United States.' Secondly, they distinguish two or more causes for events but fail to recognize interaction between (among) causes. For example, 'Gorbachev hopes to increase Soviet productivity by cracking down on laziness and corruption on the one hand and offering incentives for improved labour efficiency and quality control on the other.' Thirdly, they acknowledge that decision making involves making difficult choices in which no option is better than its alternatives on all possible criteria. For example, 'Mr Bush supports the President's request for funding SDI because he deems it critical not to fall behind the Soviets in anti-ballistic missile technology. He recognizes, however, that the SDI programme will be extremely expensive and may trigger a new destabilizing round in the arms race.'

The intermediate level of 4 is the threshold for scoring passages that imply the recognition of integration as well as clearly evidencing differentiation. At this initial stage, the author must indicate that several perspectives or dimensions exist and also hint that they interact. For example, the author may state that further information is needed before explicit statements about the relationship between alternatives could be specified, may present alternatives in a way suggesting that there is tension between them, may indicate the probability of interactive outcomes, and the like.

To assign a score of 5, the coder must decide not only that the response indicates awareness of alternative interpretations or perspectives on an issue, but also that the response clearly indicates the use of integrative rules for understanding the underlying sources of these different ways of looking at the world or for understanding the conditions under which one or another way of looking at the world is more appropriate. Integration could take the form of mutual influence, synthesis, and negotiation or compromise. Three typical specific indications that a score of 5 should be assigned are as follows. Firstly, there are explicit attempts to explain why reasonable persons view an issue in different ways. For example, 'Soviet and American nuclear forces have offsetting strengths and weaknesses. The Soviets have advantages in the number of land-based ICBMs and throw weight; the Americans have advantages in the number and accuracy of submarine-based ICBMs and in accuracy of land-based ICBMs. Arms control negotiations are extremely difficult because of the tendency of each side to focus on those aspects of the strategic equation in which it is inferior and, as a result, to suspect the other side of bad faith and striving for superiority.' Secondly, there is recognition that one needs to take into account the interactive and not just the separate effects of the causes of events. For example, 'The Nixon-Kissinger policy of detente consisted of both carrots (trade inducements for "good" Soviet behaviour) and sticks (a more confrontational American policy posture in response to 'bad' Soviet behaviour). The Jackson-Banik amendment took away many of the carrots; Watergate and American's post-Vietnam malaise took away many of the sticks. The combination of these events killed detente.' Thirdly, there is recognition that decision making involves trade-offs in which one must assess the relative importance of competing values (how much of value x I am willing to give up for this amount of value y). For instance, 'Developing weapons systems with first-strike potential may increase the credibility of America's commitment to extended deterrence (the nuclear umbrella over America's allies). It may also, however, reduce crisis stability – by increasing the incentives for the Soviets to use their ICBMs before those missiles are destroyed in an American attack. The key question is whether our commitment to extended deterrence raises the risk of nuclear war in a crisis to an intolerable level.'

The score of 6 involves signs of a high-level interaction indicating the working of several levels of concepts. Alternatives are expressed as plans, processes or courses of action; there is indication of several moving components viewed as systems or networks. The recognition of at least two such components, and how they affect each other or the system, is the criterion for a score of 6. Alternatives are accepted, compared and integrated so as to describe one or more outcomes, frequently on the basis of global overviews or organizational principles.

The score of 7 requires an overarching thesis or conclusion pertaining not only to the existence but also to the nature of the relationship or connectedness between alternatives. These alternatives are clearly described and held in simultaneous focus. Outcomes are compared; the conditions necessitating a global view, and that view itself, are described. For example, 'Although progress is being made toward ensuring peace between the superpowers, there are shortcomings within this generally significant achievement. One of the many reasons for this is the competing demands of peace and security. We must concern ourselves with the intricacies of resolving this dilemma. In the Soviet Union, a strong military hierarchy and the memory of the devastation caused by World War II must be balanced with the growing desire of the population for an improved standard of living – perspectives that imply different policies for the management of the economy and power. In the United States, a wide diversity of political and economic priorities must be combined with the accommodation of the views of allied nations whose own widely varied needs the leader of the alliance must harmonize. The question is how the leaders of the two countries, working within this intricate network of the world economic and political allegiances, can accurately judge each other's needs and limitations while at the same time balancing the competing demands of groups within their own nations.'

Empirical example: cognitive adaptation versus rhetorical style

The very first study to apply integrative complexity scoring to archival materials (Suedfeld and Rank, 1976) set out to test a hypothesis related to changes in complexity as an adaptive response to changes in the environment. The hypothesis was that revolutionary leaders had to view the world through a simplifying filter: the movement was all good, the government all bad; others were allies or enemies; events that favoured the revolution were to be fostered and commended, those that did not were to be opposed and denounced.

However, once the revolutionary movement was victorious, and its leaders themselves became the government, demands changed. In most cases, a large proportion of the population had been either opposed or neutral (passive) during the revolution; these people and groups now had to be treated in such a way as to minimize their opposition or scepticism. Foreign governments that had not supported the revolution still had to be dealt with. Problems of rebuilding the domestic economy and foreign trade, revamping policies in agriculture, education, security and so on had to be developed and 'sold' to the population. These goals could not be reached with simple undifferentiated and unintegrated approaches. Consequently, continued success would require the leader to move to a more complex integrative mode.

Analysing the speeches and writings of 19 revolutionary leaders, from Oliver Cromwell to Fidel Castro, the researchers found that there was indeed a difference as predicted. Successful leaders (those who remained in power until natural death or an unforced retirement) showed a mean change from 1.67 before the victory of the revolution to 3.65 afterwards; unsuccessful ones (those who were deposed, executed, imprisoned or otherwise driven from office) changed from 2.37 to 2.22. Individual scores showed that low levels of complexity before victory were just as important as high levels after it. The authors hypothesized that integratively complex revolutionaries tend to be perceived by their colleagues as insufficiently devoted to the cause. After all, a rebel who professes to see some good in the government against which he is fighting may have his fervour doubted.

The following examples illustrate the fairly high levels of integrative complexity at which two successful revolutionaries – Cromwell and Castro – functioned after gaining power. The Cromwell passage argues for tolerance of different viewpoints and notes the unfortunate consequences that may flow from intolerance (score value of 3):

> Sir, the State, in choosing men to serve it, takes no notice of their opinions; if they be willing faithfully to serve it – that satisfies. I advised you formerly to bear with men of different minds from yourself: if you had done it when I advised you to it, I think you would not have had so many stumblingblocks in your way. It may be you judge otherwise; but I tell you my mind. I desire you would receive this man into your favour and good opinion. I believe, if he follow my counsel, he will deserve no other but respect from you. Take heed of being sharp, or too easily sharpened by others, against those to whom you can object little but that they square not with you in every opinion concerning matters of religion.

The Castro passage also reveals cognitive differentiation, although in a different way. In praising Che Guevara, Castro distinguishes among a variety of Guevara's achievements and character traits (his experience as a soldier and the fruits of his intelligence; his skill as a writer and the profundity of his thought):

> And because of this he has left future generations not only his experience, his knowledge as an outstanding soldier but also, at the same time, the fruits of his intelligence. He wrote with the virtuosity of a master of our language. His narratives of war are incomparable. The depth of his thinking is impressive. He never wrote about anything with less than extraordinary profundity; and we have no doubt that some of his writings will pass on to posterity as classic documents of revolutionary thought. And thus, as fruits of that vigorous and profound intelligence, he left us an infinity of memories, an infinity of narratives that, without his work, without his efforts, might have been lost forever.

These data do not indicate, however, whether the change in successful leaders was deliberately managed by them (that is, whether the leaders themselves were aware and in control of the change). The position taken by Suedfeld and Rank (1976) was that structure is not likely to be manipulated because it is less salient than content. Further studies showed changes in the opposite direction (from high to low levels) with societal stress, particularly impending war, among both governmental leaders and other eminent individuals such as scientists and writers (Porter and Suedfeld, 1981; Suedfeld, 1981, 1985a; Suedfeld and Piedrahita, 1984). The *disruptive stress* hypothesis advanced by Suedfeld and his colleagues (for example Suedfeld, 1978b, 1985b) explained these shifts on the basis that environmental stressors such as information overload, time pressure, danger to important values and the like, which frequently also lead to individual stresses such as fatigue and anxiety, reduce the complexity of information processing.

An alternative view was proposed by Tetlock and his group, based on findings that in some circumstances the change in integrative complexity was so rapid as to imply deliberate impression management or at least changes in *rhetorical style*, rather than adjustments in the actual level of information processing. For example, eventually victorious US presidential candidates (somewhat analogous to pre-victory revolutionaries, in the sense that they were in opposition) showed lower levels of integrative complexity in policy statements during an election than they did immediately after assuming office (Tetlock, 1981b). Tetlock argued that simple rhetoric helps to rally support for attacks on existing policies, whereas complex reasoning is often most useful in defending those policies.

Another study, using as the data base the speeches of US senators during periods when control of Congress shifted between liberals and conservatives, provided mixed support for the rhetorical style argument (Tetlock, Hannum and Micheletti, 1984). The prediction was that each side would show higher complexity when it was in control than when it was in the minority. The results showed reductions in complexity among liberal and moderate senators when the control of the Senate moved to the conservatives; but there was no corresponding increase among conservatives during these periods.

Thus, the question is not yet answered. On the one hand, stress-related decreases in complexity have been found among individuals who have no particular reason to adjust their rhetoric, since they have no direct role in either attacking or defending a particular policy; on the other, the rapidity and strategic nature of the change cast some doubt on explanations involving major shifts in cognitive style. Of course, there are no data showing the time requirements for such shifts to occur. It may even be that the question is not answerable, since cognitive and rhetorical style may be so confounded as to defy separation (cf. Tetlock and Manstead, 1985); but some suggestive studies can at least be imagined. One might, for example, analyse speeches delivered by the same person, on the same topic, to hostile and friendly audiences in rapid succession on several occasions. The two hypotheses lead to contrary predictions: disruptive stress would cause lower complexity when one is addressing one's opponents (assuming that the issue is important to the speaker, the audience is both important and strongly hostile, and so on); the rhetorical style hypothesis would posit higher complexity when defending one's policy before its critics. The same situation could be simulated in an experimental context: individuals could be asked to argue for particular policy positions to audiences with supportive, hostile or ambiguous views. Again, the disruptive stress hypothesis would predict simpler, and the rhetorical style hypothesis more complex, arguments when individuals address hostile audiences. Other aspects of persuasive rhetoric could also be explicitly measured (for example, one- versus two-sided, extreme or moderate, firm or conciliatory arguments). Experimental studies would also permit more refined tests of individual difference and situational boundary conditions for the applicability of the competing hypotheses. For instance, modifications of rhetorical style may be more often a valid explanation for complexity changes among persons high in self-monitoring (Snyder, 1979); the degree to which subjects feel personally committed to the policies they are asked to defend may partly determine whether they rely on simple versus complex styles of rhetoric to defend those policies (cf. Staw, 1980).

Advantages and disadvantages

The advantages of the integrative complexity approach reflect some of the reasons for its development. Complexity is related to information processing and problem solving in almost any area of life. While conceptual complexity may indeed exist as a stable (or relatively stable) personality trait, the construct is not necessary for examining the level of complexity at which people function. The great range of subjects studied with this approach, which includes historical figures, politicians, generals, distinguished scientists, novelists, business executives and diplomats as well as more standard research populations, is only one index of its versatility and applicability.

One example is the accessibility for research of individuals who cannot be reached by more intrusive methodologies. Thus, for example, studies based on the archival scoring of integrative complexity have included as subjects such people as Queen Elizabeth I, Oliver Cromwell and George Washington. The ability to assess the integrative complexity of long-dead historical personages is only one issue; another is the fact that contemporary leaders who are not likely to accede to requests for research participation can also be reached. Tetlock's study of US presidents, and Suedfeld's research on such individuals as Fidel Castro and Andrei Gromyko, exemplify this point. Several checks on the validity of scoring translations from the original language (by comparing the scores from translations and from the original) have affirmed that the level of complexity is not significantly affected, at least in the case of official, authorized or scholarly translations.

The archival measurement of integrative complexity uses random sampling of the available materials. Information that might serve to identify specific individuals, periods and other variables crucial to a particular hypothesis can to a great extent be eliminated or obscured. These two features make the technique less susceptible to experimenter bias than most content analyses. As a contrast, we may consider psychohistorical techniques. Psychohistorians typically look for crucial events in the subject's childhood and family life, which when associated with the person's adult behaviour are tested against certain psychodynamic hypotheses about such relationships. One of the most frequent criticisms of psychohistory is that some incidents in childhood are emphasized while others are ignored, and that the researchers are likely to pay more attention to those incidents that fit psychodynamic preconceptions. As a result, the total early experience of the subject may be seriously distorted. This problem is exacerbated by the fact that very few if any biographies or autobiographies provide equal detail about the various periods or experiences of the subject, tending to mention dramatic incidents and to ignore many others. Whether the resultant characterization of the person's childhood is valid has been severely questioned (for example Greenstein, 1975; Tetlock, Crosby and Crosby, 1981). By contrast, in the integrative complexity scoring procedure a person who does not know the hypothesis locates the corpus from which samples are to be drawn, and then by the use of a random numbers procedure selects the sample to be scored. Once this is done, such information as specific names and dates is removed to the greatest possible extent before the samples are actually scored by another person. Ideally, the scorers are also unfamiliar with the specific hypothesis being tested.

The integrative complexity approach does not assume that cognitive behaviour is rigid. In fact, it can monitor changes in the level of complexity characterizing a subject's behaviour quite finely. For example, written materials may be produced throughout several days or weeks of a particular decision process or crisis situation; in many cases, these are precisely dated and researchers can trace changes day by day. When the event involved is also well documented, as in historical and some autobiographical records, one can further establish the relationships between such changes in integrative complexity and the developing situation in which the source is functioning.

It should also be remembered that the theory and the research methodology are neutral as to content. Thus, the same position on any particular issue may be held at any level of complexity; conversely, the same level of complexity may underlie diametrically opposed views. This relative freedom from content bias makes integrative complexity measures more objective and wider in applicability; but perhaps its most important advantage is that it is less subject to either deliberate or unconscious manipulation. Suedfeld, Tetlock and Ramirez (1977) demonstrated this in the case of speeches about the Middle East problem in the UN General Assembly. During periods of growing crisis, several months before major wars broke out in the area, the speeches of the delegates were as full as ever of references to the importance of peace and their own country's dedication to maintaining it; in fact, one content analysis of these speeches had indicated that such professions appeared to intensify in the several months prior to each outbreak of war. Overt content is easily selected by the source to convey the message desired; but levels of integrative complexity, which in the speeches showed consistent and dramatic decreases during the periods leading up to war, implied a hardening of positions, a reduced willingness to consider more than one point of view as legitimate, and the other characteristics we associate with integrative simplicity. In the aura of international crisis, these same characteristics seem likely to be associated with the probability of a breakdown in peaceful negotiations.

Unlike some content analytic techniques, integrative complexity scoring can be reliably performed on a relatively small data base, which makes it easier to perform replications and reliability checks. When compared with such massive analyses as, for example, those of Holsti on governmental documents just prior to World War I, the effort and time required to score a sample of paragraphs for complexity are relatively small. It would be very difficult to perform complete content analyses on, for example, the documents produced before and after the success of several revolutions between the seventeenth and twentieth centuries, as was done in the study by Suedfeld and Rank (1976). Nor, if one wants to eliminate the possibility that a particular score or analyst is inaccurate, is it very difficult to select another random sample from the same data base and have it scored by one or more other trained raters.

Given the nature of sample selection, one also need not worry unduly if the archives are not entirely complete. Whereas in content analysis one or a few documents may be crucial, and their unavailability may distort the data and conclusions, this is not likely to happen in the case of integrative complexity scoring. When gaps exist, the remaining material stands on its own; when the gap may be only part of the document (although in terms of content a crucial part), the rest of the passages may be sufficient to establish complexity level.

We now turn to the disadvantages of the procedure. One drawback is that the process of becoming a trained scorer is still difficult. It requires participation in a scoring workshop or seminar, most of which last at least one week and frequently more. Furthermore, such seminars are at the moment available in only two major places, the University of California at Berkeley and the University of British Columbia. It should be mentioned that there is work going on at present to develop a training system and scoring manual through which individuals can learn the procedure at a distance, and then submit samples of scored test materials to establish their reliability as raters.

It is generally impossible to establish whether changes in complexity are causes or effects of environmental or situational developments (or even whether that dichotomy is applicable). For example, there is a replicated finding of decreasing integrative complexity in the public position statements of governments prior to the outbreak of war (Suedfeld and Tetlock, 1977; Suedfeld, Tetlock and Ramirez, 1977; Tetlock, 1985). It is probable that the worsening of a crisis and the reduction of complexity are cyclically interactive: as the crisis worsens and stress increases, it disrupts the complexity of integrative functioning, which in turn leads to statements and decisions that further exacerbate the situation. But while this hypothesis seems intuitively plausible, there is no way to test whether it is accurate. One may equally well argue that the decrease in complexity is merely a consequence and symptom of the deteriorating situation; or conversely, that the situation gets worse because the protagonists are taking increasingly simple positions.

Tetlock's argument that the level of integrative complexity may be manipulated as an impression management strategy may further complicate the relationship between complexity and situational factors. Although this hypothesis still requires further research, perhaps in a more direct methodology (for example, one that allows the researcher to find out whether subjects are intuitively aware of the level of complexity at which they operate), it is certainly one that needs to be kept in mind as a warning in research relating public events to cognitive processes.

Another problem is that one does not always know the actual author of particular materials. This is especially true with documents produced by anonymous writers, even when there are strong historical guesses as to the real source; and for material possibly or definitely produced by speech writers and other assistants. Some studies have shown no reliable differences between the latter kinds of material and those known to have been produced personally by the subject being studied. It may be argued that any major leader will insist that he or she feel personally comfortable with a speech produced by someone else before endorsing it. Speech writers and ghost writers are probably selected with that criterion in mind, and their submissions have been known in many cases to be rejected or edited accordingly. Still, the potential problems raised by the use of such assistance cannot be definitely dismissed in every instance.

In some cases, written material has not survived to make complexity scoring possible. Recall, for example, Suedfeld and Rank's (1976) data showing that revolutionary leaders who evidenced low levels of complexity during the revolution and then attained significantly higher levels when they were in governmental office tended to remain powerful longer than those who failed to make such a shift. It would be interesting to know whether the former group had showed high or low levels of complexity prior to being involved in a revolution; however, for most of them no correspondence or other writings are available from the pre-revolutionary period. Similar cases arise with illiterate leaders, non-literate societies or subgroups, and individuals whose materials were produced in a relatively little-known language and have not been translated.

Where do we go from here?
The integrative complexity coding system is a cost-effective and well-validated methodological tool for testing psychological hypotheses in a remarkable range of contexts: domestic and international politics, literature, science and business. The price of this empirical productivity has, however, been a degree of conceptual confusion. Data generation has outpaced theory generation – a state of affairs reminiscent of the cognitive dissonance literature in the late 1960s. We now have numerous interesting demonstrations of individual difference and situational correlates of integrative complexity of functioning. We know, for example, that the integrative complexity of verbal behaviour is influenced by the personality of the perceiver (demonstrations of significant consistency across times and issues), the issue domain under consideration (demonstrations of the impact of value conflict), one's political role (demonstrations of the impact of changes in role or political audience), and environmental stressors (demonstrations of the impact of information load and threat). Determinants of integrative complexity can be viewed from a correspondingly wide variety of theoretical perspectives: psychodynamic theories of political belief systems (for example Adorno et al., 1950; McClosky, 1967; Stone, 1980), information processing theories of cognitive functioning under stress (for example Schroder, Driver and Streufert, 1967) or under value conflict (for example Janis and Mann, 1977), and theories of impression management and self-presentation (for example Tetlock and Manstead, 1985).

We know little about the conditions under which these very different theoretical points of view are more or less useful. It has been easier to build up a differentiated body of empirical knowledge than it has been to come up with integrative theoretical principles. The major challenge now, however, is theoretical integration. It may not be possible to resolve the theoretical dichotomies that social psychologists often try to impose on their data (for example, impression management versus intrapsychic, cognition versus motivation); but it is possible to organize the observed covariates of integrative complexity into empirically defensible and theoretically meaningful categories. Much remains to be learned about the stability and consistency of individual differences in integrative complexity. Why is the complexity of some individuals much more stable across situations than others? Much remains to be learned about person-situation interactions in integrative complexity. Why, for example, do marked individual differences exist in the cognitive strategies that people use to cope with accountability demands and value conflict? We doubt that archival research by itself will be able to answer such questions. Laboratory studies will be necessary to isolate key variables and to test critical hypotheses. But we are optimistic that a research programme that builds on the distinctive strengths of both the archival and the experimental traditions will advance our understanding of the antecedents, mediators and consequences of integrative complexity.

5

Structures of belief and justification

Charles Antaki

In this chapter I want to describe one way to get at how people organize their explanations – how they set them out and how they defend them. The technique I shall be reporting is a compromise between getting at someone's completely natural and spontaneous explanation (if such a thing could exist) and the demands of standardization and convenience. It is also a compromise between on the one hand getting a complete catalogue of everything a person could say in an explanation, and on the other being satisfied with the reductionist programme favoured by standard social cognitive techniques. It is best used for looking at the explanations people give for events they care about and know about; it's a technique that encourages a certain rationality, and a certain commitment to a clear and definite view of the event under discussion.

Theoretical background

The point I want to champion is that people's explanations are coherent *wholes*, more or less well structured in and of themselves. Your explanation of (say) your choice of holiday destination or your position on nuclear weapons will have ramifications, elaborations, justifications; the causal links in the explanation will be more or less secure, and the whole thing will be more or less well moored in the network of your beliefs about life in general.

This notion of an articulated causal belief structure may seem reasonable enough, but it is rather a change from the tradition in experimental social psychology. Attribution theory – the umbrella term for experiments on ordinary explanation – is very far from being interested in the subparts of a person's explanation structure or how they knit together. On the contrary, the strength of the attributionist position is the way it reduces the complexity of ordinary explanation to a small set of clear conceptual categories. The attributionist is less interested in the building blocks of your explanation of (say) unemployment than in how the whole collection could be boiled down to two or three dimensions of meaning.

Reducing explanations to simple causal categories
Those who followed Heider (1958) had the thrifty idea of reducing the complexity of ordinary explanation to a manageable number of categories of cause. There is far more to Heider than this reductionism, but that has been his legacy for all practical purposes. What Heider did was not to say that causes were necessary or sufficient, enabling or inhibitory, counterfactual or abnormal; his intention was not to philosophize ordinary explanation, but rather to find philosophical distinctions in ordinary talk. His prime gift to attribution theorists was to point to a profound difference between causes that the individual perceived to be located within agents of action and those perceived to be located outside them. Broadly speaking, all ordinary explanations of social behaviour – and non-social behaviour – could be ranged somewhere along the line from internal to external.

The idea of distilling an explanation, and the idea of distilling it down to a point on an internal–external line, found (for reasons we need not go into here) a responsive chord in the mood of developing cognitive social psychology. Apart from anything else, it gave a blessedly simple dependent measure which could be used to chart the output of a complex social judgement. By the late 1970s the literature was alive with hundreds of experiments designed to discover just what made an explainer choose one point rather than another on the internal–external line. The guiding models of Jones and Davis (1965) and of Kelley (1973) suggested that rational information was important; and indeed, so it was. To caricature, but not unfairly: if a respondent was told that John consistently laughed at a certain comedian, and at many other comedians, that information disposed the respondent to judge the cause of that event to be internal to John.

The value of this reductive programme depended on two things: firstly, that the internal–external division to which explanation had been boiled down was a sensible and productive one; and secondly, that not too much of the flavour of ordinary explanation was destroyed in the process.

It would be foolish not to concede that the internal–external distinction is a profound one. As Totman (1982) points out, it is enshrined in our legal and moral worlds; it would be astonishing if it had no psychological counterpart. As to sense, then, the programme passes. Productivity? Once again, it seems obvious enough that, in some circumstances, the single most important thing about an explanation is indeed what it 'all boils down to'. Say two students fail a class test. Both give long and elaborate accounts of the whys and wherefores of the failure. We ask them to boil it down to one thing. Jane says 'My alarm clock didn't wake me up in time'; John says 'I'm just no good at maths.' From that stark difference we know that Jane is likely to do better next time, since clocks can be changed; John is not, since presumably ability cannot. Here the single-category explanation does us well enough; there is, in fact, a large literature on how such explanations affect work and happiness in class (see Weiner, 1986) and are implicated in depression (see for example Peterson and Seligman, 1984).

But what have attributionists lost by the reduction? Firstly, they have lost sight of how people *reason* in making their explanations. No one needs to reason or 'show their working' in an attribution experiment. Indeed no one is allowed to. All the working is assumed to be done by the hypothetical constructs (the analysis of covariance and so on) that are the business of Jones and Davis's and Kelley's models. The reasoner has been displaced by her or his cognitive system. What is lost is respondents' evidence, backing, the justification of their causal beliefs. Attribution theory can be a theory about cognitive processing, but it can never be a theory of ordinary reasoning.

Secondly, reduction means stripping away the *context* of explanations – to whom they are given, by whom and for what purpose. Reduction to a cognitive product denies the possibility of explanations as social processes with a point and a purpose. Respondents have been freed of their need to persuade, and they have, in any case, been denied a language in which that persuasion could be done. Attributions on rating scales are offered to nobody, they are in a reductive language foreign to the respondent, and they force the respondent to use a vocabulary of thought which, for all its occasional predictive value, is on the whole a travesty of the richness of ordinary expression. Put the explainer in a social context where she or he wants to explain something important to someone, and you will not see a bald and vulnerable attribution to internal or external cause. You will see argument, defence, justification, and a display of a complicated and articulate explanation.

The structure of beliefs and warrants
What, then, should we be doing if we want to get at people's reasoning, and at the social goals of their explanations? Clearly the first step is just to listen to what they say, and record it as faithfully as possible. We could stop there and do content analyses

of what concepts they use. That would be a perfectly reasonable start, but I think one can do more.

We could sketch ourselves an idealized picture of what an articulated explanation could look like. The criteria would be that it showed how the person reasoned, and that it had a place for the social purposes that the person had in mind. Then, armed with this sketch, we could do some empirical data collection and try out the data against the ideal model. Let us take a look at what the model should feature.

Structure. When one says that individuals have a certain structure to their beliefs, one is saying that there is some network of (at its loosest) association or (at its tightest) logical implication among a certain set of their views of the world. This kind of idea is most familiar in psychologists' personality theories, where the paradigm case of (say) an authoritarian personality (in the terms of Adorno et al., 1950) was thought to believe in X *and* Y *and* Z. But note that in this sense structure here is really no more than a *constellation*; and the pattern, like the Great Bear or the Plough, is in the eye of the expert beholder. The kind of structure I have in mind is the structure that the persons *themselves* see. At its most basic, it will be something like 'the toe bone is connected to the (pause) foot bone, the foot bone is connected to the (pause) shin bone' and so on. It doesn't have to be anatomically accurate to be what the person genuinely believes.

Justification. Once one allows that respondents can make something of organizing their own beliefs, one asks what they might want to use to cement crude belief statements together (*why* is the toe bone connected to the foot bone?). In some discourses, the justification for claiming that A caused B will be a mechanical one; in another discourse, it will be a motivational one; and so on. But whatever our respondents say, they will want – if they want to abide by canons of rationality – to say *something* about why they think the two beliefs are linked.

We now have a very rough sketch of what might be in an ordinary explanation. Let us now have a look at some data to fill in some of the detail.

Empirical examples

I shall give two illustrations of what one can do with the idea that a person's explanation has a reasonably elaborate causal skeleton which is fleshed out with justification. One example is from a study in which respondents talked, and I constructed their explanatory structure from the transcripts of taped speech; the other is from a study where the respondents wrote down the structure themselves.

Example 1: conversational structures
In the first case, I talked to members of the Social Democratic Party (SDP) about their decision to join the party, their explanations of current social problems, and the state of the political scene in Britain. All were academics who were articulate, thoughtful and – by virtue of their membership of a consciously 'new' political grouping – keen to account at length about such political matters. Here is a longish extract, in which JG explains British unemployment.

CA: What from your point of view are the causes of unemployment?
JG: I'm sure the world recession has had a lot to do with it, and I think on top of that the very tight monetary policies of the government have exaggerated this to some extent. Whether one can believe half the effect being caused by the world recession I'm not sure. I would like to know much more about economics, but when I think that the professional economists themselves can't find a uniform approach I wonder if I ever will.
CA: Let's take the world recession first. Obviously one is speculating here, but how would you unpack the causes of the world recession?
JG: I don't honestly know. What happens in this country largely stems from what happens in the States. We're very dependent – just as we are for the weather, incidentally. I think there have been similar monetarist policies, which Ronald Reagan possibly copied from Mrs Thatcher. I'm not sure, but they were fairly adjacent in timing, so that's perhaps unfair. But fairly restrictive policies causing high interest rates and so on.
CA: What would the Reagan intention be, in having those restrictive practices?
JG: I think he wanted to some extent to undo the social fabric of the state ... by that I mean social medicine, these sorts of things; [that] is my impression. To save money – you know, on the good housekeeping type of theory of Mrs Thatcher. That's my impression of it.
CA: Let's move to Mrs Thatcher and the government policy. You were saying that government policy has had some effect on unemployment. What is the government policy in your perception?
JG: I think principally it's designed round the good housekeeping idea of only having so much money to spend, and I've never really followed this through to the bitter end, so I can't claim to understand it. Because people talk about the ability to borrow without making the country any worse off and certainly, from what little I know of business, businesses borrow money in order to expand and produce more and thereby make more money, and I can't help feeling that the country must have a similar sort of

ability to do this. Where you draw the line, of course, I don't feel that I know enough to say, except that I have this gut feeling that Mrs Thatcher has drawn the line too low.

CA: Do you think she's drawn it even from her own point of view on rational lines?

JG: I think she's following Geoffrey Howe in this. I suspect that he's the man who has really drawn the lines, and she seems to have great trust in him – possibly alone of her cabinet – and I don't altogether trust Sir Geoffrey Howe's logic. Again I'm not an economist enough to know whether this is wrong or not. I suppose I ought to say that what opinions I have on economics are based on reading *The Guardian* more than anything else. That gives away a lot, doesn't it?

CA: One can read *The Guardian* with very different interpretations. The way I've set it down here it looks as if one's attributing government policy, if pushed, to Howe's analysis?

JG: Yes, I think that wouldn't be too unfair. I have a personal dislike of Mrs Thatcher for what I consider her dictatorial, overbearing manner, but that's something separate in a way.

Here we are, then, with a bare transcript. If we were attributionists looking for attributional categories, we would be concerned to boil down the words to a point where we could see clearly where JG fell on our causal dimensions. This would be, as I noted above, the sensible thing to do in some circumstances; and, if we felt the circumstances were right, we would turn to the sophisticated and sensitive work exemplified by Harvey, Turnquist and Agostinelli in chapter 3 to guide us.

However, rather than pinning JG down to the attributionists' language, let us instead take him at his own estimate. How does he see the structure of the causes of unemployment? What is the skeleton, at least, of his reasoning?

Causal structure. Stripping away everything else, JG's causal story is that unemployment is caused by two kinds of thing: world recession and government policies. The world recession is caused ('largely') by events in the US; specifically, restrictive monetarist policies. These in turn are caused by President Reagan's intention to reduce public spending. On the other hand (or down the other path), government policy ('good housekeeping') is determined by the Prime Minister, who in turn is being guided by Geoffrey Howe (the Chancellor of the Exchequer at the time).

If we set all that out diagramatically, it would look like Figure 5.1. You can see that the reduction to the skeleton of causal structure does some violence to the subtlety of JG's expression, and others would treat it quite differently: see especially the contributions by Heritage (chapter 9), Wetherell and Potter (chapter 12), Parker

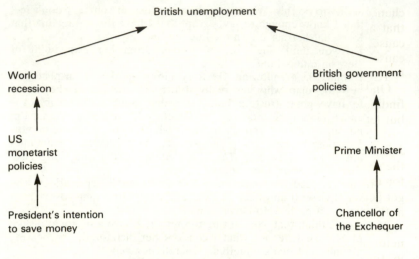

Figure 5.1   *A diagram of the causal structure in a respondent's explanation of British unemployment (the causes read upwards)*

(chapter 13) and Billig (chapter 14). But let us keep to it for now and come back to subtleties in a moment.

Suppose we then went through the same kind of skeleton stripping in a large sample of similar transcripts of people's explanations of unemployment. We would have in front of us a large set of diagrams of causal structures. We could then ask some interesting questions. Are some people's structures more articulated than other people's? Do people use lots of causes in a single, unwinding string, or do they see (as JG does) two or more independent paths of causes leading up to the event? Do some types of cause occur more reliably closer to the event than others? Do some types of cause predict other types of cause? If there is a tendency to attribute unemployment 'externally', does it appear in causes near the top of the paths, or in fundamental causes at the bottom of paths?

I don't want to foreclose on all the possible questions, but I can answer one or two of them on the basis of the study from which JG's transcript actually comes (Antaki, 1985). The academic SDP respondents I talked to were more likely to put things to do with persons or society right at the bottom of their causal pathways. Groups (like 'the Conservative Party' or 'left-wing radicals' or 'traditional economists') would appear anywhere; person causes ('Mrs Thatcher') and society causes ('world trade', 'free collective bargaining'), on the other hand, appeared proportionately more often as termini. There was a significant relationship among the types of causes in any path; one could predict, with greater than chance accuracy, what cause was coming next. The pattern was that a personal cause would be unpacked into a further personal cause, a societal cause into another societal cause, and a group cause into a group cause. There were few examples of society to personal steps, or vice versa.

One could spend time interpreting any of these structural findings, generating ideas to test with new samples of structures; but let us leave it there.

Justifications. So much for demonstrating the idea of looking at the skeletal structure in a transcript. The next thing to do is to look for the way the explanation proceeds at an interpersonal level to get across whatever social purposes the interaction requires. What is JG up to, and how does it emerge in his words?

As you can see from the transcript, JG is doing much more than neutrally reporting the bare skeleton of the diagram. Other chapters in this volume – see especially Parker (chapter 13), Heritage (chapter 9) and Leudar and Antaki (chapter 10) – make much more of the obviously interactive nature of what is going on, and some things look obvious on a first pass. JG occasionally depreciates his competence to answer the question ('I've never really followed this through to the bitter end, so I can't claim to understand it'; 'I would like to know much more about economics, but ... I wonder if I ever will'; 'I don't honestly know'). He is nevertheless cooperative and articulate in answering the probes and he is at pains to distance himself from merely emotional reactions ('I have a personal dislike for Mrs Thatcher ... but that's something separate in a way').

Such aspects of the data paint a more vivid picture of JG's image of the world. We can capture some of that vividness, I think, by making space in our diagram for the *justificatory links*, or *warrants*, that he makes between his causal claims. The idea of warrants is described by Draper in chapter 2, and more thoroughly laid out by Voss in chapter 6. The idea we need to note here is that we are taking it that JG is giving reasons or justifications for the causal claims that he is making.

Take the claim that world recession is caused by US economic policies ('What happens in this country largely stems from what happens in the States'). The warrant he gives is a meteorological analogy: 'We're very dependent – just as we are for the weather, incidentally.' The use of an analogy is neat, but JG is clearly not fully confident that it will do; he adds 'incidentally' at the end of the sentence to pull away from a full commitment. The tone continues in his warrant for claiming that Reagan 'possibly copies from Mrs Thatcher': 'I'm not sure, but they were fairly adjacent in timing.' Here there is a stronger, more rational piece of warranting: adjacency in time, on a Humean model of causality, is consistent with A causing B. On the other hand, JG immediately stands back: 'That's perhaps unfair.'

It is clear that JG's warrants of his causal beliefs are at the mercy, in this interaction at least, of worries about his competence to give them. Nevertheless, he does back up what he says, so we can begin to read off a little bit about what kind of evidence he thinks appropriate to various claims, what authorities he might be citing, and what kind of reasoning he thinks appropriate to display to this particular interlocutor. (Of course, at home or in the pub he might use quite a different discourse.) As we said above when looking at JG's structure, one could collect data on all of these things from more people like JG (in this case, middle-class members of the SDP) to get a feel for the justifications they consensually use. Carrying on further with this example of a project, one might then compare them with Conservative or Labour voters, or with working-class SDP members, and discover interesting things about the kinds of evidence different groups invoke to back up their beliefs about causes.

The drawback to the conversational method is that it requires a fair degree of subjective interpretation both in identifying the respondent's causal structure, and then in spotting just what it is that is meant to count as evidence or warrant for the various causal links. It goes without saying that this kind of subjectivity can go horribly wrong; in interpreting JG's talk, I might simply have misunderstood what he meant, made one or two spurious links, and got the whole structure of causes and justifications quite wrong.

The alternative is to get the respondents themselves to make the causal links – on a piece of paper, if necessary – and to say clearly and specifically what warrant they have for making each link in the structure.

Example 2: written structures

How shall we get our respondents to write down their explanations? One could ask them to write an essay. But we would still have the problem of seeing through to the skeleton underneath the idiosyncrasies of expression. And it would hardly help at all in making the justifications any clearer: people do not typically write 'and I think that's the case because ... '. No; if we have decided that we are interested in structure and justification (and we have first checked that such things really are there in people's explanation), then we shall have to ask for them explicitly.

Let us look at a procedure that turns the conversation into an explicit pencil-and-paper task. I asked students at Manchester University to explain to me the causes of the students' occupation of university buildings (the occupation and its aftermath was at the time a live issue, attracting a good deal of media attention and causing strong feeling around the university).

Once the students had been recruited, they were left to complete the task in their own time and at their own pace. Each person was given an envelope containing the instructions. First you had to write down, on one card per cause, as many causes as you wanted to explain the occupation. Then you had to take those cards and arrange them so that they showed which causes caused which other causes, and how they all related to the causing of the occupation itself. This meant shuffling the cards about on a table or something of the sort. Then the respondent drew the pattern he or she had made on to a blank sheet of paper, with an arrow between every cause–effect pair (notice that the instructions did not mention paths, steps, branching or anything else; the respondent was entirely free to write as many cards as she or he wanted, to put them in any causal order, to branch them in any way, and so on). All this, of course, was merely breaking down the task of drawing out a causal structure in the respondent's own words.

To get at his or her justifications for causal beliefs, the next thing the student had to do was to write down, on a separate card, the justification for each link in the causal structure. The instruction for this was simply to say: 'Why you think there was that causal connection.'

What the respondent gave me, then, was a sheet of paper on which was drawn his or her own causal structure, some cards describing the causes and some cards describing their justifications. I could then reconstitute the diagram and the cards into a full-blown causal structure. The general form of the structure was a chronological narrative. The start of the event was located at the visit of an allegedly racist Home Office minister, which was known as the 'Waddington affair' after the violence of the police protection tactics. The next phase was the university's action in disciplining four students who had been involved in the demonstration, and the last phase was the students' union's decision to protest against the disciplining.

Figure 5.2 shows part of one typical respondent's causal skeleton. It shows one causal link, and what the respondent said about why she thought the antecedent caused the effect.

Causal structure. If we wanted to concentrate on the structure of the explanations of the students' occupation, we could ask

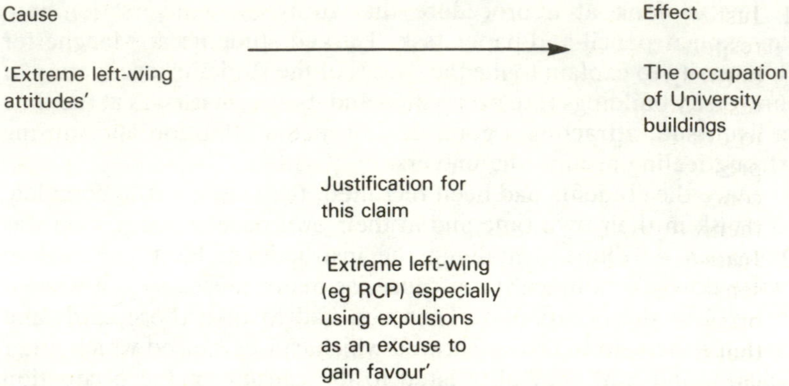

Cause	Effect
'Extreme left-wing attitudes' →	The occupation of University buildings

Justification for
this claim

'Extreme left-wing
(eg RCP) especially
using expulsions
as an excuse to
gain favour'

Figure 5.2   *Part of a respondent's explanation structure showing the justification of a causal claim*

all the types of question of the students that we asked of the SDP members in the previous study: for example, whether people who were for or against the occupation gave different structures (they didn't, although they put different causes at different points in similar structures); and so on.

Justifications. But let us concentrate instead on the justifications, since the value of this paper-and-pencil technique is that they are now very clear. In the diagram, the justification appears next to the cause–effect pair. Our respondent claimed that 'Extreme left-wing attitudes' caused the occupation of the university buildings, and writes, in defence of the claim: 'Extreme left wing, e.g. RCP [Revolutionary Communist Party] especially using expulsions as an excuse to gain favour.'

What does one do with these justifications once one has them written down clearly by the respondent in this fashion? Clearly one has to do some kind of paraphrasing to get the sense of what was meant. In this case, what the student seems to mean is that she feels justified in claiming that left-wing attitudes caused the occupation by the fact that, as she saw it, the ostensible 'expulsion' issue was merely an excuse for the activist policies of an extreme minority.

One can search among the whole corpus of justifications to see if some kind of identifiable categories of justification emerge. In this particular study, what emerged was that the respondents used four kinds of warrant to justify the claims they made:

1 Justifying the link by revealing an extra cause. Here the respondents revealed an extra level of cause that mediated between the two steps they had set down. For example, many respondents thought that 'outside pressure' caused the university to discipline students. Their justification was to say that outside pressure brought by government caused the universities to be concerned with their image of campus discipline, which caused them to make an example of this particular case.

2 Justifying the use of terminology. Here the respondents made sense of their use of a description of the state of affairs brought about by the cause. One quite common claim was that the university's action had caused the 'loss of student union autonomy'. A student making this claim might give, as a warrant, something that would make it clear that what happened was genuinely a loss of autonomy – for example, 'For the university to discipline the students was to encroach on the union's traditional right to apply its own discipline.'

3 Justifying by unpacking a hidden aspect of the cause. Here the respondent would be revealing a new or unsuspected aspect of the cause which made the link with the consequent clearer. For example, one respondent claimed that 'Dissatisfaction with government policies' caused a history of incidents. Her warrant was to unpack the cause to reveal that there was 'general student anger at the way government is running down the educational system and especially treatment of students'.

4 Historical background. Occasionally the respondent would use the opportunity to write a paragraph or so's worth of background information which covered a good deal of ground, and was difficult to melt down into one particular category of cause.

It must be said, however, that identifying a statement as being unequivocally one or other of the above justifications was hard. Partly this was because of the compact, almost telegraphic style adopted by most of the respondents. But it was partly attributable to the possibility that the respondents simply could not cope with the instruction formally to justify their claims. Respondents knew that something had to be written about the links they had made, and every respondent accordingly wrote something. One respondent was clearly *au fait* with what was asked of her, and produced responses of the form 'A justified B in virtue of the fact that C is a precondition of B, and A brought about C.' But this was unusual. What is likely is that the formality of articulating what is normally a highly implicit part of dialogue was just too contrived, and made some respondents produce spurious responses in an unsuccessful effort to bring into conscious expression the warrants that they silently invoked in more normal talk.

Advantages and disadvantages

As I mentioned at the start of the chapter, the advantage of this way of working with explanations is that it respects people's ability – in fact their right – to organize their explanations in ways that a reductive approach would simply not allow. The respondents are using their own language in which to express their thoughts; they are expressing as many causes as they like; they are putting them into whatever organization they like (within the boundary, of course, of causation); and they are showing their justifications in whatever sense they feel is appropriate.

One thing I would like *not* to do is to make any strong claim that this way of working reveals people's cognitive representation of a causal sequence. This is the point of view expressed by Kelley (1983) and by Bowerman (1981), who want to claim that people store representations of causal sequences in something that looks, at first blush, rather like the tree structures in Figure 5.1. That view is a regression to thinking of people's explanations in a social vacuum. Here the point is that the structure is thought up for a specific purpose and is addressed to a specific person. I would have no particular commitment to expecting to see the very same structure again, and I would fully expect the same person to draw up quite a different structure, with different causes differently justified, when they were doing it for someone else, or less formally, and so on. That is not to say that what they say to me is meaningless; far from it. There is nothing meaningless in saying that these students (for example) expressed themselves to a lecturer in a certain way (and that they varied in how they expressed themselves according to, say, whether they were for or against the occupation). The point is to acknowledge, and make part of the story, that this was how they addressed themselves to one particular person at one particular time, and that they might well address themselves differently to each other, to the police, and so on.

On the debit side there is the question of validity. I started off by saying that we must respect ordinary talk; yet I have presented a paper-and-pencil task quite different from the ebb and flow of conversation. I have to admit that this is a problem. There is little doubt that the technique encourages a rationality that may not be there in other media, and requires of the respondent a certain commitment to understanding the event under discussion and to looking as if they understand it – which might, again, not be the case with a different medium. Moreover, the technique is perhaps too committed to what Harré and Secord (1972) call the 'open souls doctrine': taking what respondents say too literally and making little allowance for, amongst other things, irony, facetiousness, exaggeration and the complex use of metaphor and allusion. It is perhaps too rigidly literal in its treatment of what people say to be a good net for catching subtleties of explanations in actual exchanges. But it has useful qualities for explanations and accounts which can be expressed more formally.

6

Problem solving and reasoning in ill-structured domains

James F. Voss

Theoretical background

In the most recent decades psychological research has been in a period of transition and, with respect to the study of higher mental processes, the transition has included an increase in research on problem solving and reasoning. Moreover, the transition has involved both conceptual and methodological trends. Conceptual trends have included attempts to develop an understanding of mental structure and function. Expressions commonly used in relation to this concern are 'representations', 'declarative knowledge', 'procedural knowledge', and 'strategies'. Methodologically, procedures have been developed which enable the investigator to study mental processes in a relatively wide variety of task situations. This chapter is concerned with one type of task situation that is found in the study of problem solving and reasoning, namely that of collecting and analysing verbal protocols, and in particular with protocols that are collected in relation to ill-structured problems.

The collection of protocols is of course not new. Ericcson and Simon (1984) have summarized research involving protocol analysis, considering the virtues of the procedure as well as its limitations. However, the current interest in protocol collection was given strong impetus by the development of computer simulation techniques, for investigators wanted to relate the solution steps found in the protocol to a model of those processes (for example Newell, Shaw and Simon, 1958). Newell and Simon's book *Human Problem Solving* (1972) contains examples of protocol analysis taken from a number of domains, including geometry and cryptarithmetic. Moreover, the protocols presented are portrayed in terms of problem behaviour graphs; such graphs represent the step-by-step development of the solution.

The problems typically used by Newell and Simon (1972) as well as by a number of other investigators were *well structured*: that is, the goal of the problem was well defined, the 'givens' of the problem were presented in the problem statement, and the constraints of the problem were provided in the problem statement or were known to the solver. Problems that are well structured include solving algebra or other mathematics problems, puzzle problems, and physics problems such as those found in undergraduate textbooks. Furthermore, the solutions of well-structured problems typically have been determined, and they have consensual agreement in the sense that the experts in the field agree upon a particular solution.

In contrast to well-structured problems, in *ill-structured problems* the goals are vaguely defined, the constraints may not be stated but may be generated in the course of the solution, and the givens may be minimal. (Because the extent to which the goals, constraints and givens of a problem may vary, the well-structured/ill-structured distinction should be viewed as a continuum rather than a dichotomy.) In addition, ill-structured problems typically do not have solutions which have consensual agreement among experts in the field. Ill-structured problems tend to be found in fields such as social policy, political science, sociology and, to some extent, economics, although 'cutting edge' research in the natural sciences also involves dealing with ill-structured problems.

An additional aspect of the information processing model involves the use of the concepts of task environment and problem space. The task environment consists of the situational context of the problem. The problem space consists of a mental space of the solver which contains all possible states of the problem, correct or incorrect, the problem operators, and the problem constraints. In addition, the solver's understanding of the problem statement constitutes the initial state of the problem, while reaching the goal – that is, solving the problem – constitutes the final state of the problem solution. Thus, according to this view, the problem solving process consists of the solver proceeding from one state of the problem to the next until the goal is achieved. Moreover, the movement from state to state is presumed to take place via the use of an operator. For example, considering the problem of adding a column of numbers, the solver would use the operator 'add' and apply it to each number as the individual was cumulatively adding the column.

In the solving of more complex problems, and especially in the case of the ill-structured problems, the solver develops a representation of the problem and subsequently provides a solution to the problem. In physics, for example, the solver, especially the expert solver, may read a problem, interpret it by examining the concepts and relations of the problem (perhaps by constructing a drawing), and conclude that the problem is perhaps a 'kinetics' problem (cf. Larkin et al., 1980). Such a classification constitutes the representation of the problem, and upon classifying the problem the expert solver then applies the appropriate equations. With respect to ill-structured problems, developing the problem representation may be quite complex, with the solver delineating the causes of the problem as well as its constraints. The solution then consists of providing a solution and justifying it; justification occurs as the solver indicates why the proposed solution will work and considers the possible difficulties of the proposed solution and how these difficulties may be met.

Analysing protocols of solutions to ill-structured problems

The question of how to analyse protocols obtained in the solving of ill-structured problems does not have a simple answer. In our work on this issue (Voss et al., 1983; Voss, Tyler and Yengo, 1983) we spent considerable time trying to capture the contents and structure of the protocol, approaching the question via use of a number of different methods. The expert protocols are relatively lengthy and, having been working in the area of text comprehension, we were predisposed to use a form of propositional analysis. However, it became clear quite quickly that such an analysis would not capture the organization and structure of the protocol. We tried other means such as classifying sentences in terms of their content, but this also was not fruitful. Moreover, from a problem solving perspective we tried to determine whether particular strategies were used such as 'top down, breadth first', but this also failed to capture the protocol's structure and contents.

A more positive outcome occurred when we applied Toulmin's (1958) model to the protocols. Toulmin's model consists of taking a single assertion and viewing it in terms of a datum and a claim component. For example, consider: 'A Soviet–United States arms agreement will likely produce a reduction of the United States troops in West Germany.' The *datum* involves the occurrence of an arms agreement, while the *claim* is the effect that presumably will be produced by the datum. In addition, the Toulmin model includes the concepts of warrant and backing. The *warrant* is what enables a person to make the claim; it is a sort of minor premise. In many cases warrants are not stated explicitly; the argument structure then embraces what Aristotle terms an 'enthymeme'. However, support for the assertion and hence the warrant is often provided in the form of backing. *Backing* refers to some type of supportive statement which may take the form of a fact or an assumption. Thus, in the present example, one may state that the need for United States troops in West Germany would be reduced.

The final two components of the Toulmin model are the qualifier and the counter-argument. *Qualifying* involves asserting that the datum–claim relationship holds only under a particular set of conditions. Expressions typically used in such a case are 'under such conditions', 'given that' or 'in these circumstances'. The *counter-argument* refers to a content which raises a counter-position to the datum–claim relationship, and it is often signalled by 'but' or 'however'. In the present example a counter-argument would be that with a decrease in nuclear arms there would be an increased need for conventional forces.

The unit of analysis in the Toulmin model is the single assertion. Applying it to our protocol analysis, we made two assumptions which extended the model to cover argument structures longer than one statement. One assumption was that the claim of one assertion could serve as the datum of another assertion. The second assumption was that backing could consist of datum–claim assertions. These two assumptions thus permitted us to delineate argument chains (cf. Voss, Tyler and Yengo, 1983).

While the adaptation of the Toulmin model constituted a significant step in the protocol analysis effort, it also became apparent that one thing the Toulmin-type analysis did not do is capture the problem solving nature of the protocol. Furthermore, reading of the protocols made it clear that the solution was being driven by use of general problem solving strategies. In order to capture this, we viewed the protocols in terms of goals and subgoals and examined them in relation to the strategies used to accomplish the goals. What became apparent from this analysis is that, in solving ill-structured problems, the solution process was driven by a problem solving control structure and an argument or reasoning structure which was subordinate to and driven by the problem solving structure. Moreover, the strategies employed in the solving of ill-structured problems were found to be largely those described by Newell (1980) as weak problem solving methods, for example: analogy; generate and test; means–ends analysis; decomposition; and problem conversion.

Given our experience in the analysis of protocols generated in the solving of ill-structured problems, three conclusions regarding how much analyses should be conducted may be stated. These conclusions do not constitute a formal system; nor can we even state that there is a single way to analyse. Yet the conclusions seem to be warranted.

Firstly, the analysis of protocols collected in relation to the solving of ill-structured problems must be *model driven*. By model driven we mean that the analyser needs to make some basic assumption about the model of protocol structure. The protocol contents do not 'jump out' at the analyser, clearly indicating the structure and content organization. This is an extremely important point. When individuals collect a protocol and then ask how to analyse it, they often expect that a magical coding system can be employed which makes the cogent components obvious.

A question then that may be raised is how the model of protocol structure should be developed. The answer is that as a starting point the investigator should look at the goals of the study. Sometimes the investigator may want the protocol to provide nothing more than an answer to a question. In this case the analysis may be relatively effortless, although we have observed individuals over-analysing the protocols, attempting to squeeze out information irrelevant to the issue at hand. At other times individuals may want to develop a highly detailed analysis of structure and content. This goal requires a detailed exposition of the model. Such a process, moreover, is likely to be iterative, proceeding until one believes the structure and contents are successfully captured. In fact, the need to be iterative is more the rule than the exception.

Secondly, *reliability* is of course an important issue. One needs to be able to develop a coding system which permits analysis by two or more individuals to yield equivalent outcomes. To accomplish this task we have found that the best procedure is to structure the analysis as much as possible into basic categorizations and rules. This is also an iterative procedure in that categorizations and rules need to be generated until the contents and structure are appropriately and hopefully sufficiently described. When one is finally satisfied that the coding system is well articulated, then reliability may be established. This is done by having two or more individuals analyse a large sample of protocol contents. Providing training or practice to individuals naive to the coding system is not uncommon, with reliability checks being made after such training.

Thirdly, whenever publishing work related to protocol analysis, the reader should be provided with an *original protocol* or segments thereof as well as the analysis of the protocol, so that the reader may follow the logic (or the lack thereof) of the protocol analysis. If it is not feasible to print such an account, then an address should be provided to which the reader can write in order to obtain copies of the original protocols and the analyses thereof. This is important because what we do not need in the field of protocol analysis is an increasing multiplicity of protocol analyses by which the reader must accept on faith what was done. Such a state of affairs will destroy the scientific credibility of the entire endeavour.

Taking into account these three principles, the general conclusions are that the analysis of protocols in the context of the solving of ill-structured problems is model driven, a fact that makes it incumbent upon the investigator to think about the nature of the questions that are being addressed. In addition, once a model is determined that is useful, the investigator must maintain the criteria of reliability and communicability.

Empirical example

A protocol of the Voss et al. (1983) study is presented below. The protocol was generated by a US expert on Soviet Union affairs who was responding to the question of how he would improve crop production in the Soviet Union if he were head of the Ministry of Agriculture of that country. The whole protocol is reproduced so that we can see the extent of integration and elaboration of the respondent's problem solving.

I think that as minister of agriculture, one has to start out with the realization that there are certain kinds of special agriculture constraints within which you are going to work. The first one, the most obvious one, is that by almost every count only 10 per cent of the land in the Soviet Union is arable. This is normally what is called the blackland in the Ukraine and surrounding areas. And secondly, even in that arable 10 per cent of the total land surface, you still have climate for instance, over which you have no direct control. So that is sort of the overall parameter in which we are working.

Now, we have traditionally used in the Soviet Union three kinds of policies to increase agricultural production. Of course, agricultural production has been our Achilles' heel and something that we have inherited from the time the tsars freed the serfs. Even before then, the agricultural production was low because historically the aristocracy had no need to fend for itself, as it turned to the tsar for its support and hence never, like the English aristocracy for instance, introduced modern methods of fertilization, never went to enclosures or consolidations of lands, never experimented with crop rotation. That was passed on to the peasants and throughout the period when the peasants had been freed to do what they willed with the land. They are responding with the old, rather inefficient ways. At any rate, we have had three different ways by which we have tried to increase agricultural production.

The first one might be labelled 'exhortation'. The Soviet approach to agricultural production is to mount campaigns continually to call for more effort on the part of the peasants and agricultural workers, and to put more effort into their labour activities for agricultural production. Those things are mounted periodically. Quite frankly, I think that they are a waste of time and energy and they really, as minister of agriculture I must say, that they really do nothing more than give the party a sense of false importance, because it is normally incumbent upon the party to develop these ideological indoctrination campaigns and the notion of mind over matter, in this case, has not paid off; and it leaves the party with the belief that ideological, and if you will excuse the term, spiritual policies can overcome objective limitations. So, I would not emphasize exhortation very much.

It seems to me that the second way that we traditionally go about trying to increase agricultural production is through constant reorganization that leads to confusion, that leads to mismanagement and that has forced a mind set upon the peasant agricultural worker of sort of laying back and waiting because this too will also pass. We have gone through collectives, state farms, and machine tractor stations. Our latest attempt at reorganization – which has knocked down, by the way, the number of collectives from about 250 000 to 30 000 in the last five years – is through the development of what are called agroindustrial complexes, in which the former collective farmer becomes a wage earner.

So, I think we have to tend to the nature of agricultural production. I want to say one thing, and I have to recognize that this is clear as day, and that is that in all of these cases more or less except for stringent ideological periods we have always allowed the private crop to exist even though we take it to be a much more primitive, less historically progressive form of agricultural production. We must realize that in terms of our food staples, even until today, roughly 40 per cent of the food staples are grown on the private plots.

The third thing that we have done – and this is where I would like to start off in terms of turning around agricultural production – the third thing we have done is we have tried to mechanize, and I want to use that in the broad sense because it is not the word I want, we have tried to mechanize industrial production. Not just mechanize it but also introduce scientific advances in Soviet production.

I think as a starting point as minister of agriculture, my first aim would be to get monies to invest in this further mechanization and further application of scientific techniques of agriculture, to agriculture situations. Even though we have mechanized to some extent, it has been a rather crude form of mechanization. It has been rather low level. It is not coherent, it is not consistent, it is – we have the same old problem that we, if we develop tractors or we produce tractors, we produce a thousand tractors, we have no parts to service them when they break down. We do not have adequate transportation supplies or transportation networks to carry the product we do have to the urban markets. We have been woefully lacking in a methodical application of fertilizers to our agricultural sectors in society. We are much more like a Third World than an industrial world in terms of the lack of use of fertilization. We still do not have very scientific management in terms of crop rotation, and because of all this we still have a rather labour intensive agricultural production system and therefore production per unit is very marginal.

First of all, what I would like to do is to – I would have to fight very strongly in the party and the government – to redirect the investment ration going to agriculture over heavy industry and even light industry in the way it has been in the past. Though we have in the last ten years shifted investment politics so that more and more is coming into agriculture and away from industrial production *per se*, it still is not anywhere near the break even point, even though for both international political and domestic reasons, agriculture is our Achilles' heel. If we simply do not produce enough we will become more and more vulnerable to dependency upon the West for agricultural production and we will, if we do not have enough foodstuffs internally, develop a more unstable regime. There will be lack of support. We have developed a programme where the support from the people is going to stem at least in some basic way from demand satisfaction, and yet we have not been able to satisfy a lot of the basic food demands of large parts of our population.

So, I would first have to fight in decision making circles, to once and for all recognize that the construction of socialism is the construction of an entire society that is self-sufficient and does not have to depend upon especially potential adversaries for crucial parts of its basic resources. That means that we have a high enough industrial base, we have the war technology equivalent to the West, we must now redirect in a major way our investment policy towards agriculture, towards mechanization, towards the infrastructure around mechanization, towards the transportation programme, towards the plastic bag programme so that whenever the damn fertilizer is packaged it does not sit out in the lot as it does. We lose one-half of our fertilizers because it rains on paper packages. What I mean by infrastructure, there is a whole series of secondary enterprises that we have to make. Secondly, we have to develop an education programme among the agricultural workers to teach them the more rational use of mechanization, mechanized planting and harvesting and fertilizer and crop rotation. Even in this day and age it's shocking how little they know and how backward many of our farmers are. As minister of agriculture, I would like to say as an aside, since I probably will be defecting to the West with the next ballet, that I blame the party for this. The party has always insisted that the management of state farms and even the collectives be people who have strong party credentials and who, quite frankly, do not know anything about agriculture. So, I would like to see the development of a special institute that trains managers of agricultural enterprises and trains them in the most up-to-date, modern techniques. Even if we start without investment policy, we start to reap the benefits of fertilizing and mechanization if we have administrators in these three kinds of farms: we have now the agroindustrial enterprises, which are becoming the largest; the state farms; and the smaller and smaller number of collectives. If we do not have the right agricultural managers, all the most modern techniques and methods of farming will go out the window.

The second thing that I must do is to raise, rather dramatically, the wage levels of the agricultural worker. Ideology aside, and I want to be pragmatic for a minute, what we have is one hell of a large agricultural working class. We can call them collective farmers, we can call them state farmers, but there, it is an agricultural working class. And it compares shockingly low in terms of wages, in terms of security, in terms of insurance, in terms of welfare benefits, in terms of living conditions. It is like a second class, a lower class, an underclass compared with the urbanized working class in our country. We are not going to get anywhere in terms of agricultural production until we, the state, show them that we consider them equal citizens to the urban proletariat and we treat them equally in terms of our service, welfare, insurance and wage policies. Again, this is going to rankle with the ideological facts of those people in the party who for some reason see agricultural production as a free, as a traditional kind of production, and I guess we would like to make synthetic foods so they would not have to have farmers. But, to deal with the problem so that we do not increase our vulnerability, our dependency upon the West, we are simply going to have to raise the agricultural worker to the same level and bring him in as a full citizen, both participating in policies the same as our other citizens and also sharing the distribution of goodies and rewards in our society to the same extent.

The third thing that I would do would be to work out a system whereby the private plots are not considered a temporary historical phase but are an integral part of our agricultural system. Whether we like it or not, that is where we get a lot of our foodstuffs, and I think that we could work it into our system so that the agricultural, agroindustrial enterprises we are now calling the private lands could be given to those farmers who are most productive as an incentive to work even harder for the agroindustrial enterprise. As well, I think we need – maybe I mentioned it before but I am going to go over it again – as well, I think we need strong investment, not only in the day-to-day things that increase production, we also need more investment in research and technology. So that is one area to deal with.

The second area that I think that we have to deal with is the question of what are the marginal payoffs for trying to increase the amount of arable land. I think that by doing a series of studies we can identify those lands where a massive irrigation would bring them up almost to the productive level of the blacklands, and I would target especially those where just moderate irrigation or little irrigation would be needed to bring them up to such a level of production and I would develop a very, very extensive irrigation network for those lands. I think irrigation is a major problem that we really have not dealt with adequately, sufficiently, coherently, and in a centralized manner, believe it or not.

The third area that I think we have to think about is not only the private plots, but also the use of the private market as a mechanism, as an incentive mechanism for further agricultural production. Frankly, right now, a farmer that works on a collective and has a little private plot on the side and sells produce privately in the market makes more from the little bit of tilling of the private plot and the sales on the market than he does from his full day's work on the collective. If we are going to get rid of this private notion of agriculture, then we have to make collective work much more rewarding, even if it means further subsidization by giving inflatably high, artificially high prices to our collectives, to the state farm workers, to the agroindustrial enterprises, to those workers and subsidized foodstuffs. We have one hell of a problem because what we have been doing is (given how low the productivity is per person) we have been paying them wages – even they are low by urban working class standards – we have been paying them wages that are higher than the prices that we get for the food when we sell it to our people in the urban areas. We have been subsidizing our whole food programme to the tune of 20 or 30 per cent. We have to increase that subsidy if we want to get that production up to the point where at some point we would not need a subsidy at all.

As previously noted, our model assumed that the protocols had two structures, a general problem solving structure and a reasoning structure, the former being assumed to 'drive' the reasoning structure. Table 6.1 presents the operators used in reference to each of these structures. An *operator* here is a link between statements; for example, 'Historically, the aristocracy had no need to fend for itself' is given as a reason (RREA) for 'Agricultural production (being) low'. The first three G operators listed in table 6.1 are the basic problem solving operators and are self-explanatory. The GIPS operator was applied when the solver represents the problem in relation to how it is to be solved. The GSUP operator was applied when a subproblem or constraint had already been identified, and the GEVA operator was applied in reference to specific solutions which are accepted or rejected.

Table 6.1   *Operators of the problem solving and reasoning structures*

Problem solving operators (G Structure)		Reasoning structure operators (R structure)	
GCON	State constraint	RARG	State argument
GSUB	State subproblem	RSAS	State assertion
GSOL	State solution	RFAC	State fact
GIPS	Interpret problem statement	RPSC	Present specific case
GSUP	Provide support	RREA	State reason
GEVA	Evaluate	ROUT	State outcome
GSUM	Summarize	RCOM	Compare and/or contrast
		RELA	Elaborate and/or clarify
		RCON	State conclusion
		RQUA	State qualifier

The most cogent operator of the R structure is that of stating an argument (RARG), which frequently is a stated subproblem or constraint. The use of other operators then follows, including RSAS, which also involves statement of an argument but the argument is not part of the problem solving structure. The RFAC, RPSC and RREA operators are used to support a previous statement, while the ROUT operator is used when an outcome of a previously stated action is described. The RCOM and the RELA operators are self-evident, while the RCON operator is used in stating a conclusion, which in turn usually ends a line of argument. The RQUA operator produces a qualification of the preceding statement.

Given the above operators, the protocol analysis began with segmentation of the protocol into *idea units*, with each unit typically consisting of one sentence. Following segmentation, our version of the problem behaviour graph was constructed. This was done by determining the operator that applied as the solver moved from one

Table 6.2   *Contents of analysed protocol of box 1*

1 GIPS

(RARG) Historically, agriculture has been a problem in the Soviet Union

(RFAC) Problem has been inherited from the time the tsars freed the serfs

(RFAC) Agricultural production was low even before then

    (RREA) Historically, the aristocracy had no need to fend for itself

    (RCOM) Was not like English aristocracy

        (RPSC)   Never introduced modern methods of fertilization

        (RPSC)   Never went to enclosures or consolidation of land

        (RPSC)   Never experimented with crop rotation

(RFAC) Agriculture problem was passed on to peasants so they could do
what they willed with the land

    (ROUT) They responded with old, inefficient ways

(RFAC) USSR had three different policies to increase agricultural production

    (RPSC)   Exhortation

        (RELA)   Campaign for more effort on the part of the peasants

        (RCON)   Was waste of time and energy

            (RREA)   Only gave the party a sense of false importance

(RREA) It is incumbent upon the party to develop these campaigns (but they haven't paid off)

(RREA) Party believes that ideological policies can overcome objective limitations

(RCON) I would not use exhortation

(RPSC) Reorganization

(ROUT) Leads to confusion, mismanagement, makes peasants laid back

(RPSC) Reorganized collective state farms, machine tractor stations

(RPSC) Now have agroindustrial complexes, reducing number of collectives and making farmer a wage earner

(RQUA) Have always allowed private crops to exist

(RQUA) Except in astringent ideological periods

(RELA) It is taken to be a more primitive form of production

(RFAC) Private crops account for 40 per cent of food staples

(RPSC) Mechanization

(RCON) This is where I would start my solution

(RELA) Have tried to mechanize agricultural production more

(RELA) Tried to introduce scientific advances in agricultural production

Table 6.3   *Contents of analysed protocol of boxes II, III and IV*

II GEVA

(RARG) Mechanization low level, crude, inconsistent

    (RPSC) If we make tractors, then we have no repair parts

    (RPSC) Inadequate transportation supplies

    (RPSC) Inadequate transportation networks to carry produce to market

    (RPSC) Woefully lacking in methodical application of fertilizers

        (RCOM) More like a Third World country in application of fertilizer

    (RPSC) No scientific management of crop rotation

    (ROUT) Because of all this, we have labour intensive system

        (ROUT) Production per unit is very marginal

    (RSAS) Would have to fight to redirect investment into agriculture over heavy and light industry

        (RQUA) Over last ten years investment policies have shifted to agriculture more

        (RQUA) Though still not near break even point

            (RQUA) Though internationally, politically, and domestically, agriculture is Achilles' heel

        (RREA) If not enough produced, will become more dependent on West

        (RREA) If not enough produced, will develop less stable regime

            (ROUT) Will lack support

(RREA) Have developed programme where support from people comes from demand satisfaction

(RQUA) But still haven't been able to satisfy force demands

III GEVA

(RARG) Support infrastructure around mechanization

(RPSC) Support transportation programme

(RPSC) Support plastic bag programme

(RFAC) Lose when it sits out in paper bags

(RELA) Support series of secondary enterprises

IV GEVA

(RARG) Need to teach agriculture workers rational use of mechanization

(RELA) Mechanized planting, harvesting, fertilizing and crop rotation

(RREA) Farmers are backward

(RREA) Blame the party for this

(RREA) Management are people that have strong party credentials, and don't know about agriculture

(RCON) Need special institute to train managers

(RREA) If don't have right managers, investment in agriculture useless

Table 6.4 *Contents of analysed protocol of boxes V, VI, VII and VIII*

V GEVA

(RARG) Large agricultural working class which compares low in wages, security, insurance, welfare benefits, and living conditions

(RELA) Can call them collective farmers or state farmers, it is the working class

(RCOM) It's like a lower class compared with the urban working class

(RSAS) Won't get anywhere in terms of production until the state shows them that we consider them equal citizens to the urban proletariat

(ROUT) This will rankle some party members

(RREA) Because they see agricultural production as a free and traditional kind of production

(RCON) But we have to do it

(RREA) So we don't increase our vulnerability to and dependency on the West

(RCON) Simply going to have to raise agricultural worker to same level and make him full citizen sharing in the distribution of rewards

VI GEVA

(RARG) Make private plots integral part of system

(RREA) Because it is where a lot of foodstuffs come from

(RPSC) Use as incentive for farmers to work harder

VII GEVA

(RARG) Identify lands to irrigate

(RREA) To raise levels of production

(RELA) Target areas where little to moderate irrigation would be needed

(RELA) Develop extensive irrigation system there

(RREA) Irrigation is major problem not dealt with adequately, sufficiently, coherently, or in centralized manner

VIII GEVA

(RARG) Have to make collectives more rewarding

(RREA) Now worker gets more from private plot than whole day's work on collective

(RPSC) Subsidize collectives to give artificially high prices

(RREA) To get rid of private notion of agriculture

(RFAC) Wages paid are lower than urban working class

(RFAC) Have been paying wages higher than what is received from food

(RFAC) Have been subsidizing 20–30 per cent

(RCON) Have to subsidize until production is up enough not to have to subsidize idea unit to the next, the idea units thus representing the respective states of the problem as the solver proceeds along the solution path. The analysis of the protocol in terms of the states and operators is provided by the problem behaviour graph presented in figure 6.1. The reader may compare the protocol, as presented in paragraph form, with figure 6.1. The protocol begins with a statement of constraints, followed by interpretation of the problem statement. The problem is represented in GSUB and the solution is presented GSOL. The reader is asked to note that the contents of the boxes that have brackets are broken down and presented in tables 6.2–6.4. The boxes containing brackets are denoted by roman numerals I–VIII. One other aspect of the protocols is that a dashed line describes an implicit statement, as indicated by the contents.

Advantages and disadvantages

A theoretical issue that may be raised is how the protocol contents should be interpreted. To what extent, for example, do the contents reflect the knowledge structures of the individual? We have gathered data germane to this question, and the most reasonable answer is that the protocol contents indicate how the individual would solve the problem at that particular time in that context. Two results provide for a more complete answer.

We did request that a few experts return approximately two weeks after their initial session. We asked one to solve the problem again and the other to recall his solution. What we found is that the solutions were shorter, but that they maintained the general structure. What was different in content, but not structure, was the argument development. The experts, for instance, did not remember very well what they had provided as examples.

In another case an expert on Central America agreed to attend a graduate seminar, at which time he was given two problems and asked to provide a 'think aloud' protocol to each of them in the presence of the class. He received one problem and provided a solution, then received the second problem and provided a solution. One of the problems essentially asked him to suggest a new US policy regarding El Salvador if he were a US State Department official. (This was before the US preoccupation with Nicaragua.) He began with the solution phase, basically without the verbalization of a representation phase. When he had finished, I asked him why he did not discuss the causes of the problem and related matters. He immediately answered that, first of all, from the problem statement one could infer that the current policy was not working because the problem asked for a change. Secondly, he pointed out that he had

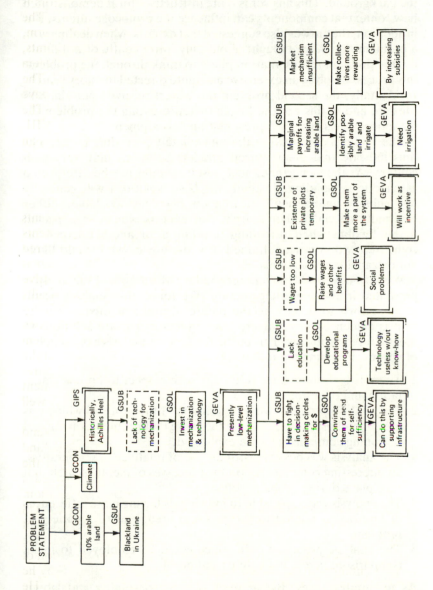

Figure 6.1   *Graph of the protocol presented in text*

been giving much thought to the problem, having appeared on TV and given speeches on the issue, and he felt he was well aware of the background. This answer is quite instructive, for it demonstrated how contextual components can influence the protocol contents. But in addition, the answer also suggested that experts, when dealing with a problem they have thought about only infrequently or not at all, use the problem representation phase to think through the problem; this process involves an extensive and quite directed memory search. Incidentally, the second problem this expert received pertained to Mexico, and in this case he began by representing the problem via the more typical type of representation development.

The findings described in the immediately preceding paragraphs thus indicate that ill-structured problem solutions may vary with context. At the same time, such results should not be interpreted as chaotic responding. Instead, the basic solutions will generally not change unless new information becomes available, either externally or via further search. But experts would be expected to be flexible when providing a solution to another expert as compared with a novice. Indeed, it is the novice who would likely not be capable of such flexibility.

We turn now to the advantages and disadvantages of the analysis presented in the preceding section. We found this analysis useful in our efforts to determine the nature of problem solving activity as it is evidenced in relatively long protocols that are solutions to ill-structured problems. This particular type of analysis has a number of virtues, including the following:

1   There is high inter-rater reliability with respect to both segmentation and operator classification.
2   The analysis provided for a description of the protocol which was meaningful psychologically, in the sense that problem solving and reasoning components were explicated.
3   The analysis was possible with the use of relatively few operators, an interesting commentary on the processes of mental search that take place during problem solving.
4   The analysis was applicable to individuals having large differences of knowledge related to the problem area, and to a variety of problems.
5   The analysis produced data which could be employed to make comparisons across individuals and problems.

As to disadvantages, the analysis is time consuming and labour intensive, especially in the earlier phases. In addition, the analysis provides one type of data, and the investigator may readily want to look at the protocol in different ways to address other questions.

It is important to reiterate a point made earlier in this chapter, namely, that the presented analysis is appropriate only if the goals of the investigator are essentially the same as we had in developing the analysis. To illustrate this point, we recently completed some work in which we collected protocols that were answers to questions in economics (Voss et al., in press). The participants were naive (having no formal training in economics) or novices (having had one or two courses in economics). One question asked for factors that can influence a change in interest rates. One person began his response with: 'I guess, from an idealistic viewpoint, I look at interest rates as the cost of money. Again, it's a supply and demand type of thing. If money is in short supply, it costs more.' In that particular study we were interested not in providing the sentence-by-sentence analysis of a protocol, as described in this chapter, but in specific questions such as 'Did the individual transform the problem', 'Did the individual use any type of rule at arriving at an answer?' Thus our purpose led us to a different type of analysis. Of particular interest is the fact that it is often necessary to study the protocols in order to consider the nature of the model that will provide for extracting the most interesting information. Our experience suggests that, as stated, protocol analysis is model driven and serves not as an end in itself but as a tool to address issues of interest to the investigator.

Note

Preparation of this chapter was supported by a grant of the Office of Educational Research and Improvement of the United States Department of Education for establishing the Center for the Study of Learning at the Learning Research and Development Center of the University of Pittsburgh. The viewpoints expressed in this chapter are not necessarily those of any of these organizations.

7

Narrative structures in social explanation

Mary M. Gergen

In this chapter, I would like to present the idea of accounts as *stories* – not random sequences of action and reaction, but coherent unfolding narratives of human conduct. The idea of looking for narrative structures has a long history in literary theory, of course, and even in the social sciences it can be traced back to the early 1920s (and specifically to the seminal ideas of the Russian folklorist, Vladimir Propp). Nevertheless social psychology has been somewhat immune to this way of thinking, and we can start by having a look at why this might be so.

Theoretical background

The origin of the study of social explanation in social psychology was based on the notion that explanations developed out of a common-sense psychology. As conceptualized by Fritz Heider (1958), everyday explanations were integral to the ordinary business of getting along with others. Heider's ideas were later pressed into conformity with the dominant experimental paradigm in social psychology, and what had been a rather loosely construed approach to everyday explanation became reconstructed as tightly organized theories of cognitive process (Antaki and Lewis, 1986). As fitted the laboratory mode of operation, studies of 'causal attribution' became decontextualized simulacra of everyday life, bound only to the brief time frame of an experiment. Variables were developed that classified explanations into the internal versus external and actor versus observer cells. The area of attribution theory flourished, and helped cognitive social psychology achieve its present hegemony. From the 1960s to the present, attribution research has exerted a powerful influence on the field (cf. Kelley, 1973; Jones and Nisbett, 1971; Ross, 1977; and see chapter 3 in this book).

Criticisms of the experimental paradigm and the associated array of mechanistic theories have been widely voiced in recent years. One particularly relevant line of criticism has challenged the ahistorical and decontextualized nature of traditional inquiry (Gergen, 1982). Such inquiry remains generally blind to temporal transformation in phenomena, and it is removed from concerns with the sociocultural contexts of the people under study. A number of efforts to surmount these problems are contained in the book *Historical Social Psychology* (Gergen and Gergen, 1984). This contains a variety of efforts by European and American scholars to analyse cross-time or diachronic social processes. This attempt to develop a contextually embedded form of analysis has led in a variety of directions, one of the most important of which is inquiry into everyday explanations of human action.

The focus of this chapter is on the analysis of narrative explanation. For many scholars narratives are seen as providing a sense of coherence and directionality in one's life (cf. Cohler, 1979; Kohli, 1981). As the psychologists de Waele and Harré (1979) have indicated, life events are made intelligible by locating them in a sequence or 'unfolding process'. If events are not tied to a larger story they lose significance. So, for example, if someone mentions that it snowed 10 inches on 14 February, this remains an inconsequential fact until connected to a story about one's efforts to travel that day to meet a loved one and the end of the relationship precipitated by the failed tryst. Narratives are often shaped so that culturally valued activities and endpoints are highlighted for self and others. Events that are encapsulated in stories are presumed to have some significance in the lives of the characters and those who tell and hear the story. For example, Rosaldo (1986) has suggested that the anthropologist may gain an understanding of which activities have great importance to the people by listening to the stories that are told and retold among themselves. Joseph Campbell (1956) has suggested that the most basic myth for humankind, or 'monomyth' as he calls it, is the story of the hero who overcomes obstacles to reach some transcendent goal. A similar claim for a universal plot was made by Lord Raglan (1956). While these myths are framed out

---

[1]One might well question to what extent the requirements of what defines a well-made story or a universal plot are not influences by androcentric forces in society. For example, metaphorically speaking, the ideal Western narrative follows the dramatic form of the prototypical male performance during intercourse – linear motion, with increasing intensity, directed to an endpoint, with a climax and fade-out. One might envision a prototypical narrative form based on female sexuality that might be less goal directed and more episodic and have less emphasis on a climax and more on the foreplay, that is, the process of the interactions.

of a peculiarly male perspective (the lone male hero leaves home), the basic story is a well-known framework frequently employed by people to lend meaning to their lives.[1]

The concern with narrative account of human action is shared by scholars throughout the social sciences and humanities. The social significance of myths, legends and tribal stories has been a focal consideration for folklorists (Propp, 1968; Young, 1987), anthropologists (Campbell, 1956; Rosaldo, 1986), political theorists (Tololyan, in press), psychiatric investigators (Spence, 1982), developmental psychologists (Bettelheim, 1976) and philosophers (MacIntyre, 1981). Of particular relevance, a number of investigators have discussed the ways in which narratives define reality for groups of people. Narratives are seen as critical to the ways in which people understand themselves and their lives, past and present, and how their futures might be (Sarbin, 1986; White, 1980). Tololyan (in press), for example, has analysed the lives of Armenian terrorists; he argues that their plans and activities are the result of being imbued in a cultural tradition where the stories, songs and religious litanies create heroes of young martyrs who die fighting for the honour of the Armenian people. Tololyan believes that the culture's narratives are primary factors in promoting present day terrorist activity among the Armenians.

Our own line of inquiry has extended this concern with the importance of narratives in people's constructions of their lives (Gergen and Gergen, 1983). From our perspective, traditions of story telling, dramatic performance, literature and the like have generated a range of culturally shared forms of emplotment, or narrative forms. When the individual attempts to understand him/herself, these culturally embedded forms furnish a repertoire of sense making devices. It is through embedding one's actions within one or more of these forms that one's actions take on meaning; they belong to a person with a certain past, heading in a certain direction, and with a future that will represent an extension of this past (Gergen and Gergen, in press). Yet, as we have also proposed, narrative constructions are not the mere product of cultural history. The particular form that they acquire for any person is an outgrowth of the social relationships in which one is currently embedded (Gergen, in press). One's narratives typically include the positioning of others in relationship to self. Without their particular functioning within the narrative, one's own position or identity is threatened. Likewise, others' self-narratives contain constructions of other individuals embedded in their mutual social surrounds. Thus, the narrative constructions within a community of interlocutors may be viewed as a communal achievement. Finally, these narrative constructions appear to have a variety of functions over and above rendering the individual's actions sensible both to him/herself and others. For example, narratives may reinforce or alter others' self-perceptions. Being a worthy friend, for instance, must be supported in the narratives of one's friends. Other functions of the narrative will be treated later.

Individuals will typically possess a variety of narrative potentials, which may variously be deployed as occasions permit or invite. Narrative presentations may thus be used to signal a future set of actions, to indicate positive potentials, to invite others' nurturance, to generate a sense of drama, and so on. In each case, these social functions are prepared by the accumulated lore of cultural history.

Theoretical analysis of narrative lines
A certain number of our analyses have been concerned with the way in which narratives structure individual lives. However, to carry out such an analysis a preliminary elucidation of the major narrative forms available within the culture is required. A narrative that is nonsensical to its listeners is a failure. In order to be intelligible a narrative must conform to certain rules of what constitutes a reasonable story within the culture. As our analyses have shown, basic to a good story in Western culture is the establishment of a valued *endpoint* or goal toward which the action in the story is directed. For example, stories about winning the lottery, being promoted or getting married might all be seen as having positively valued endpoints, while those about breaking an arm, losing a bet or separating from a friend may all be seen as having negatively valued endpoints. A coherent narrative line is achieved by selecting and ordering events around this endpoint. Events not influencing the course of action related to the endpoint are usually not included in the well-made story.

Events within the narrative abide by culturally prescribed notions of order. Often they are arranged chronologically. If events are randomly described, the narrative may not be seen as credible (Lippman, 1986). Events in the story are also described evaluatively with respect to the goal or endpoint. Events that lead toward the achievement of a valued endpoint are positively evaluated, and those that lead away from it are negatively evaluated. Other subtle rules of what constitutes a realistic narrative have been elaborated but are unnecessary to our present purposes.

Yet these various ingredients only tell us what is required for an account to possess a storied sense. Still required is a framework for describing how these various components are organized to yield the range of plots which we today consider sensible or intelligible. For example, if someone were to describe her life story as one in which each positive event was followed by a negative event, and vice versa, the narrative would be viewed with suspicion by contemporary listeners. Such a story would seem unreasonable by current social standards, as would a story in which one wonderful success followed unceasingly upon the preceding one, or one catastrophe followed upon another without end. How then, are we to characterize the major narrative forms derived from our cultural heritage?

Some help in answering this question is furnished by traditional accounts of emplotment. The early Greeks formulated the basic difference between the tragedy and the comedy. Tragedy involved the sudden demise of a noble person through the elaboration of some 'tragic flaw' that this person possessed. Oedipus and Antigone were both tragic characters in the Greek sense. Comedy was often about less socially elevated persons. After confrontation by the characters with various mishaps, the plot was resolved with a 'happy ending'. Aristophanes' play, *Lysistrata*, is exemplary. While the terms 'tragedy' and 'comedy' remain vital today, the concepts have also undergone shifts in meaning. Today we tend to think of tragedy as involving a sad ending, regardless of how it has occurred, and comedy as being humorous, usually with a happy ending. The social class origins of the characters is also less relevant in contemporary drama but not entirely erased, as tragic characters are generally more respectable than comic ones.

Northrup Frye (1957) has provided a more elaborate theoretical summary of narrative forms. He describes four basic forms of narrative related to the cyclical changes of the seasons. Spring is represented by the comedy. Here we find a challenge or threat which is overcome to yield social harmony and a happy ending, as in the Greek formulation. Summer is the season of the romance, defined as a series of episodes within which a major protagonist is faced with numerous challenges and threats. These obstacles are overcome, and the protagonist emerges victorious. The autumn dramatic form is the tragedy. The happy days of summer are overturned, as the approach of winter and the death of living things is forewarned. The tragic form is similar to the ancient Greek one. Winter is the season of satire. Beyond hope, these narratives are the representations of unrealized expectations and dreams.

From the present perspective, the traditional typologies of narrative form seem unsystematic. While they do pinpoint traditions of importance, the types have either little relationship with each other or, in the case of Frye, the relationship through seasonal variations seems more poetic than analytic. In the earlier analysis, narrative construction was said to require the establishment of an endpoint or a goal, with events selected so as to make the goal more or less probable. In this context it is possible to view each event in a narrative as moving through a two-dimensional evaluative space. For example, as one succeeds in approaching the valued goal over time, the story becomes more positive; as one goes through a series of negatively valued steps toward a negative endpoint, the story moves in a negative direction. All narrative plots may be converted from a story form to a linear form with respect to their evaluative shifts over time. These linear forms are called *story lines*. Examples of these are shown in a later section.

By conceptualizing narratives in this way, one can begin to see variations in narrative form, from the rudimentary to the more complex. On the simple level, consider the *stability narrative*. This narrative is characterized by an unchanging story line with respect to the evaluative dimension. As depicted in figure 7.1, the stability narrative (N_1 in the figure) might be, for example, the story of a highly successful business trip where everything was perfect from start to finish. The reverse narrative, in which nothing went right, would be represented by a negative stability narrative N_2).

The stability narratives may be contrasted with two other simple narratives. Within these, the narrative may be structured in such a way that things get continuously better or worse over time. When the events become increasingly positive over time, the narrative may be called a *progressive narrative*. When they are increasingly negative over time, it may be called a *regressive narrative* (see figure 7.2). The individual who describes a rise from mailroom clerk to president of the corporation, with no detours or set-backs, would be telling a *progressive narrative*. Conversely, the once wealthy heiress

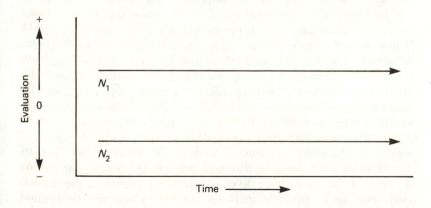

Figure 7.1   *Stability narratives*

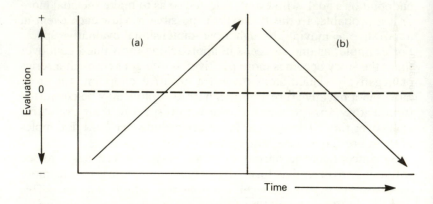

Figure 7.2　*(a) Progressive and (b) regressive narrative forms*

who describes a steady procession of events leading to the gutter is constructing a regressive narrative.

These three prototypes – stability, progressive and regressive – exhaust the basic vocabulary of possible narrative projections over time. They are the rudimentary forms from which more complex variations are constructed. The classic forms described above, such as the Greek tragedy and comedy, are derived from these three simple forms. The tragedy is the story of the rapid downfall of one who holds a high place in society. A positively evaluated stability narrative is followed by a rapidly descending regressive narrative. The comedy begins with a regressive narrative followed by a progressive one. That is, life events become problematic and then, through a succession of events, happiness is finally achieved. When a progressive narrative is followed by a positive stability narrative, the well-known fairytale ending of 'happily-ever-after' is obtained. The romance, usually the tale of a heroic character who overcomes obstacles, may be diagrammed as a series of regressive and progressive story lines. The satire, we may note, involves a particular style of depiction emphasizing ridicule or parody and is not, in fact, another type of narrative form. Figure 7.3 illustrates the narrative forms of tragedy, comedy, happily-ever-after and romance.

We may also use these graphic representations to speak to issues of dramatic tension. The way in which many people characterize their lives is flat and unexciting; others can create a sense of drama in their lives, even when events in themselves may seem to be of little intrinsic interest. The dramatic tension that shapes these experiences of life may be attributed to the type of story line followed within the self-narratives. In particular,

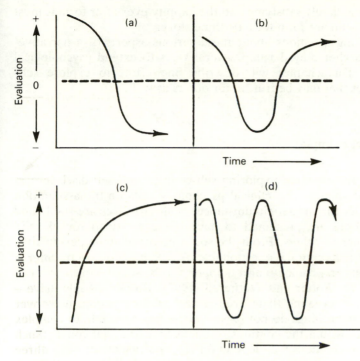

Figure 7.3 *(a) tragedy, (b) comedy, (c) happily-ever-after and (d) romantic saga*

drama is first injected into a story line by increasing the incline of the slope in either the upward or downward direction. The steeper the incline of the story line, the more sharply events change in their evaluation. This shift is, in part, responsible for increased dramatic impact. Thus, within Western culture, the stability narratives would be the least dramatic and perhaps most boring of narrative forms. The tragedy is highly compelling because of the radical shift as the regressive narrative unfolds.

A second contribution to dramatic impact can be traced to the direction of the story line. In particular, alterations in the direction of the slope line are important ingredients of dramatic tension. In this sense the comedy has dramatic power because the downward trend of the regressive narrative is, at a critical point, abruptly shifted to a progressive narrative. This point also creates a break in the emotional tension generated by the previous downward slope of the line. During the final progressive phase emotional satisfaction can be achieved, while in the tragedy this process must be delayed until the narrative is ended. Thus the comedy is most immediately satisfying and the happily-ever-after form is most soothing – an apt form for a bedtime story.

By asking questions about these various aspects of a narrative, the researcher may develop several ways to extend psychological inquiry. This chapter will describe one effort to explore self-narratives that may be fruitful for others as well.

Empirical example

Most of the research exploring self-concept and self-disclosure in social, personality and clinical psychology rests on the assumption that, under the proper circumstances, self-narratives are stable and true. People are presumed to have the capacity to reveal valid biographies to others. From the social constructionist perspective, this basic assumption is questionable. A recent critique of traditional personality psychology also supports this social constructionist perspective (Potter and Wetherell, 1987). Rather, people are not capable of revealing their 'true selves' or their actual life stories because such things do not exist. People are only able to construe their lives within the confines of linguistic and social conventions. These constructions will depend on their particular situation at the moment. The social constructionist position challenges established wisdom from a theoretical perspective. Thus, the data one gathers when collecting self-narratives are viewed not as kernels of truth about a person's life, but as temporary constructions of what seems most appropriate from the perspective of the narrator at that time. (This is not to say that the same narrative may never again be repeated, but merely that it need not be considered foundational.)

What is constrained for the narrator is the form that a narrative must take. As illustrated in the introduction to this chapter, narratives are composed of a limited vocabulary of forms. Story tellers may individuate their narratives by being more or less dramatic about various events, but even these shifts in evaluative dimensions and alterations in story line are regulated by social conventions. In the study to be reported here, college students were asked to create narrative expositions of their lives. We were interested in finding out whether there were any trends in how this group of people in late adolescence would tell the story of their lives, and also to see how consistent they were in their descriptions of their overall lives, and of various subelements of their lives. The study was also designed to experiment with a story line methodology, which will be illustrated below.

Acquisition of the data
A major purpose of the study was to explore the social constructionist view of self-narratives, the use of narrative forms among
late adolescents, and in addition the utility of a protocol developed
around the story line method of constructing a self-narrative. To
these ends, a group of 29 undergraduate students, ages 18–21,
was asked to respond to a questionnaire entitled 'Constructing the
past'. The introduction to the questionnaire stated that the study
was 'concerned with the construction of personal history – how we
look back (and ahead) on our lives and make sense of events in
relationship to each other'. In section I of the protocol respondents
were asked to recall the happiest times in their lives, and their 'most
unhappy times'. This section of the questionnaire was included so
that the students would be put in a frame of mind to think over
their pasts, and to recall the high and low points of this time. It
was preparatory to section II of the survey, in which subjects drew
a story line to describe their 'feelings of generalized well-being' from
birth to age 20+, followed by a brief description of the highest and
lowest points. An example of this appears in figure 7.4.

In section III respondents were asked to create additional story
lines reflecting their relationships with their mothers, fathers and
with their academic work, along with descriptions of the highest
and lowest points in each of these domains. The latter areas were
selected because they seemed to be aspects of students' lives that
would be central to their overall feelings of well-being. Thus,
comparisons and contrasts could be made between the various story
lines for each of the respondents. In section IV of the questionnaire,
respondents plotted their generalized feelings of well-being on two
graphs, one for the day of the study and the other for their future
life, from age 20 to beyond 80. An example of an anticipated
future graph appears in figure 7.5.

The protocols designed with the story line method proved to
be very useful in summarizing the feelings of the sample over
time. Previous research using free-form responses to open-ended
questions had proved difficult to transform into narrative forms
because of the subjective nature of the data, and the complexity
of trying to graph the narratives on to a two-dimensional space
(Gergen, 1980). In this study the respondents had accomplished
this task for the researchers.

Interpreting the data
There are several possibilities for analysing these data. Given
that the number of respondents was small, the major attempt was
to assess what types of narrative form seemed most common to

II. *Trajectory of the past.* Below you will find a grid on which you can begin with
the earliest period you can remember and draw a continuous line to the present.
This line would indicate, for each period, how you now remember your feelings
of generalized well-being. The more positive the feelings the more upward the
displacement of the 'life-line'; the more negative the feelings the more
downward the displacement.

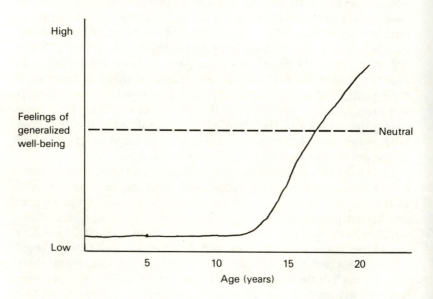

Brief description of highest point:

I didn't really begin to like myself until I was about 15 years old. I was very shy until I
entered a boarding school and became more active with other people.

Brief description of lowest point:

I was very shy. Much anger because I didn't have a 'live-in' father. I blamed father
for my being over-weight. I was very withdrawn and I had few friends my age with
whom I was close.

Figure 7.4 *Trajectory of the past (protocol section II),
and descriptions of high and low parts*

IV. *Anticipated future.* Can you now indicate briefly what you think future years may hold in terms of feelings of generalized well-being. Can you project your 'life-line' into the future?

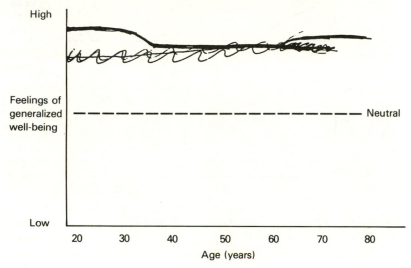

Figure 7.5   *Future trajectory of life graph*

people in the study. It was also possible to explore multiplicities of narrative forms. In addition, attention was given to questions of how well the protocol was designed for the study and where there were problems in its construction.

Many possible hypotheses were feasible when contemplating the narrative form of these story lines. One might expect that these young adults would portray themselves as part of a happily-ever-after story, having reached a happy plateau from which they will live out their lives. Or one might conjecture that the participants would characterize themselves as living out a romantic saga, overcoming one obstacle after another. Perhaps, more pessimistically, these students might see themselves as actors in a tragic drama, on the edge of a chasm, heading into a nuclear calamity. To explore this question an attempt was made to derive the average self-narrative from the story lines of their past lives. To do this, each point at

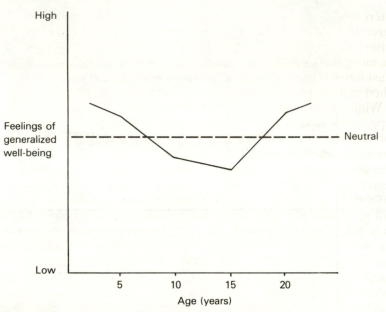

Figure 7.6   *Composite self-narrative for the sample:*
generalized well-being, birth to 20+

five-year intervals on the story line labelled 'generalized feeling of
well-being' for their lives since birth was converted to a numerical
value for each respondent. The displacement of each story line from
the neutral midpoint was computed at each five-year interval. The
resultant story line was the composite representation of all the story
lines for the sample of 29 respondents. In figure 7.6 this story line
is reproduced. As is evident, the general narrative form disclosed
by this analysis was none of those mentioned above. Rather, for
the first 20 years, the most common story line approximates the
comedy form of narrative. The basic story as revealed through this
assessment is that life was quite good as a child, but problems
occurred during adolescence, which were resolved during the college
years. The overall form averaged out to represent the typical myth
of Americans that childhood is idyllic, adolescence is a time of
turmoil, and college days are halcyon.

   In this light it is interesting to take account of the highest
and lowest points related to each of the narrative forms. As these
accounts revealed, these events were highly diverse. High points
included falling in love, travelling abroad, and finding Christ. Low
points included parents' divorcing, moving, and death of a pet. The

interesting point here is that while these young adults tended to agree that adolescence was a miserable period, the content of the misery varied greatly. This suggests that the participants seemed to be more influenced by the narrative form that prescribes how life must have been for a young adult than by any specific set of events. Their facts served to justify the preselected narrative form.

While the average student's narrative fitted the comedy proto-type, only nine of the 29 participants fully adopted the popular form. Fourteen of the respondents' story lines deviated from the composite in that they had additional hills and valleys in their narratives. The remaining six students used simpler progressive or regressive narratives, with story lines either rising or falling steadily from early childhood. In the protocol reproduced in figure 7.4, you will note that the period from birth to early teen years is described as a low stability narrative followed by a progressive narrative. As the data indicate, at least two-thirds of the respondents had some variation on the comedy form. Because there are many versions of the narrative form appropriate to Western culture, one may hypothesize that young adults have within their narrative repertoire many versions of their childhoods, which they may be able to produce if the circumstances are appropriate. This research and similar studies with young adults have indicated that projections of generalized well-being into the future show a much more consistent happily-ever-after prototype after age 25, with a regressive downturn at life's end.

As was mentioned above, the narrative form which a person uses for telling a story is selected for specific occasions or functions. Multiple narrative forms characterize an individual's story telling repertoire. We might conjecture, for example, that a narrative that is shaped as a romance, with the narrator overcoming obstacles to achieve a goal, is an attempt to present the narrator as a hero who lives in a world of treachery or danger. The listeners are expected to be enthralled and admiring of such a protagonist. The tragedy may be designed to elicit sympathy, and the comedy a companionate spirit of solidarity and harmony.

Different stimuli may bring to the fore different narrative forms. This was discovered in looking over the story lines for the sample protocol for relations with mother, father and school work (not shown here). Here we found many divergent slopes in the story lines. The miserable childhood which is depicted in the 'feelings of generalized well-being' in the past is not found in the story lines related to mother or school work. The narrative line for mother seems to be a form of comedy quite unrelated in its temporal pattern to the story line for generalized well-being, except in the resolution phase after age 15. Life with mother was fairly positive until the teenage years, and then after a strong negative period became even better than ever. This form echoes the most popular narrative form used by the sample group. The school work narrative line shows two positive stability narratives, separated by a dramatic reversal around age 10. This is a different pattern from the other three story lines.

Only in the relations with father story line is there a parallel with the generalized well-being line. Yet, when the respondent described his or her most unhappy times in the first section of the questionnaire, father is not mentioned at all. Later when describing the lowest points on the generalized well-being story line, the respondent mentions several factors, including being shy and without friends, in addition to not having a 'live-in' father (figure 7.4). The respondent also implicates his or her father in the description of low points, as he or she writes 'I blamed father for my being overweight.' In this section of the protocol, the story of childhood seems strongly focused on father. The father is made responsible for much childhood misery, including the respondent's weight. The point to be emphasized here, however, is that this rendition of childhood is simply one version among many possible. At another time and in another place the construction might be reorganized into some other form.

Within the studies in which I have been involved, the major thrust of the analyses has been to look at the narrative forms that seem preferred by the group, and to look at the diversity of forms used. It is clear from this sample that a model form was utilized, and that diversity could be found not only between group members, but also within each protocol.

It would seem that many other uses might be made of this story line methodology, depending on the purposes of the researcher. For example, in the case of a clinician looking for means of helping a client, the protocol might prove a useful starting point for assessing areas of life in which the person has described himself or herself as unhappy. In addition certain relationships might appear to be more problematic than others. In the protocol shown in figure 7.4 and 7.5 the narrative points to problems with father more than mother. The act of construing the narrative might also be looked upon as a therapeutic exercise. As Donald Spence (1982) has suggested, the central mission of the therapist and the patient is to construct a narrative of the patient's life story. The story line might be one form of endeavour for the illustrating of this agreement.

Another analysis of the individual protocol might take account of the number of reversals in the slope of the story lines and the steepness of the slopes. Respondents who deviated greatly from the average profile (figure 7.6) might be expected to perceive their lives as more dramatic and intense than the average person. In looking at the protocol presented herein (figures 7.4 and 7.5), it seems clear that the respondent views his or her past life as changing rather dramatically in generalized well-being around age 13, for example, and as becoming very stable in the 20s, with only a slight decrement after age 30.

Further research with different groups of respondents of various ages, backgrounds and interests should reveal some differences in overall self-narratives. One can envision research in which various subgroups of youth, for example, might reveal group differences in expectations concerning life satisfactions. For example, if a group of adolescents consistently perceives that well-being peaks at 18, and is downhill thereafter, the notion of delayed gratification might be very repugnant to them.

Within various social groups the 'cultural clocks' – that is, the times at which people are expected to do certain things such as marry and have children – should help formulate certain parameters for how self-narratives are shaped (Neugarten and Hagstad, 1976). Research among pre-menopausal women indicated, for example, that they had begun to formulate expectations of how their lives would be after menopause, and what they would expect to look like, feel and do for the next 20 years (Gergen, in press). These attitudes are based to a great degree on what the popular culture portrays about the older woman. With an elderly population the narrative form also seems to be influenced by the culture's beliefs about the aged. The tendency to accept a declining level of involvement and activity seemed to echo the notion of disengagement from society that often is expected of elderly people (Gergen, 1980; Gergen and Gergen, 1983).

The last portion of the protocol explored two other narrative dimensions: the feelings of generalized well-being for the day, and feelings of generalized well-being for the future life of the individual. Of course, story lines could also be created for other periods or for other aspects as well. The feelings of daily well-being could easily be analysed as to the type of narrative form it portrayed. The analysis could be useful in giving one a sense of the emotional context in which the other narratives were being constructed. The daily story line also gives a baseline for how dramatic the person may be as a story teller. A very changeable line for one day might indicate instability in other narrative lines. The story line that projects into the distant future can be analysed in terms of preferred cultural forms, of individual variation and of mental health and well-being. One protocol contained a story line that ended abruptly at 30, with the word 'dead' scrawled next to it. When asked about this story line later, the narrator said that he had had a premonition when he was younger that he would die in a car crash at that time, and so he was planning his life around this belief. Of course we cannot be certain from this story line or his explanation just what interpretation to give to this person's expectations for the future. People have multiple narrative forms about what happens in adulthood, and they are capable of drawing more than one story line, depending on the situation. For example, college students rarely include marital discord or divorce in their future life story lines, but if they were to create two or three different versions of their future story lines, some would be likely to include these rather normal but unpleasant episodes.

Advantages and disadvantages

Within traditional paradigms of psychology, the study of personality and the self stands in stark contrast to the narrative approach. Within what I will call the psychometric approach to personality, the assumption is made that people have fairly stable and predictable personalities and behavioural patterns. It is also assumed that through quantitative methods the dimensions of the personality and the self-concept can be obtained. The research is usually focused within a narrow time span, and results in data that are ahistorical and decontextualized numerical representations of the subjects. The resultant scores are then often correlated with other variables to predict behavioural tendencies. This psychometric approach relies on a natural science model of psychology, in which the basic goals of the science are the creation of universal laws and the prediction and control of people.

In contrast, the social constructionist approach assumes that people's self-narratives are social products. They are not seen as enduring, stable fixtures of a pre-existing nature, but as temporary constructions that are shaped by such important factors as literary conventions, social norms, the context of the narration and self-determined social goals. Self-narratives are not viewed in the same light as a traditional psychologist might view a personality profile. Narratives are not seen as representations of the 'real self' underlying the story. The narrativist gives up the certainty of the psychometrician by taking this perspective. While this seems to be a disadvantage, the failure of the psychometrics approach to find generalizable laws regarding the prediction of behaviour from personality traits makes the loss less significant. At base, the change from a natural science foundation to a human sciences approach is a matter of intellectual preference and conviction. But once inside the latter paradigm, the use of a narratives methodology becomes more appropriate for the study of lives.

There are potentially many ways in which to explore the narratives of lives. One of the most common approaches is to ask people to give written or oral biographies of their lives, or parts of them. A derivation of this approach is to ask for narratives that cover certain topics or periods. For example, in a study of the social explanations of the elderly (Gergen and Gergen, in press) respondents were asked to state why they were more or less involved in some activity than they used to be. In terms of analysis, written or oral narratives have as advantages being rich in detail, individualized, flexible, revealing of personal judgements of importance, targeted to sensitive areas that might be avoided otherwise, and potentially complex in structure. As disadvantages, biographies can vary greatly in their elaboration. The level of motivation, of comprehension and of verbal skills in the respondent makes a great deal of difference in how the biographies are formed. In oral biographies, especially, respondents can lose their train of thought. It is also somewhat problematic for the analyst to know how to assess the biography. It is difficult, for example, to know whether an unhappy childhood story is seen by the respondent as unhappier than an unhappy period in adolescence. The researcher must make many judgements concerning the relationships among various episodes in a biographic protocol. The biography form does not easily produce such comparisons.

This chapter has emphasized the use of the graphic story line to reveal the evaluative dimension of one's life and relationships with others. A cardinal advantage of this approach is that subjective appraisals of life events can be converted to dimensions that are quantifiable. Thus, as was demonstrated with the lives of this college sample, narratives can be compared and combined. While not designed to be a precise mathematical instrument, story lines can also reveal perceived peaks and valleys in people's lives, and their relative impact on the narrator. For example, one can tell at a glance whether parents' divorcing is now viewed as more or less painful than a bad love affair. Story lines are also useful for conducting dialogues with narrators about their lives. For therapists and counsellors, for example, the interpretation of the story lines by their authors would be potentially a very useful guide. The inclusion of questions within the protocol that ask for specific events that marked the high and low points helps to draw attention to certain critical events in the person's life, as they are now perceived.

The story line is also relatively quick and easy to fill out, and may be perceived by the respondent as an interesting and creative mode of self-expression. It is not as dependent on excellent verbal skills as biographies are. Also, it is not as threatening to the participant as filling out a questionnaire that asks about intimate details of one's sexual life, for example. Narrators have a sense of control over how they will be perceived by others. Of course, some psychologists may perceive this as a flaw in the instrument.

As for limitations, the story line may encourage too much glossing over of events and the details of life. A year could be filled with extreme highs and lows, and these might be averaged out to look like a mediocre year. Some years may also be much more important than others to the narrator. The advantages of the story line in terms of administration and utilization may be also at the base of the disadvantages of brevity and compression. The story line may also be limited because some respondents might find the task unusual and hard to understand. Also narrators might create story lines without reflection.

While each type of methodology in studying narratives has limitations as well as advantages, the challenge of the approach is an interesting and exciting one for increasing numbers of psychologists. New innovations are forthcoming, and modifications in existing forms may improve their capacities for eliciting life stories. Contributions from other sources, such as those in other chapters of this volume, should increase the means for exploring the narratives of lives.

PART III

ACCOUNTS IN CONTEXT

8

Accounts on trial: oral arguments in traffic court

Michael J. Cody and Margaret L. McLaughlin

We propose in this chapter to examine the notion of *accounting*, which we take to be the way in which *failure events* are managed in social interaction. Early treatments of accounts tended to be descriptive and classificatory, focusing on the development of a taxonomy of forms which accounts take when allegations of untoward behaviour arise in everyday social encounters. For example, Scott and Lyman (1968) offered an extensive treatment of two kinds of accounts, *excuses* and *justifications*, and paid particular attention to their wide variation in substantive form. Excuses and justifications were distinguished on the basis of their treatment of two issues: (1) whether or not a putative 'offence' had indeed occurred, and (2) whether or not the person called upon to give an account was in fact 'responsible' for its occurrence. An excuse was held to take the form 'I committed the offence, but I was not responsible', and a justification the form 'I am responsible, but I deny that an offence was committed.' Thus a person accused of failing to appear for an appointment in a timely fashion might excuse himself by claiming that he had been the victim of a flat tyre, or justify the tardiness by claiming that the one who had been 'kept waiting' had not in fact been specific about the time they were to meet.

Theoretical background

More recent work in the taxonomic vein, such as that by Schonbach (1980, 1985, 1986), attempts to extend the catalogue of accounting types to forms other than excuses and justifications. Schonbach

(1980) added the categories *concession* and *refusal* to deal with, respectively, admissions and denials of guilt (responsibility). Concessions in their pure form are confessional; that is, the offender admits to having been late, having been drunk, having failed to take appropriate action, and so forth. Such admissions of guilt may or may not be accompanied by apologies, expressions of remorse, offers of restitution and the like. Refusals as a response to an allegation of untoward action may entail the flat denial by the one reproached that she committed the act in question, or may take the form of a refusal to acknowledge the other's right to reproach. Schonbach has recently (1985) revised and expanded his taxonomy of accounts, although he retains the four 'cardinal categories' of his earlier work: concessions, excuses, justifications and refusals. He revises the 'received' definition of excuse and incorporates the notion of theme. In the 1985 paper, Schonbach defines excuse as 'any account which admits the occurrence of a failure event and some involvement of the actor in it, but pleads for mitigation in judgment on the basis of various arguments including, but not limited to, claims of impairment and hence reduced causal responsibility' (p.10). Justification is defined conventionally as a 'strategy by which the actor accepts causal responsibility for the event in question, but asserts that it was legitimate or at least permissible under the given circumstances' (Schonbach, 1985:11). Schonbach also introduces into the ongoing discussion of accounts the notion of themes, for example 'appeal to loyalties', 'influence of powerful agents' or 'situational constraints', which can be exploited as a resource for constructing more than one kind of account. Thus, for example, the theme 'provocation by the accuser' could be used to fashion either an excuse ('I was so upset by what you said that I wasn't myself when I hit you') or a justification ('You deserved it after what you said to me').

Much of the current work on accounts is concerned with the *functional utility* of accounting to the individual; that is, scholars have begun to examine how (and/or if) excuses and justifications work. Some researchers have been interested primarily in the role of accounts, particularly excuses, in the retrospective (and sometimes anticipatory) redefinition of events with dispreferred outcomes. Backman (1985) has examined the relationships among self-identity, self-presentation and moral decision making: specifically, the role of the anticipatory construction and rehearsal of accounts in 'defensively reinterpreting' (Rest, 1984) a morally problematic situation so as to make the circumstances surrounding the actor's choice appear to be mitigating. The actor's search is for situational definitions that will 'blunt the effects of anticipated censure from the self or others, either by reducing the strength of the rules operating in the situation or by providing a basis for accounts or explanations' (Backman, 1985: 268).

Snyder and his colleagues have also been interested in the utility and efficacy of accounts, particularly excuses. Their attention has been on the *process* of making excuses; Snyder and Higgins (1986) define this process as one of 'shifting causal attributions for negative personal outcomes from sources that are relatively more central to the person's sense of self to sources that are relatively less central' (p. 2). Snyder and Higgins focus primarily on the role of excuses in the maintenance of self-esteem. After an extensive survey of the relevant literature, their assessment of the evidence is that the availability of excuses (from whatever source, including one's own resources) can significantly reduce the effects of negative outcomes on self-esteem. For example, being able to claim that a task was too difficult or that one's friends would also perform poorly could serve to restore self-esteem, or prevent losses resulting from an intellectual failure. Snyder and Higgins (1986: 9) maintain that it is the so-called EVS pattern of excuse-making, that is, attributing negative outcomes to external (extra-individual), unstable (variable) and specific factors rather than internal, stable and global ones (the ISG pattern), which is facilitative. The EVS pattern has been found to be associated with improved outcomes in psychotherapy, better long-term health, and superior athletic performance. Similarly, Tedeschi and Norman (1985) proposed that accounts can be viewed as 'defensive mechanisms' which are used by the individual to maintain an appropriate public image.

In our own research (Cody and McLaughlin, 1985; McLaughlin, Cody and O'Hair, 1983; McLaughlin, Cody and Rosenstein, 1983) we have been interested in how accounts work in an interactional context; that is, how parties to a failure event work collaboratively to effect repair. We have now conducted four studies on accounting episodes. Our first study (McLaughlin, Cody and O'Hair, 1983) was a survey in which 278 undergraduate subjects provided retrospective reports on a failure event. Our second study involved the analysis of accounting episodes in 50 half-hour recorded conversations between strangers (McLaughlin, Cody and Rosenstein, 1983). Our third study was again a survey of 156 drivers in Texas, New Mexico and Oklahoma, who were asked to recall instances in which they had been stopped by a police officer for a traffic offence. In our fourth study, which we report here, we observed 375 cases of account giving in four traffic courts in the greater Los Angeles area. Our work has led us to two major conclusions about the way in which accounts unfold in social interaction.

Our first conclusion is that accounting sequences have a canonical form (Cody and McLaughlin, 1985; Remler, 1978; Schonbach, 1980, 1985). At a minimum, the sequences consist of three 'slots' which may or may not all be explicitly filled. Firstly, there is a slot for a *reproach*, in which a party taking offence communicates to an actor by some means (possibly non-verbal), or the actor perceives through his or her own guilt, anxiety or social astuteness, that something is amiss. The second slot in the canonical sequence is for an *account*. The right or obligation to talk in this slot is assigned to the party reproached, whose job it is to produce a reply or remedy conditionally relevant (Schegloff, 1972) to the form of the reproach employed in the particular context. (One may of course provide an account for another just as one may answer her or his own question, and thus effect closure as far as the requirements of functional coherence are concerned, but this is clearly not the normative case.) The third slot in the accounting sequence calls for an *evaluation*, in which the initiator of the reproach reports his or her assessment of the offending party's account. This canonical sequence, variations of which have been reported elsewhere (the misapprehension sequence by Jefferson, 1972; the corrective interchange by Goffman, 1971; the account episode by Schonbach, 1980, 1985, 1986; and the remedial episode by Morris, 1985), may incorporate additional steps such as a precipitating failure event or an acknowledgement of the evaluation.

Our second conclusion is that the steps or slots in the canonical form of the accounting sequence relate to one another in some predictable ways, such that certain types of reproaches are more likely to induce certain types of accounts, and similarly with accounts and evaluations. A construct we have invoked in describing this is the *aggravation–mitigation continuum* (Labov and Fanshel, 1977). Reproaches, accounts and evaluations can be arrayed along a continuum such that at one end are clustered forms which will tend to exacerbate the tension already generated by the failure event, and at the other are forms which will tend to defuse or ameliorate the situation. For example, a reproach in which a truculent attitude on the part of the offending party is projected ('Just try to deny that you were flirting with that woman!') we would fully expect to provoke an account in kind ('I don't have to deny it; we're not married and I can flirt with whomever I please!'). We have found in general that aggravating antecedents lead to aggravating replies; such a relationship could be attributed to reciprocity norms, topical relevance constraints, or the 'interlocking preconditions' (Cody and McLaughlin, 1985; Searle, 1975) of the illocutionary acts (challenge/reply) embedded in the utterances. Similarly, we have found that more mitigating forms of reproaches and accounts are likely to be met in kind. For example, in our study of drivers in south-west USA (Cody and McLaughlin, 1985), more mitigating accounts were likely to lead to 'honouring' (being let off without a ticket). In our study of conversations between strangers (McLaughlin, Cody and Rosenstein, 1983), reproachers honoured accounts or withdrew their reproaches more frequently when the accounts took the more mitigating forms of concession or excuse. This evidence in favour of matching response levels has been stronger for aggravating reproaches and accounts than it has been for the more mitigating ones (see in particular Cody and McLaughlin, 1983).

The various forms in which accounts appear may be ordered with some consistency with respect to the aggravation–mitigation continuum (and thus with respect to the probability of being honoured). However, what is mitigating in an interpersonal context may be *aggravating* in a legal one. Our studies indicate that in dealing with failure events in interpersonal contexts, concessions (admissions of guilt, apologies, offers of restitution) are the most mitigating, followed by excuses, justifications and refusals. However, in our study of drivers stopped for traffic offences we found that admissions of guilt were likely to have an aggravating effect (lead to ticketing). The critical issue here is that the patrolman does not enter into the accounting episode as an individual but rather as a representative of the state (city, county), and his obligation toward a guilt admission is qualitatively different from a friend's or lover's (Cody and McLaughlin, 1985).

Our fourth study, which we use as our empirical example, is (like our third) an examination of account giving in a situation in which the reproacher (or recipient of the account) is acting as such in an official capacity. Our expectation was that in the courtroom context, excuses would be the most mitigating (least likely to result in penalties), followed by justifications, refusals and concessions (guilt admissions). However, Coleman (1976), in his study of courtroom control and grievance accounts, brought up two points which might argue against the predicted order. Firstly, the refusal strategy of some defendants is to bring documents or develop 'logical proofs' that they could not have committed the act with which they had been charged; for example, a defendant might present to the court a bill showing that his car had been in a repair shop all day on the day he had been ticketed for a parking violation. Such an account qualifies as a refusal under our category scheme, but would probably not be perceived as aggravating and might well result in honouring. A second issue raised by Coleman is the need of the presiding judge to keep things moving along; the requirements for the rapid processing of cases might dispose the judge to look with more favour on the defendant who utters a quick 'no contest' than one who insists on delivering a lengthy excuse.

Special considerations aside, however, we anticipated that the proposed ordering of account forms with respect to the likelihood of penalty would be robust. In as much as the mitigation level of an utterance or series of utterances is carried by non-verbal as well as verbal factors, we incorporated into our study a number of variables related to the accounter's apparent level of remorse, degree of anxiety, amount of anger and so forth.

Empirical example: courtroom observation

In this example of analysing accounts, we present in some detail a study of accounts given in traffic court. Fifty-six undergraduates at the University of Southern California worked in pairs as observers at one of four traffic courts in the greater Los Angeles area. Observers had trained to satisfactory reliability levels (median $r > 0.80$) on taped versions of the half-hour television programme. 'The People's Court'. Observers recorded for each of 375 cases the location, date and time of the session, and the name of the presiding judge; the sex and approximate age of the defendant; a brief description of the statements made in the courtroom by the defendant, arresting officer and judge; the severity of the offence (ranging from drunk driving and excessive speeding to jaywalking and 'fix-it' tickets (to repair light bulbs etc); and the nature of the outcome, namely no penalty (dismissal), partial penalty (traffic school, dismissal of some but not all counts, community service or reduction of the normal fines) or full penalty (guilty as charged). Observers also rated characteristics of the defendant's self-presentation on nine-step bipolar scales: confidence (fast speech rate, no or few silent/filled pauses, air of confidence); concreteness of account (contained details of actions, motives, decisions and so on); extroversion and dynamism (animation, high energy level, erect posture, forceful gestures); anxiety (nervous gesturing, pacing, speech errors, adaptors, random body movement); apologetic voice quality; non-verbal expression of regret (dejected body position, lowered head, 'sad' expression and so on); politeness; and anger.

Coding of defendants' accounts
All observer summaries were read by three coders, each of whom had read Coleman (1976), Cody and McLaughlin (1985) and Scott and Lyman (1968). Preliminary examination of the observers' summaries of the defendants' courtroom statements by two coders (who

conducted the first reading of the essays) indicated that for the most part the observation categories emerging in previous investigations (concession, excuse, justification and refusal) were appropriate for the classification of accounts in traffic court, with one significant exception. The *refusal* category obtained in the earlier studies (McLaughlin, Cody and O'Hair, 1983; McLaughlin, Cody and Rosenstein, 1983) was manifested in three very distinct forms in the defendants' courtroom statements. We have called these categories challenges ($n = 21$), denies offence ($n = 53$) and logical proofs ($n = 48$; following from Coleman, 1976).

In using a *challenge*, the defendant rejected the claim that an offence had taken place on the grounds that the reproacher (arresting officer) was unfair, unprofessional or inexperienced. In some cases the defendant was verbally abusive of the police officer and/or aggressive towards the judge. Examples are as follows:

Defendant: I am a good tax-paying citizen and I should not be getting a ticket in this speed trap.

Defendant: I might have been going 60, but I was not going anything like 70. I think the officer added those extra miles on just to make me more upset.

Defendant: Not guilty, your honour [*answering the judge's question*]. The police officer was going in the other direction. He could not have known my speed and I was flowing with the traffic. The officer pulled me over just because I drive a red Porsche and it looks like it's going fast.

Refusals which we classified as *denies offence* simply involved a flat assertion that an offence had not occurred. Although the defendant may have taken issue with the arresting officer's characterization of the action as an offence, there were no assaults on the officer's integrity or motivation. Conversely, there was no true physical proof of the defendant's claim. For example, a man charged with 'driving on the sidewalk' and 'soliciting a prostitute' made the following response:

Defendant: I was asking directions from a woman at the bus stop and had no idea she was a prostitute. I was not on the sidewalk [but] had pulled into the gas station.

In another example:

Defendant: The light may have been yellow, but it was not red when I made the turn. ... The officer's view was obstructed by other cars.

In a very distinctive form of refusal, *logical proofs*, the defendant attempted to demonstrate his or her innocence through logical argument, often bolstered by physical evidence:

> Defendant: Well, your honour, the road was mismarked and the car behind me was motioning me to turn right, across the line [*from the left lane of two lanes heading north*]. I brought the pictures of the area, and I went to the city planner who agreed that the area was mismarked and under investigation for a change.

> Defendant: Your honour, I can't be guilty because they painted the kerb red after I parked there.

> Judge: This sounds like a cartoon!

> Defendant: Here are papers from the city showing that the kerb was painted the day I got ticketed.

> Defendant: The cop said the moped was unfit for two people, but I have the specific manual here that states the moped is designed for one or two passengers.

The *concessions* category ($n = 74$) subsumed those cases in which the actor admitted guilt or stated that she or he would not contest the ticket. Concessions could include apologies, offers of restitution and promises that the behaviour would not recur, and pleading for leniency, or might simply consist of a response such as 'no contest' or 'guilty, your honour' to the judge's question 'How do you plead?' The defendant's first two utterances in the exchange below are typical of the category:

> Judge: Reckless driving. What is your plea?
> Defendant: Guilty as charged.
> Judge: Were you under the influence of alcohol at the time of the arrest?
> Defendant: I had two beers at dinner.
> Judge: Oh, the old 'just two beers' story.
> Defendant: Yes, your honour.
> Judge: Well, the charge will stand, but I want you to attend 12 AA meetings, and [take] a $406 fine [and] 36 months' summary probation.
> Defendant: Isn't that a little bit harsh?
> Judge: Not for someone who is a threat to other drivers on the road.

Excuses, as was the case in our earlier studies, were the most popular form of account ($n = 134$). Defendants attributed their offences to (among other factors) accident, misinformation, lack of knowledge, lack of ability, illness and the behaviour of others:

Defendant: There was a car to the left of me, and the pedestrian was on the west side; the car on my left was ahead of me, therefore obstructing my view.

Defendant: The car was parked in the no-parking zone because [it] had a flat tyre.

Defendant: I was driving a new Mercedes that was shipped from Europe. It doesn't show you speed in m.p.h., it shows it in kilometres [per hour].

Defendant: I didn't see the sign because it was dull and I didn't have my glasses on.

Not surprisingly, fewer defendants in court attempted to *justify* their behaviour ($n = 45$). In this variation the accounter admits that he or she engaged in the behaviour described by the arresting officer, but argues that the behaviour should be condoned because others were doing it, it was done for a good reason, and so on:

Defendant: I left my curling iron on, and was rushing to get home to turn it off before the house burnt (sic) down.

Defendant: I was driving on the 118. I became very tired and almost fell asleep, so I pulled over and went to sleep. I was aware the ramp was closed, and parked there for that reason. After my nap, it would not have been safe for myself and other drivers if I had backed up on to the freeway, so I felt it was much safer for me to go up and over to the ramp to re-enter. I was doing what I thought was safest.

Defendant: I was late for work, and everyone else seemed to be going just as fast as I was, so I didn't think I was speeding.

Defendant: [*accused of drunk driving*]: It was my thirtieth wedding anniversary and we had a party. I only live around the corner.

One of the two coders who had conducted the preliminary reading of the 375 essays, as well as the first author, coded the essays into the respective six categories while blind to the assignments made by the other coder. The agreement was highest for concessions (98 per cent) and lowest for justifications (83 per cent), and averaged 89 per cent. The two coders met and reached mutual agreement for the essays on which they had initially disagreed.

Analysis
The quantitative approach allowed us to compare the relative efficacy of the different account types. Logical proofs were by far the most effective means of avoiding the imposition of a penalty,

whereas a concession was virtually certain to result in a penalty's being assessed (see table 8.1).

Interestingly, there were no significant univariate linear relationships between defendant characteristics and the imposition of a partial penalty. Twenty-three per cent of the sample received 'no penalty', 24% 'partial penalty' and 52% received 'full penalty' ('guilty as charged'). The fact that there were no significant correlations with the partial penalty category reflected the catch-all nature of the category: poor defendants unable to pay a fine were assigned community service; defendants (even those with excessive speeding charges) were granted traffic court (as an alternative to payment) if they had clean driving records for over a year and had not been to traffic court in the last three years; and some judges routinely reduced the fine on excessive parking tickets (one defendant had over $2000 in unpaid parking tickets) and some speeding tickets. For the rest of the analyses, we compare 'no penalty' (23 per cent) defendants with penalized ones (76 per cent). However, the correlations indicate that full penalties were associated with the severity of the offence, the vagueness of the defendant's account, and a plea of guilty/no contest. Escaping penalty altogether was positively associated with lesser severity of the offence, concreteness of the account, defendant's extroversion and the use of logical proofs, and negatively associated with anger and concession of guilt.

To tease out more subtle aspects of the data, a multiple discriminant analysis (MDA) was conducted with the six account types as levels of the dependent variable (groups) and the outcome and defendant characteristic variates as predictors. A non-stepwise procedure was carried out over the entire predictor set. The first two of five discriminant functions were significant. Function 1, on which the only substantial loading was the dichotomously coded variable 'no penalty', served primarily to contrast defendants using logical proofs (group mean = 1.62) and defendants using concession (group mean = -0.87). Function 1, with an eigenvalue of 0.50 and a Wilks's lambda of 0.53, accounted for 69.59 per cent of the between groups variance (chi-square (d.f. = 60) = 225.55, $p = 0.00$). Function 2, on which the variable 'confidence' had a large negative loading, and the variable 'apologetic' a large positive one, served chiefly to contrast users of challenge (group mean = -0.75) and denies offence (group mean = -0.49) with the other categories of message type. Function 2, with an eigenvalue of 0.10 and a Wilks's lambda of 0.81, accounted for 14.79 per cent of the variance (chi-square (d.f. = 44) = 77.09, $p = 0.001$), bringing the cumulative variance accounted for to 84.39 per cent. One may conclude from the MDA that defendants using logical proofs are

Table 8.1   *Rank order of account types with respect to imposition of penalty*

Rank	Type of account	n	Proportion of defendants not penalized*
1	Logical proofs	48	0.75[a,b,c,d,e]
2	Excuse	134	0.25[a,f,g,h]
3	Denies offence	53	0.19[b,i,j,k]
4	Justification	45	0.09[c,f,i,l]
5	Challenges	21	0.09[d,g,j,m]
6	Concession	74	0.03[e,h,k,l,m]

*Proportions with common superscripts are significantly different from each other, p less than 0.05.

likely to escape penalty and those using concession are not, and that defendants using challenge or denying the offence are likely to be perceived as confident and unapologetic.

Advantages and disadvantages

Our earlier work (Cody and McLaughlin, 1985; McLaughlin, Cody and O'Hair, 1983) relied on survey data. We have shifted emphasis in recent years away from survey data in favour of observing behaviour in natural settings (whenever possible, ethical and legal). Two of many important reasons will be discussed here. Firstly, observational data are not likely to be as biased as *recalled* data. If we have social actors recall episodes of account giving, some episodes are likely to be perceived (and/or reinterpreted) in such a way as to enhance or increase self-esteem (or, at least, the actor may avoid threats to his or her self-esteem) (see Snyder and Higgins, 1986 for sample research). One estimate of the type of biased reporting that one can expect was provided in a recent summary of research on compliance-gaining goals (Cody, Canary and Smith, in press). A typology of goals was proposed, based on Rule and Bisanz's work (1987; Rule, Bisanz and Kohn, 1985), including goals such as 'obtain permission', 'gain assistance' (which included both favours and selfish requests – those in which the actor argued that his or her goal should be pursued at the cost of the target's goal), 'give advice', 'change relationships', 'enforce obligation' etc. To assess frequency of success of different goals, Cody, Canary and Smith conducted a survey in which respondents were asked to recall from communication episodes all types of goals they could remember pursuing, and a diary study (whose respondents kept diaries over a 12 week period). Some of the differences in methods were attributable to qualitatively different types of environments (that is, actors made fewer attempts to obtain permission from parents once in college; instead, 'gain assistance' goals increased in frequency). However, two substantive differences occurred, when comparing methods, that could be attributable to biased reporting: (1) in the recall data, actors reported extremely high success rates in 'change relationships' goals (83 per cent), but not in the diary method (62 per cent successful); (2) in the diary data, actors made selfish requests routinely of others, but such requests were rarely reported in the recall data. In essence, actors do not want to admit that they were not in control of relational changes (initiations, escalation and, perhaps most importantly, de-escalations: consult Hill, Rubin and Peplau, 1976), and do not like to admit how frequently they make selfish requests of others. With respect to the present data, most (76 per cent) of the defendants failed to avoid penalty. One would expect that they would have to attribute the failure to some type of cause external to their own limited or inappropriate way of influencing representatives of the court. Hence, data in this goal situation lend themselves easily to biased reporting (the judge was prejudiced, there wasn't time for a full explanation, mine was the first case heard and he was trying to set an example, and so on).

A second issue relevant to recalled versus observational data deals with the reliance on likelihood-of-use rating scales. Although none of our own work and, fortunately, few studies in accounting have relied on likelihood-of-use data, this is not the case in research in compliance gaining generally or in related work on relational disengagement. Likelihood-of-use scales are seven-step Likert-type measures that assess the actor's self-reported probability of using a particular type of tactic or approach in a particular influence situation. This approach suffers from at least two limitations. Firstly, we gain little new insight about communication phenomena by limiting the range of responses that can be made (consider, for example, the different types of 'logical proofs' we recorded; see above). Secondly, rating scales provide biased estimates of what people actually say and do because of *question threat* (see discussion in Cody, 1982). That is, actors do not want to endorse an extreme position that might make them look bad to the experimenter. Such biased reporting has appeared in studies of relational disengagement (Cody, 1982), in which actors who used blatantly rude tactics according to their essays on 'How I disengaged' rated the same type of tactics as only moderately high in their own likelihood of use (see also Burleson et al., 1986; Seibold et al., 1986 concerning the issue of likelihood-of-use scales).

One problem with the study reported here has to do with generalizability. While similar (if not exactly the same) results are to be expected at other traffic courts in the USA, the goal and the environment are so specific and unique that these findings are not likely to be generalizable across many types of goals or contexts. In most interpersonal environments (as in McLaughlin, Cody and O'Hair, 1983; McLaughlin, Cody and Rosenstein, 1983), we anticipate that concessions, apologies and excuses would lead to more honouring than logical proofs (except, perhaps, if one's friends and family were all judges or lawyers). There are situations which could aptly be described as hybrids. They are similar to the traffic court and patrolman studies in that they involve explaining oneself to a *representative* of an institution, but similar to the interpersonal studies in that they require the accounter to explain himself to someone who may know him well and with whom he can anticipate further encounters. We think in this context of situations such as: explaining to the local librarian why junior's book is three weeks overdue; accounting to the principal for one's tardiness; explaining one's absence from the faculty meeting to a department chair; explaining to an editor why one's reviews are late; and so on. We would anticipate that neither our courtroom findings nor the findings from our earlier studies on accounting in interpersonal relationships would precisely suffice to predict patterns in these contexts.

Other limitations to this study are primarily methodological in nature. If we focus attention on how we coded the defendants' oral arguments to explain their alleged offences, more worthwhile information would have been obtained if we also interviewed defendants about their plans to influence the judge and their thoughts on what evidence and argument they believed to be persuasive in this context, and solicited their accounts for why they failed or succeeded in their courtroom experience. If we focus attention on the outcomes of the trials, we would (if we repeated the study) probably sample more cases from fewer judges and make a comparison of the judges' evaluations. Some of our observers, for example, felt that one judge was particularly lenient on the unemployed defendant who claimed that he or she was unable to pay the fine: the judge frequently and automatically assigned such defendants a relatively small number of hours of community service. Another judge seemed to be particularly impressed when a professional (doctor, lawyer, etc.) appeared in court with records and documents and used the blackboard (obviously showing considerable planning) to contest a $40 or $50 fine. A fully developed model of courtroom outcomes of the kind studied here should take such biases into consideration. Finally, when replicating this study we propose that some attention be given to the apparent *strength* of evidence. Based on the results of this study, we recommend that a defendant use logical proofs (with supporting physical evidence) to avoid penalties. However, some pieces of evidence may lack persuasiveness. For example, a woman was ticketed for parking in a no-parking zone, and she claimed that she could not tell whether the kerb was painted red or not:

Defendant: Also, I took photos. [*to prove the red paint was faded*]

Judge: Well, let's have them here. [*The judge studied these photos for a long while*]. Nope! These sure look red enough to me. Guilty as charged.

9

Explanations as accounts:
a conversation analytic perspective

John Heritage

In this chapter I will discuss some central aspects of explanations or accounts as treated using conversation analysis. My concern will be with accounts which are *naturally occurring* in conversation rather than elicited by an investigator. I will focus on the use of accounts in *ordinary conversation* rather than some more specific or specialized location in social space such as a hospital, a school or a courtroom. And I will largely concentrate on accounts which are addressed to, or explain, some current action going on in the conversation, rather than accounts that focus on events that are wholly external to the conversation in which they occur (though see Cody and McLaughlin in chapter 8 for an approach to the latter type of data). The central conceptual focus of this discussion will fall on the role of accounts in relation to conversational organization and social solidarity.

Theoretical background

Conversation analysis has developed over the past 15 years as a subdiscipline within the wider intellectual framework of ethnomethodology (Garfinkel, 1967). Primarily concerned with social action and its underlying reasoning, its focus has been descriptive and naturalistic rather than explanatory or experimental. Practitioners have aimed, in the first instance, to describe *how* common-sense reasoning and social action work, rather than to develop explanations in advance of detailed description. As the reference to reasoning suggests, Garfinkel and his collaborators have formed part of the recent 'cognitive revolution' in the social sciences but, as a sociologist, Garfinkel's preoccupation was with how social actors can achieve a shared or common apprehension of the social world. He proposed that every aspect of a cognitively shared social world depends on a multiplicity of tacit (taken for granted) methods of reasoning. These methods, he argued, are both socially organized and socially shared and they are ceaselessly used during every waking moment to recognize ordinary social objects and events.

In order to demonstrate his claims, Garfinkel devised numerous procedures which were designed to engineer drastic departures from ordinary expectations and understandings about social behaviour. The results clearly showed the extent to which the shared nature of ordinary understandings is dependent on the joint application of shared methods of reasoning. His work also demonstrated that the application of these methods by social actors has a *normative* background: those who departed from the use of these methods were met with anger and demands that they explain themselves and their actions. His investigations thus displayed the inherent *morality* of social cognition and that the sense making procedures we all use are themselves part of the moral order (Garfinkel, 1963, 1967; Heritage, 1984).

Garfinkel concluded that shared methods of reasoning generate continuously updated implicit understandings of what is happening in social contexts – a 'running index', as it were, of what is happening in a social event. It is through the creation of this running index that social activity is rendered intelligible or, as Garfinkel puts it, 'account-able'. To make sense, the overt descriptions and explanations (or accounts) which actors provide for their actions must articulate with these already established implicit understandings.

Both ethnomethodology and conversation analysis are thus concerned with two levels of 'accountability'. On the one hand, there is the taken-for-granted level of reasoning through which a running index of action and interaction is created and sustained. On the other, there is the level of overt explanation in which social actors give accounts of what they are doing in terms of reasons, motives or causes. In this chapter I shall mostly be concerned with the latter level. But I shall later show that an understanding of the properties of accounts at this second level cannot be fully achieved without reference to how the running index works.

Methods of analysing sequencing in conversational interaction

Conversation analysis (henceforth CA) has developed primarily as an approach to investigating the normative structures of reasoning which are involved in understanding and producing courses of intelligible interaction. The objective is to describe the procedures by which speakers produce their own behaviour and understand and deal with the behaviour of others. The central resource for analysis is interaction itself. Interaction forms such a resource because during its course the parties, whether intentionally or not, implicitly display their understanding and analysis of what is happening as it happens. These implicit displays are embedded in the participants' own actions. CA represents the development of an analytic technology that capitalizes on this fact. Its central focus is on the analysis of sequences of interaction and of turns within sequences. Thus CA is centrally concerned with the study of the sequential organization of interaction and of the reasoning that is inherently embedded within it.

A central assumption of interactional sequencing is that, unless otherwise signalled, each turn is addressed to the matters raised by the turn preceding it. The most powerful expression of this assumption arises in the form of *adjacency pairs* (Schegloff, 1968; Schegloff and Sacks, 1973), in which the production of a first conversational action or first pair part (for example, a greeting, a question, an invitation, a request, an offer and so on) both projects and requires the production of a second (for example, a return greeting, an answer and so on). This projection and requirement is *normative* in character. Thus a questioner, for example, whose question has not been answered will usually have the right to repeat it or to request that the intended respondent answers it, to sanction the non-respondent, or to draw sanctionable inferences from the respondent's lack of response. It is in terms of adjacency pair rules, which relate a first to a second action, that speakers can influence or even constrain the conduct of their coparticipants.

However, rules that relate first to second actions are not just important resources by which interactants can shape the trajectory of sequences of action. They are also important resources through which interactants can grasp how others understand their actions. Consider the following example. (Note that in each example the convention is to indicate where the talk comes from. In this case it is SBL, which is the code for a large number of telephone calls collected in Santa Barbara, California. Fuller details of these conventions can be found in Atkinson and Heritage, 1984). In this example a speaker B responds to a question:

(1) (SBL:10:12)
    A: Why don't you come and see me some⌜times.
    B: ⌊I would like to.

Here B's response exhibits an analysis of A's question. Specifically, in being shaped as an 'acceptance', it treats A's initial question as an *invitation* geared to the *future*, and this treatment is plainly available both to A and to us (the analysts). However, suppose that B had responded as follows:

(2)   (Invented variation on (1))
      A: Why don't you come and <u>see</u> me sometimes.
      B: I'm sorry. I've been terribly tied up lately.

Given that this response takes the form of an 'apology', it would be clear to A (and to analysts) that B had understood A's question as a *complaint* directed at B's conduct in the *past*. The relationship between actions in sequence thus provides an interpretative resource both for participants and for those who are concerned with the scientific analysis of interaction, because each action in a sequence inherently displays its producer's interpretation of the prior actions in the sequence.

Using the sequential organization of action as a data resource in this way has allowed CA to unravel many complexities in the organization of actions and sequences and in the reasoning that informs their construction and interpretation. In developing these analyses, CA has made a number of assumptions. These are:

1   Interaction is structurally organized.
2   The significance of each turn at talk is doubly contextual in that (a) each turn is shaped by the context of prior talk and (b) each turn establishes a context to which the next turn will be oriented.
3   No order of detail in interaction can be dismissed *a priori* as irrelevant to the parties' understandings of what is occurring (see Heritage, 1985, forthcoming for further details).

These assumptions have strongly shaped CA's approach to data and its analysis, to which we now turn.

Data collection and analysis
CA is primarily concerned with analysis of the organization of mundane social action. Researchers have proceeded by collecting materials from ordinary conversational interaction which is as uncontaminated as possible by social scientific intervention. These materials are invariably collected using audiotape or videotape. Audiotape is particularly suitable for the telephone medium where, because there is no visual channel available to the participants, there is no need for researchers to have access to a video recording. In collecting data from face-to-face interaction, video recording is by far the most appropriate means.

This emphasis on the use of tape as a means of collecting data from natural settings is based on the following considerations. First and foremost, the analysis of interaction in detail cannot proceed without repeated reviewing of materials. The use of note taking or on-the-spot coding of behaviour cannot allow the researcher to recover the details of original materials, and is indeed already analysis in itself. Naturally occurring data are strongly preferred to the development of data generated through the use of role plays or experimental techniques because, although these methods are undoubtedly valuable, they tend to restrict both the range and the authenticity of the data that they generate, no matter how cleverly they are contrived.

In place of these methods, CA has adopted the naturalist's strategy of building up large collections of data from as many natural sites as possible. Like a good collection of naturalist's specimens, these growing data bases contain many variations of particular types of interactional events whose features can be systematically compared. Analysts constantly seek for new variants and may focus their searches on particular settings in the expectation of finding them.

Once possessed of a corpus of data, CA operates in the first instance using inductive search procedures. An analyst who is interested, for example, in how invitations are accepted or rejected will begin by building up a collection of invitations and will attempt to establish regularities in the organization of positive and negative responses to them. At the core of this task is the demonstration that these regularities are methodically produced and oriented to by the participants as normative organizations of action.

To achieve this end, 'deviant case analysis' is commonly used. This means taking cases where the established pattern is departed from and showing the ways in which the participants, through their actions, orient to these departures. If both dimensions of the analysis can be adequately accomplished, then the empirical task of showing that a particular normative organization is operative in interaction (that is, underlying both the production of and reasoning about a particular social action or sequence of actions) will have been achieved. Beyond this point, there is the theoretical task of specifying the role which the organization that has been discovered plays in the communicative and social matrix of interaction.

In what follows a brief demonstration of these tasks will be accomplished using explanations or accounts in social interaction as illustrative material. It is emphasized, however that this is an illustrative sketch and is not to be treated as a full-blown analysis.

Empirical examples

We begin by delimiting the domain of interest. Our focus will be on the use of explanations or accounts that are provided in the immediate context of the activities they account for. We thus ignore narrative explanations of events that are external to the conversation in which the account occurs, and explanations which are external to the particular sequence of conversational interaction in which the account occurs. Those kinds of explanations would have to be treated in different ways.

Establishing a pattern

Our subject matter has already been the object of considerable philosophical and social scientific exegesis (for example Antaki, 1981; Gilbert and Abell, 1983; Mills, 1940; Peters, 1958; Scott and Lyman, 1968). This literature converges in the judgement that explanations and accounts are routinely provided or demanded in contexts where projected or required behaviour does not occur. A comparison of our case (1) (repeated here) with another case will begin to illustrate this phenomenon:

(1)   (SBL:10:12)
    A: Why don't you come and see me some⌐times.
    B: ⌐I would like to.

In this case the invitation, which projects an acceptance, gets a simple unvarnished acceptance. No account is provided for the acceptance. In effect, the acceptance is treated as projected or 'provided for' by the invitation. By contrast in (3), which is taken from the same conversation, a subsequent and more specific invitation is rejected in an elaborated fashion.

(3)   (SBL:10:14)
    A: Uh if you'd care to come over and visit a little while this morning I'll give you a cup of coffee.
    B: 1 → hehh Well that's awfully sweet of you,
        2 → I don't think I can make it this morning
        3 → .hh uhm I'm running an ad in the paper and-and uh I have to stay near the phone.

It can be readily observed that in (3) the rejection of the invitation is accounted for with an explanation (arrow 3). Moreover, the account is the final component of a turn that also includes an appreciation of the invitation (arrow 1) and a mitigated or 'cushioned' rejection component (arrow 2). All three features are highly characteristic of rejections of invitations and related actions and have been extensively documented elsewhere (Davidson, 1984; Wootton, 1981). These same features can be readily illustrated in relation to other domains of action, for example in responses that reject offers:

(4) (Her:OII:2:4:ST) (B's wife has slipped a disc)
    A: And we were <u>w</u>ondering if there's <u>a</u>nything we can
              do to help
    B: ⌈Well 'at's⌉
    A: ⌊I mean ⌋ can we do any shopping for her or something
              like tha:t?
              (0.7)
    B: 1 → Well that's <u>mo</u>st <u>k</u>ind Antho<u>ny</u>
        2 → .hhh At the moment no::.
        3 → Because we've still got two bo:ys at home.

And a similar, though less elaborate, pattern is observable in the context of responses to questions:

(5) (Trio:2:II:1)
    M: What happened at (.) <u>wo</u>:rk. At <u>Bull</u>ock's this evening.=
    P: =.hhhh Well I <u>don'kno</u>:::w::.

Here the question relevances the production of an answer which, in this case, is not forthcoming. In its place, the intended answerer provides an *account* (ignorance) for the absent answer. A more complex version is to be found in the following:

(6) (W:PC:1:MJ(1):18) (Concerning how boat-trains work)
    J: But the <u>trai</u>:n goes. Does th'train go o:n th'boa:t?
    M: .h .h Ooh I've no idea:. She ha:sn't sai:d.

Here the intended answerer not only accounts for her inability to respond by asserting ignorance, but also then accounts for her ignorance by reference to a third party, whose forthcoming journey is the occasion for the sequence in which this question arises.
    Here then are a range of instances in which a second speaker's failure to accomplish a projected, or looked for, action is accompanied by an explanation or account of some kind.

Deviant case analysis
The second stage of the analysis involved establishing that the provision of accounts in such contexts is treated as a normative requirement and this, it will be recalled, can be done through the analysis of deviant cases. The latter are inevitably less common than examples of the normal pattern and are often more complex to explicate.
    A relatively straightforward case is the following, in which S has announced a disastrous examination result which will prevent her from entering law school. Her coparticipant asks her if she will take the examination again using a turn design that clearly presupposes that she will.

```
(7)  (Frankel:TC:1:1:4)
     G:        So yih g'nna take it agai:n?=
     S:        =nNo.
               (0.5)
     G:  1 →   No:?
     S:        No.
               (0.3)
     G:  2 →   Why no:t.=
     S:        = .t.hhhh I don't rilly wan'to.
```

This sequence shows a number of significant features. Most notably, after S's initial and unexplained reply, G waits for fully half a second (a long time in a conversational context) for some explanatory elaboration before prompting it with a turn (arrow 1) that queries S's announced decision. S's next response is also unelaborate and G waits for a further period before initiating an overt request for an explanation. Thus G's conduct throughout the sequence evidences her belief that an explanation is due. And S's apparent reluctance to volunteer one, in effect, manoeuvres G into the overt pursuit of one.

A more complicated case involving a similar form of covert manoeuvring around an absent account is the following. This example is taken from a situation in which a group of men are engaged in sharing out goods and fittings from a store which has closed down. From time to time their talk turns to who will take possession of particular goods. M's question, which opens the example, is clearly heard as a request for a fish tank which V subsequently rejects flatly and without explanation (arrow 1):

```
(8)  (US:simplified)
     M:        What are yuh doing with that big bowl– uh tank.
               Nothing?
               (0.5)
     V:        ((Cough))
     V:        Uh::
               (1.0)
     V:  1 →   I'm not intuh selling it or giving it. That's it.
     M:        Okay.
               (1.0)
     M:  2 →   That was simple. Khhhh huh huh heh=
     V:  3 →   =Yeh.
               (0.7)
     V:  4 →   °Yeh.°
               (1.0)
     V:  5 →   Becuz selling it or giving it I::, that's (all there is)
```

Here's M's ironic remark ('That was simple) and slight laugh (arrow 2) audibly sanctions V's brusquely unaccounted for rejection. V meets it with a further reassertion of his decision (arrow 3), another *sotto voce* repetition of 'Yeh' (arrow 4) and, subsequently, the initiation of an explanation (arrow 5) that ultimately trails away into nothing. Here, subsequent to the rejection, the conduct of both parties evidences their orientation to the absent explanation.

Similarly, in the following sequence B's unexplained failure to phone his vicar (arrow 1) is waited out over a number of turns by A, who thereby gets B to offer the looked-for explanation (arrow 2) without having to request it overtly:

```
(9)  (Campbell 4:1)
     A:         Well lis:ten, (.) tiz you tidyu phone yer vicar ye:t,
                (.3)
     B:   1 →   No I ain't.
     (A): 1 →   (.hhh)
     A:         Oh:.
                (0.3)
     (A):       .hhhhh-
     A:         Ah::-::┌::
     B:   2 →          └I w'z gonna wait 'ntil you found out about....
```

Once again both parties exhibit an orientation to the moral requiredness of an account for the reported failure. In A's case, this is exhibited by not advancing the talk beyond the place where an account could be provided. In B's it is exhibited by the subsequent offering of an account in response to A's conduct.

In sum, through deviant case analysis we can determine that account giving is not merely an empirically common feature that is associated with unexpected or unlooked for actions, but is a normatively required feature of such actions. Since failures to provide accounts attract either overt or covert pursuits of them or sanctions, we can conclude that the giving of accounts in such contexts is itself a morally accountable matter.

Embedding the analysis of account giving in a
wider analytical context

So far, we have sketched some aspects of a demonstration that account giving is a normatively organized feature of sequences of interaction in which one of the parties acts in an unlooked-for way. Now we can proceed to the final analytical task mentioned earlier, namely the attempt to locate our normative organization within a larger framework. What I want to do here is to show that the short extracts we have been looking at so far can be placed in a broader context. There are more general aspects of social interaction that only emerge when one stands back and looks at a more inclusive range of issues. Here I shall sketch two broad themes: what accounts tell us about the management of self–other relationships, and their role in sustaining the underlying normative structure of social interaction.

Accounts and self–other relations
A number of the details of the organization of account giving suggest
that they are strongly sensitive to issues of 'face' (Goffman, 1955;
Brown and Levinson, 1978). Among a number of features, we will
briefly deal with the content of accounts, the internal organization
of the components of the turn containing the account, and the
temporal placement of such turns.

Content. In many of the cases shown in this chapter (for example (2),
(3), (5) and (6)), second speakers account for their failure to carry
out the proposed or required conversational action by reference to
their *inability* to do it (cf. Drew, 1984). Patently, the speakers
could have accounted for their actions in other ways. They could
have asserted an unwillingness to carry out the proposed action,
or denied either the right of the first speaker to propose it or their
own obligation to respond. It is significant, however, that the latter
accounts would all, in one way or another, have threatened the 'face'
of their co-interactants. By contrast, the accounts which invoke
inability (and in case (4) a lack of need for the help offered) all
have a 'no-fault' quality (Heritage, 1984). None of them implicates
a lack of willingness to respond in the proposed way, or challenges
the other's rights in the situation. All of the responses avoid any
threat to the other speaker, and they also avoid any threat to the
social relationship between the parties.

Internal organization of turn components. The turns that do not
accomplish a projected activity often exhibit a careful balance
between self- and other-attentiveness. Thus it can be noted that in
the rejections of the invitations and offers (examples (4) and (5)),
the speakers appreciate what is offered before they produce their
refusals. Through this temporal ordering of the components of their
responses, the refusing speakers attend to the others' viewpoint
before attending to what is relevant from their own perspective.
That this other-attentiveness is significant can be illustrated by
considering what can emerge when speakers don't show it. In the
following sequence, which is analysed in detail in Schegloff (1988),
a student returning to a group of friends has evidently failed to come
back with a promised ice-cream sandwich.

(10) (SN 4:7)
    S: You didn' get an ice-cream san'wich,
    C: →   I kno:w, hh I decided that my body didn't need it,
    S: Yes but ours di:d

Here C's conduct fails to display any element of other-attentiveness.
She does not apologise for her lapse, and her account is framed
exclusively in terms of her own desires and concerns. Indeed, in

the way that she presents the lapse as the result of a deliberate decision rather than, for example, a failure of memory, she in fact aggravates the original failure. Her self-attentive account is immediately sanctioned by a matching self-attentive riposte by S, which is purportedly produced on behalf of the group, and C subsequently remains at odds with the rest of the group until she leaves a little later with the issue still unresolved.

Temporal placement of account turns. A further dimension of other-attentiveness that is built into the structure of rejections also centres on temporal ordering. In (3) and (4) the rejection is delayed by being placed after a variety of other turn components: an appreciation component, standard pre-rejection objects like 'uh' and 'well', and, in (4), by a delay of 0.7 seconds before the turn is initiated. These delay features, which are systematically present in rejections, have been shown to create opportunities for first speakers to revise their prior actions so as to make them more acceptable (Davidson, 1984; Pomerantz, 1984; Wootton, 1981). Where such revision is successful and second speakers find that they can then go on to carry out the proposed action, they have enabled first speakers to 'save face' by being accepted after all, and they have also enabled second speakers to avoid threatening the other's face by a rejecting action. The building of delay features into the design of rejecting actions is thus also intrinsically other-attentive.

All three of these features of accounts for rejecting actions – their content, internal organization and temporal placement – converge in extracts (11) and (12) below. In (11) the invitation recipient produces an initial appreciation of the invitation (arrow 1) which is sufficient to indicate to the inviter that a rejection is in the course of being produced. In response, the inviter specifically enquires (arrow 2) about circumstances that might make the invitee *unable* to accept:

(11) (NB:II:2:14: slightly simplified)
```
     E:           Wanna come down'n 'av a bite a'lu:nch with me:?=
                  =I got s'm bee:r en stu:ff,
                  (0.2)
     N:  1 →      Wul yer ril sweet hon:, uh::m
                  (.)
     N:           ⌈l e t- I: ha(v)        ⌉
     E:  2 →      ⌊or d'yuh'av sum⌋p'n else (t')
```

Notice here that E's last utterance (arrow 2) works to save the face of both speakers. It anticipates and invites a rejection account from N rather than just leaving it to her to produce it on her own behalf. And the kind of account that it invites (that is, one based on ability) is, as we have seen, least face threatening for E herself.

A similar process is apparent in (12), with one important difference:

```
(12) (JG:II(b):8)
        G:        Whenih you uh: what nights'r you available.
            1 →   (0.4)
        M:        .k.hhhhh.⌜hh
        G:  2 →              ⌞Are you workin' nights et all'r anything?
        M:        I do: I work, hhh a number o:f nights Gene.....
```

Here the inviting party G anticipates that there will be a difficulty with the invitation simply from the delay (arrow 1) in the response from his co-interactant. In this instance, as in (11), the inviter proposes a difficulty about the invitee's ability to accept and his action again serves to save face all round.

All of the features discussed in this section are socially standard, or institutionalized, features of 'dispreferred' action sequences. The motivation for their use ultimately derives from this fact of social standardization. Speakers are treated as having the capacity to produce or avoid producing these features. They may thus find themselves being accountable for and evaluated in terms of how they design and package their utterances. Thus, given that accounts are institutionalized, the speaker who fails to provide an account may be sanctioned as wilful and self-attentive, as one who 'would not, or could not, be bothered to provide an account'. One who fails to provide a no-fault account can be construed as hostile or insinuating or, at the least, careless of the face of a co-interactant. One who disorders the relative placement of an account and an appreciation (so as to produce, for example, a rejection followed by an account followed by an appreciation) may be heard as self-centred, if not downright selfish. One who rejects something 'too quickly' may be heard as rude.

The social logic underlying these judgements is socially institutionalized along with these institutionalized features of the rejections themselves. Both are embodied in a web of moral accountability whose binding character rests on its seamlessness. Within this web of accountability, the pressures are consistently towards other-attentiveness and towards the maintenance of face, of social relationships and of social solidarity. The personal sensibilities of face are intelligible through this logic, and in turn these sensibilities motivate its maintenance as an institutional form.

Accounts and the structure of social action
Earlier in the chapter, I proposed that ethnomethodology and CA are concerned with accountability in two senses of the term. The

first is the issue of intelligibility – the running index through which interaction is given constantly updated interpretation – while the second concerns the occasions and the ways in which participants explain their actions. I also proposed that the two dimensions are deeply interwoven. In this section, I want to comment on the connections between the two levels and to suggest a social role for ordinary accounts which cuts still deeper than the maintenance of social solidarity and self–other relations. This role has to do with the maintenance of the methods or procedures through which the organization of social action is sustained.

As we have seen, CA focuses on shared methods or procedures as the central resources through which actions are both produced and understood. The maintenance of these methods is a crucial feature of maintaining both the social organization of action and the social intelligibility of action. Both dimensions stand or fall together. As we have seen, for example, the fact that answers to questions normally and properly follow the questions to which they respond is a facet of the social organization of action, but it is also a resource in the social organization of interpretation – a resource which supplies the presumptive basis on which to interpret utterances which follow questions as 'answers'. For speakers, then, this presumptive linkage between questions and answers is both primary and presuppositional on the one hand and normative on the other.

Take the following rule: after the production of a first utterance recognizable as a question, a second speaker (the addressee) should produce an utterance that is hearable as an answer to the question. This, as we have seen, is both a rule of conduct and a rule of interpretation. The role of accounts in relation to the maintenance of this rule can be approached by considering the following problem. Our rule is one of a multiplicity of methodic procedures through which social action and social interpretation proceed. But, like all rules, it is not always complied with. The fact that social rules are often not complied with could conceivably lead to a situation in which, at the social level, the rule ceased to be respected and, at the psychological level, the rule's cognitive salience was eroded. In short, the incidence of non-compliant actions might imaginably create a process of attrition in which the social reality of the rule progressively decayed. How then do accounts function to prevent this? We can begin to address this issue through the following consideration.

When a speaker remains silent in the face of a question, two major types of interpretative option are available. The first is that the rule that questions should be answered no longer makes sense of, or applies to, the current situation and that some other rule (yet to be determined) applies instead. We scarcely ever contemplate this option, let alone implement it. If we did, the social organization of action (and with it the social intelligibility of action) would have to be treated as contingent and haphazard. Rather than adopt this option, we cling to the presupposition that questions relevance answers and, in this sense, 'should' be answered.

The second interpretative option is that the silence requires explanation. It may be explained by the speaker's deafness, failure to recognize the question, rudeness, lack of willingness to answer, inability to answer without self-incrimination, or whatever. At all events, *the failure is treated as requiring explanation* and, indeed, it is a positive signal for us to initiate a search for an explanation that is appropriate to the circumstances. The explanations which may be arrived at under such circumstances are almost always negative in their implications for non-responding parties, and this factor may be a major motivation for them to produce either compliant actions or to produce their own accounts for non-compliance in order to forestall the negative conclusions which might otherwise be drawn.

It is crucial to recognize that this second interpretative option embodies the presupposition that questions relevance answers. For speakers there are only two options: either the rule linking questions and answers is complied with and the question is answered, or the lack of an answer is an exception to the rule which requires some kind of 'secondarily elaborative' explanation. In either case, the cognitive centrality of the rule is maintained by treating the rule, together with the explanations for non-compliance with the rule, as exhaustive of the full range of possible contingencies. The exceptions with their explanations thus become 'the exceptions that prove the rule' because the provision of such explanations maintains the rule's presuppositional status both as a rule of conduct and as a rule of interpretation. Once again, we encounter a closed circle of interpretation. Presuppositional rules of action and interpretation interlock with the organization of account giving to form a seamless web – a self-motivating, self-sustaining and self-reproducing normative organization of action.

Generalizing this analysis, we can suggest that rules of action and interpretation are sustained in the first instance by an accumulation of instances that exhibit compliance with them. But they are also maintained by the provision of accounts which 'explain away' instances of non-compliance in ways that, by their very provision, sustain the presuppositional status of the rules. Thus at the deepest level of cognitive and social organization, the role of accounts is intrinsically bound up with the maintenance of the methods informing social cognition and the social organization of action. Accounts function to 'repair' the ubiquitous relevance of rules of conduct by protecting them from the 'entropic' process of attrition that could otherwise arise from the incidence of non-compliant actions. Ordinary explanations of action, no matter how trivial and apparently inconsequential, thus play a crucial role in maintaining the foundations of social organization itself.

Advantages and disadvantages

While it is not easy to evaluate the usefulness of a methodology as complex and multifaceted as CA in a few words, some basic comments can be made. As already noted, CA has been developed as a methodology which is specifically geared to the analysis of the structural organization of social action. During the past 15 years or so, many hundreds of detailed studies of interactional organization have been developed using this methodology in a number of countries. This widespread use of CA techniques testifies to their 'transportability' both within and across national boundaries.

The effectiveness of CA techniques comes from their exploitation of fundamental facts about how interaction is organized. These techniques are therefore specific to the analysis of interaction. It is unlikely, for example, that CA techniques would be as effective in the analysis of explanations provided in a pencil-and-paper procedure that was relatively disengaged from interactional organization and constraints. CA analyses are also highly focused. For example, in the analysis of the provision of accounts for rejected invitations, empirical analysis might well show that, where accounts of the rejection are given to third parties as opposed to the inviting individual, many of the features of accounts sketched above would be absent or considerably modified.

In terms of its specific empirical techniques, the strengths of CA are balanced by corresponding limitations. The discussion of both can be grouped under two headings: data collection and data analysis.

Data collection

The concern for naturally occurring data has resulted in data collection techniques which, like the naturalists' specimen hunting expeditions, have so far been largely unfocused. These techniques are geared to the specific tasks of conversation analysis and, as such, have important justifications. First and foremost, CA is at present a fundamentally descriptive exercise which is concerned with the 'natural history' of social interaction. Its aim is to describe the structural organization of social interaction and its associated reasoning in as many social settings (and as many languages) as possible. The focus is on fundamental structures and the ways in which they both create and influence choices among courses of action. It is important to recognize that this task has only been seriously addressed in the past few years and that we have no reason to suppose that it will be completed in a short period. It is also important to recognize that an understanding of how the structural organization of interaction works is not a descriptive or theoretical luxury, but an essential basis on which the interpretation of a wide range of social, social psychological and communicational data may depend.

Much of CA research is focused on data derived from mundane conversational interaction, and this approach is the product of a considered analytical strategy. It is based on the recognition that ordinary conversation is the predominant medium of interaction in the social world and the primary form to which children are first exposed and through which socialization proceeds. There is thus every reason to suppose that the structures of mundane talk form a kind of benchmark against which the more specialized forms of communication, characteristic of for example the courts, the classroom, the news interview, doctor–patient interaction and so on, are recognized and experienced. This supposition has been confirmed by an increasing body of CA studies focused on these forms of institutional interaction. It is clear, therefore, that the study of ordinary conversation offers a principled approach to describing the distinctive character of these more specialized forms of interaction and also interactions involving the asymmetries of status, gender, ethnicity and so on.

There is an undeniable temptation to accelerate the investigative process by using role plays to focus the collection of data or to use experimental techniques to gain control over variables which may influence the character of interaction. However, these procedures may seriously limit the range and kind of social interaction that is produced and, more generally, may compromise the naturalness of interaction in a variety of ways.

Thus, although it can be slow and cumbersome, the CA style of data collection does hold out the hope that a full range of interactive procedures will eventually be captured. Moreover, there are other advantages to be gained from the CA approach. In particular, the taping of natural interaction creates enduring data bases of interaction which, because they have not been shaped by the constraints of a particular research design, can be reused in a variety of investigations. Any strip of interaction will contain exhibits of a very large range of different interactional phenomena which can be compared with other exhibits from other data corpora. The accumulation of data corpora into banks of data will greatly facilitate the process of comparison.

These are some of the positive features of the CA approach to data collection. These features are intrinsically associated with the fact that CA is primarily geared to the analysis of the structural organization of interaction (see Duncan and Fiske, 1977 for an account of structural versus variable analysis approaches to the analysis of interaction). They are also associated with significant limitations in the use of CA data. In particular, the data are collected without the use of experimental controls on the content of interaction or controls on the sociological or psychological characteristics of the participants. The absence of these controls may contribute to the roster of acknowledged difficulties in assessing the impact of sociological (for example, gender, ethnicity, social class and so on) and psychological (for example, personality) variables on the specific outcomes of interactions.

In sum, the data collection techniques used by CA reflect a specific set of research objectives and strategies. By their very nature, they occlude other research objectives. This is not to say that the research techniques of CA are ultimately incompatible with other approaches. On the contrary, there is every reason to anticipate the development of complementary research programmes that integrate the findings of structural and variable analysis approaches. The adoption of its chosen approach to data collection reflects CA decisions about the priority of structural analysis in the research process at present.

Data analysis
In this chapter a basic three-phase framework for data analysis has been sketched, comprising (1) the inductive search for regularity, (2) deviant case analysis and (3) theoretical integration with other findings. Once again, this framework is specifically appropriate for the analysis of normative structural organization in interaction. It cannot be applied to patterns of interaction which are not normatively organized because in such data deviant case analysis, in particular, is inappropriate.

Although this methodology can be simply stated, it is complicated to apply. The complexity and specificity of the structural organization of interaction is such as to make the mechanical application of research technologies inappropriate. Much therefore depends on the ability of the analyst to isolate regularities and pattern in data cleanly and without overgeneralization. CA data analysis has developed as an operation in which empirical advances in particular domains have increased descriptive purchase in other, related areas of investigation. For example, the discovery that response tokens (such as 'mm hm', 'yes', 'oh' and so on) are not a set of undifferentiated 'back channel' utterances, but are systematically differentiated in terms of their placements, valences and tasks, has enabled researchers to gain access to new understandings of how 'topics' in conversation are organized and shaped. Effectiveness in CA research is not guaranteed by the application of a fixed set of methodological canons, but rather by resourceful use of the corpus of current knowledge.

CA research thus involves careful attention to the contextual and sequential details of interaction. It requires extensive listening or viewing of tapes, careful transcription of interactional detail, and exhaustive analysis. These tasks are time consuming but their results have proved rewarding and influential.

Conclusion

In this chapter, I have attempted to explore some of the interests which ethnomethodologists and conversation analysts have in lay accounts and in the more generic phenomenon of interactional accountability. I have also tried to illustrate some aspects of CA methodology by examining some cases in which conversationalists account (or fail to account) for their conversational actions. And I have examined aspects of the fundamental role played in social interaction and social life by interactional accountability and the giving of accounts. From an ethnomethodological and conversation analytic point of view, the last aspects lie at the very heart of the normative organization of social life. Accounts and accountability are fundamental features of social organization itself and their foundational significance is not restricted to the domain of social interaction (Pollner, 1974, 1975, 1987; Mulkay and Gilbert, 1982; Gilbert and Mulkay, 1984; Heritage, 1984). Accordingly the topics of this book have a particular relevance for those social scientists who are concerned with the phenomena of social organization. They are also of concern to anyone who has an interest in the fact that, from the point of view of social participants, the members of the social world are *agents* who treat one another as morally and socially accountable for their actions.

10

Completion and dynamics in explanation seeking

Ivan Leudar and Charles Antaki

Theoretical background

In this chapter we want to talk about a framework for analysing what happens when speakers ask each other for explanations. This kind of dialogue is causing a degree of puzzlement in artificial intelligence and human–computer interaction circles, as some articles in, for example, Norman and Draper (1986) show. The workers in the field know that, without an explanation, the information given by a so-called 'advice system' can be sterile; but they have had severe problems in designing computers better able to volunteer explanations, or to understand the explanatory requests that users sometimes make and to give them satisfactory replies (Alvey KBS Club, 1987).

It seems that what is missing is a theory to guide the design of systems which could engage in explanatory dialogues (or, at worst, which would explain why such systems are not feasible), despite the fact that conversations have been studied intensively in psychology, sociology and linguistic pragmatics. The problem is that not enough attention is paid to the variety of dialogue types, to dynamics of conversation or to the interplay between the individual and the social, and all of these are essential in understanding explanations.

We shall outline some concepts we have been developing which would allow the study of such aspects of dialogues. We shall not say much about explanations themselves, but shall try to persuade the reader that some of the ideas of turn-of-the-century pragmatic philosophers are useful tools, especially if used in conjunction with the methods and findings of modern pragmatics.

The focus here is on the work of G.H. Mead and, in particular, on his notion of *completion*. This is developed and used in analysing how participants in dialogues construct each other's (and their own) moves as explanations, conceiving of conversations in terms of a socially distributed cognitive system. The notion of completion is also used to develop a framework for conceptualizing dialogues as dynamic processes, which is necessary if one is to understand how it is possible that a dialogue game between participants may metamorphose as they talk to each other, and if one is to understand the function of explanations in that metamorphosis.

Completion and conversation

'Activities are social in that the acts begun within the organism require their *completion* in the action of others' (Mead, 1973: 446, our italics). (We shall refer to the completion of one person's act by another person as *other-completion*; and the completion of one's own act as *self-completion*.) Mead, working in a tradition which had still not lost faith in grand theories, intended his notion of completion to cover the whole ground of human behaviour. It seems to us that Mead was basically right to postulate completion, even if he left it general and unspecified. Most intentional behaviours are not just aimed to evoke social responses, but *require* them in order to become themselves social actions. For something to qualify as a purchase, for example, the money tendered by the purchaser has to be accepted by the shopkeeper. The act may have begun with my wanting a chocolate bar, but it would fail to be a purchase until the shopkeeper took my money. The behaviour is not constituted into a purchase by the customer's intent only. For something to count as a reception at court, there has to be a monarch to receive one's homage and graciously to return one's bow. The participants have to agree on the situation and have to show evidence of that agreement in their ready completion of actions initiated by others. The homage is defined both by the intent of the supplicant and by the features of the objective context including the actions of others.

Although faith has been lost in the tradition of grand theories such as Mead's, echoes of the notion of completion are still to be found here and there in social science thinking on communication. It is at least implied in such concepts as intersubjectivity, joint action, mutual knowledge, framing and so on. One can see a clear (but unacknowledged) Meadian heritage in modern pragmatics. Conversational analysis in particular (e.g. Sacks, Schegloff and Jefferson, 1974; Schenkein, 1985; Atkinson and Heritage, 1984) seems to us a framework which makes use of the idea of external completion. This is obvious from the fact that its starting position about the analysis of conversation is premised on taking exchanges, rather than individual utterances, as units of communication: 'Utterances are in the first instance contextually understood by reference to their placement and participation in a sequence of actions. For conversation analysts, therefore, it is sequence and turns within sequences, rather than isolated sentences or utterances, that have become primary units of analysis' (Atkinson and Heritage, 1984:5). Even this, Levinson (1983: 304–5) points out, is a first approximation, and examples of much more complex units of conversational organization can be found: our discussion and examples, however, focus on two-move exchanges.

The point is that in the conversational analytic framework, individual utterances achieve their significance as moves in exchanges. In this, conversational analysis is radically opposed to speech act theory (Searle, 1969; Searle, Kiefer and Bierwish, 1980) in which the illocutionary force of speech acts is defined by their form and the propositional attitudes of their authors. The controversy is made clear in an argument put forward by Levinson (1979). He points out that a promise (one of the 'classical illocutionary acts') is not a promise unless it has been 'taken up' by the addressee. If I promise to pay you back for the meal you just bought, does what I said still stand as a promise if you tell me not to be silly, it was nothing? Well, without the uptake, I certainly would not enter into the commitment that is the point of promising.

A systematic analysis of the extent to which different acts of communication can be incomplete is lacking, although incompleteness has been argued for requests (Habermas, 1975) and the indeterminacy of communicative intent has been argued for indirect speech acts (Edmonson, 1981). Indirectness and the use of various illocutionary force indicators make it obvious that speakers in fact exercise some control over the extent to which their utterances are open (to interpretation).

In general, the argument is that at least some of the conditions necessary for an individual's action to count as a speech act cannot be satisfied without the uptake by an audience or are only satisfied on the uptake. This is one sense in which individual acts can be underdefined, open to interpretation, and requiring a completion. The conditions which a behaviour must satisfy to be an action need not be coextensive with the mentality of an individual but may be distributed over the individual and the context of her action. This argument has a close parallel in philosophical debate on whether meanings are 'in the head' (e.g. Putnam, 1975; McGinn, 1983).

Conversational analysis thus admits openness and consequently allows the significance of an utterance to be negotiated. The initial move of an adjacency pair constrains the audience to a set of completions (partially ordered for preference), and thus *partly* defines the structural identity of those completions. In fact, the deviation from the set of follow-ups is normally signalled by the audience. The adjacency pair initial move is, however, itself basically open in that some of its properties remain to be defined by the addressee's move which affirms or (reinterprets) its intended identity. What follows an offer can be an acceptance, an evasion or a refusal; what preceded an acceptance was an offer! The completion, in its own turn, interprets or reinterprets the preceding initial move. Thus one way to specify Mead's notion of completion is to use conversation analysis and say that completions can be understood in terms of exchange structure.

Empirical example

Most of the data we use come from dialogues that we arranged ourselves. The aim was to set up situations which were similar to human–machine 'dialogues'. They are rather contrived, but the purpose was to simulate the situation of someone asking a machine for an explanation, which is itself a rather peculiar situation.

In each dialogue there were two participants. One was always our confederate, who was working from the same knowledge base – in this case, 'unemployment and its causes'. We gave the confederate no instruction about unemployment, and the knowledge base was simply his own beliefs and theories about it. His goal in conversation was given as informing the other participants (one at a time!) of his views on unemployment. The other participants were naive to the purposes of the study. They were asked to try and find out the confederate's explanation of unemployment. In some dyads, respondents were of the same knowledge status as the confederate; in the others they were junior to the confederate, who was introduced as an 'expert on unemployment'.

Our data indicate that not all other-completions reflect and are determined by the exchange structure. Another level at which addressees complete messages is that of content, and the cohesion of moves is a matter of logic. Examples of *structural completion* would be a greeting being reciprocated (as in (1) below) and a question being answered (as in (2)). In both of these the second move completes the exchange structure. In (3), in addition, the pragmatic identity of the initial move is fixed: K's 'Thanks' establishes L's previous move as an (indirect) offer.

(1)
    P: Hi, I'm Pete.
    J: Hi, I'm John.

(2)
>   J: Do you think this government is to blame for the unemployment?
>   P: To some extent.

(3)
>   K: I'm starving.
>   L: I have a pound left.
>   K: Thanks.
>   L: Right.

Cases (4) and (5), on the other hand, are examples of *cognitive completion*:

(4)
>   P: I would have to ask them whether they mean that it [*new industrial revolution*] is purely a technological change.
>   J: Or a complete reorganization of society, the same way as the industrial revolution.

(5)
>   CA:(i) If you educate people in a certain, say, vocational way, then you produce a certain kind of skill and a certain resource to be used by the economy. If you don't, if you have a liberal education, for example, you have a certain range of other skills for the economy.
>   BF: (ii) So do you then believe that the education system is at fault, that it should be changed, and if it were changed, there would be less unemployment?
>   CA:(iii) I don't believe anything so direct, no. I think it's just one aspect of demographic variables, which are themselves an aspect of economic trends, which are themselves an aspect of unemployment.

These are different from the completions in (1), (2) and (3), and it is not clear how they are to be explained in terms of exchange structure. In (4), P's proposition (that the new industrial revolution is a purely technological change) was completed by J by a further proposition (that the new industrial revolution is a complete reorganization of society) and forming a disjunction (new industrial revolution is either a purely technological change or a complete reorganization of society). In (5) BF treats the argument put forward by CA as a premise and provides a conclusion, thus completing her move into an *implication* which CA subsequently rejects. In (1), (2) and (3), what was at issue was how a response completed the initial move into an adjacency pair, and the pragmatic identity of the moves was fixed. The completions in (4) and (5) are different. In (4), for example, J's move is not itself a sentence, but it completes the sentence just uttered by P into another sentence. The cohesion of the completion is not provided by exchange structure but is in this case a matter of grammar and logic. One can certainly say that in (4) there is now one new and complete statement which is distributed over two participants. In (5) the implication is at first distributed between BF and CA, although CA subsequently denies his individual commitment to it.

We seem to have moved into controversial territory by suggesting that meaning and cognition can be 'socially distributed' and not coextensive with individuals; this is at odds with 'social cognition' as currently understood in most experimental social psychology (as in for example Fiske and Taylor, 1984). The notions on relationships between cognition and individual/social divide have changed over time. The distinction between subject and environment and in particular their radical modularization was certainly not always as sharp and as taken for granted as it is nowadays (Novack, 1975). Dewey put it this way: 'The distinction [between an individual and the environment] is really a distinction due to our interest; it is an intellectual distinction. ... There is a functional unity, a unity of the life process which maintains itself in, and by means of, a continuous series of diverse changes' (Dewey, 1975: 275). We may not agree with Dewey in detail, but had the winds of social change blown in another direction we should all now be contextualists (or, according to radical critics, we should have given up the distinction altogether; see Henriques et al., 1986).

Self-completion and internal completion

Mead was obviously sensitive to the problem of individual/environment dualism and offered a solution, some aspects of which are relevant here. He claimed that individuals act as their own audiences, 'completing' internally their own utterances:

> In the human organism the pattern of the whole social act is in some sense initiated in the individual as the pattern of his act. The mechanism of this is the effect, which the gesture of the organism has upon itself, that is analogous to the effect which it has upon the other. ... When this gesture, as is the case in the vocal gesture, tends to arise in the individual who makes it *the response or responses which it calls out in the other or others*, there may appear in his organism the initiatory stages of the act of the other or others. (Mead, 1973: 446, 447, our italics)

So according to Mead, not only the addressee but also the author completes her (individual) acts.

It may simply be a fact that an individual has no option but to react to herself as another, and to this extent objectively (even though the actual perspective on herself may vary and not be accurate). The idea of internal completion may seem, nevertheless, on the face of it, rather bizarre; and if the parts we italicized are misread appropriately, does away altogether with an individual's need to communicate. And of course it would do so if the internal self-completion was exactly the same as the prospective external other-completion: but it is not. The internal self-completion is not simple; often, and probably as Mead intended it, it establishes only the type of a response, not a specific response. The question is, to what extent is internal self-completion like other-completion?

Our strategic hypothesis is that internal completions and the overt moves tie together according to the same principles of discourse structure, logic and syntax as moves tie in ordinary conversations. Our speech samples contain two kinds of relevant evidence – extended turns and false starts. These have been noted previously (for example Labov and Fanshel, 1977) and analysed under the heading 'repair'. (Levinson, 1983, chapter 6). In neither of the conversations from which examples (6) and (7) come did the audience indicate (and presumably notice) anything odd. In fact, the turns make very good sense if we assume that the speaker was completing her own overt moves internally and subsequently reacted overtly to the tensions between the moves and their completions.

Extended turns such as (6) are like ordinary conversations in that they consist of a series of recognizable moves, all of which are, however, produced (overtly) by one person without being interrupted by another person:

(6)
P: What did you think of Jill's daughter?
I: (i) She is quite interesting, isn't she? (ii) What's her name? (iii) Isobel. (iv) Right.

In this example, (i) presupposes that the identity of the person referred to by 'she' is established. Let us assume that the internal completion of (i) queries this presupposition and the speaker I discovers that he cannot specify the identity of 'she' by naming her, although her name is on the tip of his tongue. Question (ii) is supposed to resolve the tension by finding the name from the other participant P, but the fact of putting the question seems to make the name available and I provides the answer for himself in (iii). In fact, the answer is acknowledged in (iv).

The second type of evidence is sequences of false starts, as in the following:

(7)
A: (i) So what has the government – (ii) if you blame the government – (iii) you blame the government – (iv) because they haven't done the things that you think they should do, like reflation?

This text makes sense if we make a couple of assumptions. Firstly, (i) was going to be a question: 'So, what has the government done to be blamed for the unemployment?' This presupposes that the addressee actually believes that the government is to blame. Secondly, the author has completed the (intended) question (i) intrasubjectively by, for example, 'but I do not believe that the government is to blame'. In other words, the speaker is uncertain that the presupposition of (i) is shared. The tension between the presupposition of the question (i) and the intrasubjective completion is expressed in (ii), which is supposed to solve the tension. In fact the speaker answers (ii) himself and thereby resolves the uncertainty in (iii); and proceeds to answer his own original question in (iv).

The process of internal self-completion makes it possible for the speaker's intention to change in mid-sentence as she becomes aware of ways she might be misinterpreted or misunderstood; or perhaps, as she starts talking, she foresees likely rebuttals or objections. In any case, the original aim of the utterance needs to be realized in a form different from the original.

In a sense we are improvising on the ancient claim that one must treat thought processes as inner dialogue. The conception goes back to Plato, and has in psychology been particularly elaborated by Vygotsky and his followers (Wertsch, 1985). In fact, even the notion of 'the language of thought' (for example Fodor, 1975) is also broadly consistent, even if the conception of language is often rather restricted. The advance is that it seems possible to apply the findings from pragmatics to thought processes and, in fact, the position has been cogently expressed by Carlson (1983).

Mead's concept of internal completion seems to be useful but requires a careful analysis and tightening up. The problem is that he has never given a systematic account of which completions are possible and what are their consequences. Once this is attempted, the notion becomes less straightforward. The first complication is that an addressee may respond to an author's move by a variety of moves, including dispreferred ones (such as evasion or querying presuppositions). This poses a problem for extrapolating the response back into the initiator's mind. Is it possible for an initiator to ask a question and at the same time to make preparations for doing something as dispreferred as answering it untactfully? Can one issue a request and also stubbornly refuse to carry it out? In other words, are there constraints on internal completions absent in ordinary dialogues? The problem is that the evidence is likely to be selective, and only the internal completions by dispreferred moves are externally exhibited in false starts, as seems to be the case in our data. The only candidate for self-completions by a preferred move in our data is (iv) in example (6), and even then it is external rather than internal self-completion. One possible mechanism which would produce such biased external self-completions is the following. The speaker internally completes her own move and a tension may arise between the move and the completion; the function of the external self-completion is to resolve the tension. That is what we have in fact assumed in the analysis of examples (6) and (7). It may be possible to formulate a relatively general method to guide decisions on the identity of internal self-completions. We start with two assumptions.

Assumption 1 The external self-completions resolve tensions between moves and their internal self-completions.

Assumption 2 The set of possible internal self-completions (of a move) consists of the conversational moves which could follow that move in ordinary, well-formed conversations (and this is where conversation analysis helps).

On these assumptions, it is possible to determine or at least to narrow down the identity of internal self-completions. The move being completed is known and so is the external self-completion. One has to choose from the set of possible internal self-completions the one which would produce the tension resolvable by the external self-completion.

It seems to us that an analogue of the postulated process of intra-subjective completion operates observably in dialogues and was manifested in the conversations between the participants in our study. The analysis of extended turns can be complemented by analysis of dialogues, and both contribute towards a classification of kinds of tensions which produce dynamics and of their resolutions. In the next section we give some relevant examples.

Completion and dynamics in conversations

Our text suggests that inconsistencies between on the one hand a move's significance for the author, and on the other its interpretation as implicit or expressed in the completion by the addressee, are one major source of dynamics in conversation. An example of this was already given in (5). There BF's interpretation (ii) of CA's argument (i) produces a tension which is supposed to be resolved by the explanation in CA's final move (iii). Another example is as follows:

(8)
BF: (i) So what else affects unemployment?
CA:(ii) Demographics.
BF: (iii) What does that mean?
CA:(iv) Age, sex, immigration, emigration, schooling, education.

BF: (v) In what way has education led to increased unemployment?

CA:(vi) The way you put the question sounds as if you mean: 'Is it not paradoxical that you are claiming that education leads to increased unemployment?'

BF: (vii) I did not say anything about education causing more unemployment.

Here, in move (v) BF draws a conclusion that education has led to increased unemployment. CA's subsequent move (vi) challenges this inference. What happens is that one participant treats another participant's move as a premise and provides a conclusion, this resulting in a 'distributed implication'. The process is again obvious in (9): (ii) is interpreted in (iii) as a premise, and both constitute a distributed implication which is challenged in (iv).

(9)

A: (i) So how do you think one should go about reducing unemployment?

B: (ii) Well, it's ... perhaps by reducing the working hours and overtime.

A: (iii) So they would be getting less money.

B: (iv) Well, yes, but not necessarily because you could ...

Exchanges (5), (8) and (9) all contained examples of cognitive completion which helped us to understand some of the dynamic characteristics of the dialogues. Similarly, examples can be found of structural completions which play a role in dynamics, mainly where the intended pragmatic identity of a move is not affirmed in uptake. The examples suggest that some moves in conversations might be generally understood as resolving tensions between one participant's moves and their interpretations in another participant's moves. One way in which explanations operate in dialogues is to establish the communality of beliefs where completions indicate its absence, as happened in move (iii) and text (5) and move (iv) in text (9).

At the functional level of analysis the process of self-completion does not seem to be too different from the dynamics characteristic of ordinary dialogues. The characteristics of 'tension' giving rise to dynamics are, however, not exhausted by their formal descriptions.

Advantages and disadvantages

We have attempted to extend Mead's notion of completion and use it to analyse conversations. The advantage seems to be that the framework acknowledges links between individual cognition and communication and allows the treatment of some cognitive processes as socially distributed. The approach also enabled us to consider the dynamic aspects of conversations and to analyse how tensions between individual moves and their interpretations seem to motivate much of conversation dynamics.

The disadvantages are questions, as always, of level of analysis. Does the approach pay too little attention to the content of the conversation, the participants' roles, and the macro-structure of the interaction in general? The worry is that by emphasising its formal characteristics, we overlook the conversation's idiosyncratic flavour. We might also be losing sight of how the episode functions as a discourse, that is to say as a rhetorical display that has an implied or explicit social force.

Our way of thinking is not incompatible with other levels of analysis. Whatever view one takes of conversations the fact is that they work extremely well, and people's success in bringing off such a difficult exercise needs explanation. The extension helps show that at least part of the explanation lies in treating cognition as a social process. This pulls us away from a more mentalistic account of talk, and into the sort of social account where contacts with other disciplines can be made.

11

Accountability within a social order: the role of pronouns

Rom Harré

One of the most important webs within the fabric that makes up a social order is the network of accounts. Accountability may be differently conceived in different societies and rights and duties to explain oneself may be differently distributed, but the giving and receiving of explanations is probably ubiquitous. Rights and obligations to perform accounting acts are non-uniformly distributed among the various ranks and categories of societies, and are in continuous historical flux: witness the changing rights of women and children in our own society within the last century. There are the experts, the credible and untrustworthy, the penitent and the brazen, and so on. The variety of contributions to this book is in part occasioned by the variety of ways in which position in a grid of roles and status locations appears in and influences the procedures of accounting.

In this chapter I want to direct attention to the fine structure of the languages in which accounting is generally expressed. Accounts *must* be tied to the array of relevant persons, on pain of unintelligibility. Among the most effective devices by which speech is linked to speaker and listener is the system of pronouns of its equivalent. These ties are effected through the linguistic property of indexicality. Pronouns are indexical expressions since they mark the relation between speech acts and person, place and time of their utterance. The role of indexical devices has been underemphasized in Anglophone studies, since English, for a variety of historical reasons, is amongst the most indexically impoverished languages in current use. The expressions available for denoting persons in many other languages encode, to a greater or lesser degree, the social relations between speakers and listeners. And this may be so to such an extent that the very grammar of the language determines what can be said to whom. This adds an important dimension to the understanding of accounts.

Theoretical background

> A court [in Germany] has ruled that familiarity means contempt
> and has ordered a woman fruit pedlar to pay a fine of 2250
> marks for insulting a policeman during a confrontation in the market
> square. Testimony brought out that the woman continuously addressed
> the policeman as 'du', the familiar form of 'you'. The policeman used
> the formal and respectful 'Sie' and thereupon filed a complaint of insult
> and misdemeanour. The woman is appealing against the verdict. (*Herald
> Tribune*, quoted in Brown and Gillman, 1970)

This news story nicely illustrates the power that grammar has both
to express and to offend social status. The woman's explanations,
whatever they were, were not at fault. We are not told whether or
not she actually had a vendor's licence. The unacceptability of her
account turned on a choice of *pronoun*.

That languages encode social orders in the rules of their grammar
is one of the central tenets of the social constructionist approach to
the study of human psychology. But they do so in varying degrees.
The Japanese language encodes most of the Japanese social system,
whereas at the opposite pole English encodes very little. No
competent speaker of Japanese could produce an account which did
not also express the requisite condescension and deference called for
by the social relations between the persons involved. It is advisable
to begin our approach to the encoding of social relations with an
analysis of some of the Western European languages, on grounds
of both familiarity and simplicity.

A powerful influence on psycholinguistic thinking was the work
of Brown and Gillman (1970) on the grammar of pronouns. Their
theory, which I shall take as my point of departure, can be summed
up in two principles. The first is *status*: a person will use the T form to
refer to or address an inferior, and will receive the V form in return.
The second is *solidarity*: status equals who are not members of the
same 'solidarity' (that is, roughly speaking, intimate group) will use
the V form to each other, while members of a solidarity (say an Army
platoon) will use T. The generic V/T distinction is realized in different
ways in the different European languages: in French *tu* and *vous*; in
German *du* and *Sie*; and so on. The variety of ways of grammatically
marking the V form is a matter of some importance. English now has
no honorific forms, and has lost the distinction between singular and
plural in the second person. The honorific second person in Italian and
Spanish is grammatically third person (as it is in American military
speech). The explanation is simple enough. *Lei* is a contraction of
la vostra Signora, just as *Usted* is short for *vuestra Merced*. But why
the plural form should have taken on the role of the honorific is

another matter. Brown and Gillman offer three possible explanations, not necessarily mutually exclusive.

The most fanciful – though I suspect it is the one they secretly prefer – is that it derives from Diocletian's reforms. In these, though there remained two Roman Emperors, there was only one system of administration. Necessarily then when addressing the ultimate source of power one used the plural *vos*. 'Eventually', they say, 'the Latin plural was extended to other power figures', but they do not suggest why! Their second suggestion is that royalty and heads of state and family are plural in another sense: that is, they are the summation of the people. However, if the Royal 'we' is used in addressing the subjects, should not a plural 'You' be offered by them in return? Finally they suggest that anyway plurality is a metaphor for power, since no doubt two horses can pull a heavier load than one. In the absence of any hard evidence one can take one's pick.

The stability of the total system is threatened when an asymmetrical status relation exists between people who inhabit a common solidarity, such as horseman and groom, professional and amateur cricketers, and so on.

Finally it was Brown and Gillman's contention, even in the revised version of 1970, that solidarity semantics has tended to displace status semantics as the basis for the grammar of pronouns and other person deictic devices, at least in Europe. Thus there would be two coacting tendencies. There would be a tendency towards a perceived symmetry in relationships favouring VV and TT over the asymmetrical forms, and a further tendency as solidarity attains dominance to favour TT over VV. Linguistic changes involved in the disturbances of 1968 *seem* to support this thesis, as indeed to the attempts by the ideologues of the French Revolution, such as Robespierre, to impose an egalitarian grammar based on *tu*. The spirit of 1789 is still abroad. I was present at a meeting of the faculty committee, a kind of 'soviet', at Aarhus University in 1972, at which a middle aged professor, hostile to the student revolution, threw in the towel by agreeing to use the intimate pronoun and to accept it when addressed to himself. The fate of these managed changes is instructive. As in the France of Napoleon, so in the post-1968 era the simple shift to TT has not occurred. Danish has drifted back to a condition near to its pre-1968 style.

What of Brown and Gillman's theory? I believe it is a reflection of a folk theory of pronominal and other forms of address in accounts and indeed in speech in general. People seem to believe that by saying something it can be made to be so. And here we come across one of the dimensions in which the priority of linguistic relations to other social relations must be qualified. The ancient changes in English do not seem to be susceptible to so neat a sociolinguistic explanation as Brown and Gillman offer for current changes in European languages, yet it seems that their dimensions of status and solidarity can nevertheless usefully be evoked. In English up to and including the Elizabethan period, the second-person pronoun was 'ye' in the plural and 'thou' in the singular. 'You' was the accusative of 'ye', while the accusative of 'thou' was 'thee'. So one would say 'I want you to do this' as a polite alternative to the brusque 'Ye shall do it.' But 'you' drifted across the linguistic landscape to become the honorific singular, and is so used by Shakespeare. I owe a quite tidy explanation of this drift from accusative plural to nominative singular and finally to a ubiquitous second-person reference to Michael Silverstein (1985). He believes that the Norman French practice of using the plural V form was copied by the speakers of English, to create a grammatical analogue of the status/solidarity semantics. So 'thou'/'thee' would be the pronoun of solidarity and of deference, while 'ye'/'you' would be the pronoun of distance and of condescension. Drawing on Brown and Gillman, Silverstein cites Sir Edward Coke's contemptuous remark to Raleigh: 'All ... was at thy instigation, thou viper; for I "thou" thee, thou traitor.' In the mouth of such a person as the Attorney-General, 'thou' is a pronoun not of solidarity but of contempt.

The Quakers wished to repudiate both kinds of human relations expressed in the 'ye'/'you' forms, since they wanted to use that part of the language resource which would emphasize relations of intimacy (closeness on the solidarity dimension) and to delete those usages which expressed the asymmetries of deference and condescension. Curiously the Quaker authors, such as George Fox, argued the case for 'thou' and 'thee' on the basis of the impropriety of the use of a *plural* form of address for a single person. In linguistic terms Fox and others took the plural to be the marked value of 'ye'/'you'. Now we can see why 'ye'/'you' became the general forms for second-person address. Unless one adopted the 'distant' alternative one would be heard, when using the old singular solidary form, to be talking like a Quaker. But why the accusative should have displaced the nominative requires a further explanation. I have already hinted at one above. It is also characteristic of English to use indirect forms for the giving of orders, rather than drawing on specific politeness terms. In modern English 'Would you mind doing ... ' is routinely preferred to 'Please do ... '. Since the indirect forms usually have the pronoun in the accusative, the tendency to generalize to 'you' seems unsurprising. Like all honorifics, 'you' can also be used as an ironic belittling device, a usage found in Elizabethan drama. By the end of the seventeenth century 'thou' and 'thee' had disappeared outside Quaker circles, to be replaced by the ubiquitous 'you', lacking both a marked plural and an honorific counterpart. Two pseudo-plurals 'youse' and 'you-all' have drifted in and out of use, but I know of no pseudo-honorifics. Without the plural model which seems to have animated the first shift, perhaps a contracted honorific title, in the Spanish manner, could have come on the scene. 'Yug' for 'your grace' hardly has the right deferential ring! It may be, however, that the rapidly changing English social order with a rising bourgeoisie needed what Brown and Gillman calls 'a linguistic waiting room', a device which leaves social relations unspecified. Grades can then be marked with official titles.

Empirical: social relations and accountability in Japanese

The analysis of ways of encoding social relations in European languages has focused our attention on pronouns and the two social dimensions of solidarity and status. But even the more elaborate European languages provide their native speakers with a fairly limited resource for pre-empting the best positions from which to give accounts and to hear and comment on the accounts of others. The Japanese language is tied into and encodes a much more complex system of social relations than almost any other. Indeed the Japanese social order is so fully encoded in grammar that accounting must always take place within an effectively non-negotiable grid of condescension and deference. This has a profound effect on whose stories have the greater weight in the creation and re-creation of society. Since this book presents a repertoire of methods, a word is in order about the way grammatical analysis is to be undertaken. Someone like myself who neither speaks Japanese nor lives within a Japanese social world is dependent on the work of linguists. But grammar is not enough, since the burden of the argument of this chapter is the role of grammar as laying the groundwork of a social framework within which all linguistic interchanges must occur. The analyses of experts must then be examined against a kind of folk ethnography of speaking that one gleans from native speakers and explores through shrewd (one hopes) probing and eliciting of their intuitions. I have had help from a number of native speakers of Japanese, but above all from Shinya Kimura.

Harada (quoted in Bachnik, 1982) has suggested that 'no real personal pronouns exist [in Japanese] that correspond to the Indo-European personal pronouns.' This judgement seems to me to be essentially correct, though for expository convenience I shall occasionally refer to some Japanese deictic expressions as pronouns. The Japanese language provides the user with a wide range of very subtle devices for interpersonal address and reference to which all account giving must conform, but neither functionally nor etymologically are they pronouns. We have already seen that deixis, and particularly indexicality, is the dominant function of Indo-European pronouns in use, with important sociolinguistic functions facilitated by this underlying grammar. Japanese seems to occupy the opposite pole, in that the social uses are etymologically prior and deixis and indexicality are built upon them.

Three technical notions are needed to bring out the nature of the Japanese systems of person reference and address: deixis, register and cline. In an excellent discussion of these matters, Bachnik (1982) draws attention to the fact that, concerning deixis, 'we may perhaps safely assume that the deictic anchor point [indexical locus] is Ego in societies where the individual is the basic unit of social organization. But in societies where the basic unit is *not* the individual, the question of the deictic anchor point and its relation to social organization must be raised.' In Indo-European social orders it is enough to know who is the speaker and who is the person addressed. But in the Japanese social order we need to know what is the relevant speaker's group and the group of the person or persons addressed. I hope the terms 'my-group' and 'your-group', though not ideal, are sufficiently unfamiliar to bear the differentiation I want to mark.

The term *register* is used in linguistics to refer to a system of lexical items by the use of which a number of non-linguistic distinctions are represented or expressed. Japanese includes a number of registers for expressing person distinctions. Since I am arguing that social relations do not exist independently of sociolinguistic practices, I shall be taking the use of the Japanese registers to be expressive rather than representative of social relations.

Finally the term *cline* will be necessary to refer to graded sets of distinctions. A downward cline expresses successively more condescension or more self-deprecation, while an upward cline expresses more respect or self-aggrandizement. The Japanese person registers turn out to be complex systems of reciprocal and interwoven clines.

Now let us turn to some observations of word forms that express deixis, register and cline. The role of second-person address is played by a noun register created by the use of suffixes. The system involves five terminations, related in a complex pattern. The pair *-sama* and *-san* are used to express respect for the interlocutor, the former being addressed to persons of a higher-status group than the group of the speaker, and the latter for equals. Both are polite forms of address. The termination *-sensei*, which can be used alone almost like a pronoun, comes from a word for 'teacher'. However, it is widely used in addressing those to whom the speaker stands in other kinds of dependent relation than pupil. At the other end of the cline the suffix -*tyan* is an affectionate and condescending diminutive. Incidentally, it is never used reflexively of speaker – a grammatical problem for small children, who are frequently addressed as -*tyan*. Indeed, none of these suffixes can be used reflexively. Women's grammar differs in many ways from that of men in Japan, and there is a suffix -*kun* in use only amongst men.

Complementary to this register is another system used indexically by speaker. But again one must be wary of treating this as some kind of elaboration on the pronoun 'I'. Not only is the indexicality directed to the me-group, but the register includes a complex of clines of formality and informality. Combining these first-person indexicals with the second-person register of honorifics above permits an amazing variety of speech acts. Harada gives an extensive list of such words, from which I extract four. As far as I can grasp the system, the principle seems to be that the more formal the first-person term, the more respect is being shown to the addressee. I have a sense that in some way the more formal the term the more self-status is being expressed too. There is an androgynous cline with *watakushi* and *watashi* in descending order of formality. When used by women each term is one level down in formality, reflecting and expressing the overall social status of women as a group relative to men. Then at the lower end of the cline of terms usable by men are two informal words, *boku* and *ore*. *Boku* is a term of speech rather than writing. It is not so much informal as formally self-denigrating. As my Japanese informant explained, you can use it when you know inside yourself that you are quite important but wish to display public deference. Formerly reserved to the speech of men, it has now come into use among liberal and radical women. *Ore* is the true term of intimacy. It is never used on first meeting. Moreover, it would sound very odd if used by a high-status person in ordinary conversation, and indeed is never so used. However, such a person could and would use it during a drinking party, underlining the asocial nature of the temporary grouping, a kind of life out of real social time and space. The most general informal term in use by women is *atasi*. (If it is used by a man he would be identified immediately as a homosexual.)

By choice amongst these terms the speaker expresses relative status from a pole reciprocal to that expressed by the choice of second-person term. Since any speech act must be analysed as a two-term relation linking speaker and addressee, a language sensitive to relative social position of the two termini, as they are members of this or that group, must find expression. A better sense of the force of these first-person terms and a clearer grasp of their difference from say English 'I' , which always leaves the social status of the speaker *vis-à-vis* the addressee undetermined, comes from observing their range of usage. Bachnik (1982) quotes Wolfe to the effect that *watakusi* is used in lots of ways that are not indexical of speaker. In these uses the term seems to mean something like 'belonging or pertaining to this or that person'. However, there are two English first-person indexicals which do express status in the Japanese way. These are the use of 'we' in the singular (appearing at the high end of a cline in the mouth of Victorian royalty and at the low end in the mouths of the excessively self-conscious) and the use of 'one' by the 'junior royals'. I am informed by Fred Vollmer that the Norwegian *Je*, which normally appears only in one of the written forms of that language, can be used for spoken acts of self-reference by persons of high status. If used by the lowly it sounds absurd.

Two other groups of terms serve pronominal deictic functions. Kinship terms are differentiated to express the distinction between me-group and you-group, as well as to express respect. Bachnik points out that the respectful *otoosan* (father) can be used to refer to your father, to address my father and to refer to our father (when talking with siblings). But another term *titi* is used when referring to my father in talking to a member of the you-group.

The group indexicality of Japanese person terms is clearly shown by the use of the word *uchi* (etymologically 'house') as a way of making speaker reference. We must not call this 'self-reference' because it is not clear that the English concept carried by the word 'self' can be applied to the Japanese person at all. The second-person term reciprocal to *uchi* is *otaku*, etymologically 'your house'.

Summing up the principles involved in this fragment of grammar, Bachnik remarks that the 'reference/address distinction is closely related to the boundary of the speaker's group.'

The noun registers I have sketched illustrate the general principle that the Japanese language permits the expression of social distance by either advancing the status of the addressee or reducing the status of the speaker (both kinds of speech acts taken as indexical of me- or you-group) or both. Verb registers work in the same way. Again I owe to Bachnik a very clear exposition of the complexities involved. Just as in the noun registers there are always two clines at work, one from formal to informal style and the other (best called for the verb register) from exalted to humble. So the choice of verb form lies in a two-dimensional space defined by two non-orthogonal axes, one of formality and the other of deference. The axes are not orthogonal because, as we have already notice, formal style of address is adopted when speaking to one of higher-status you-group. Sliding down both clines expresses, so to say, double deference. Thus degree of closeness expressed through greater informality is also an indirect mark of degree of deference. (One notes in passing the inversion

in English forms of address in which a formal style is adopted for
addressing those lowly in an institution.)

I cite Bachnik's layout of the variants of the verb 'to go' in
illustration. We start with *iku* in the centre of the 'space'. Choosing
instead the verb form *irassyaimasu* exalts the addressee, and in a
reciprocal response the addressee can choose *mairimasu*, humbling
himself. Again starting at the 'centre' with *iku* a speaker can choose
iki-mas-u as a formal stylistic variant, leaving *ik-u* as the informal
contrast. Likewise in exalting address the particle can be inserted
to give *irassyai-mas-u* as a formal stylistic variant, leaving *irassyar-u*
as the informal. Since *mairi-mas-u* is humbling and so *already formal*
the *-mas-* cannot be omitted; you cannot be both humble and informal
in Japan. In addressing David Copperfield Uriah Heep managed
this sociolinguistic feat in English. But then we are a linguistic
community famous for our 'hypocrisy'.

In analysing first-person deixis in terms of a collective deictic
anchor I have so far shelved the problem of plural self-reference.
What devices in Japanese correspond to 'we'? Correspondence cannot
be exact since singular terms of self-reference take collective deictic
anchors. So the Japanese singular and plural self-referential devices
cannot stand in the same kind of contrast as do 'I' and 'we'. In the
following I am greatly indebted to Shinya Kimura. There are three
pluralizing devices in use in Japan. One can repeat the word, as for
example *hito-hito* (= person-person, that is people) or *yama-yama*
(= mountain-mountain, that is mountains). But these are not simple
plurals. This device accomplishes roughly what 'each' does in English.
Not all nouns can be iterated in this way. For instance *neko-neko* (=
cat-cat) is never used. The second device is the attachment of a suffix
from among *-ra*, *-tachi*, *-domo* or *-gata*. These can be added, with
minor exceptions, only to words denoting human beings or creatures
personified as such. It will come as no surprise to learn that choice
amongst these suffixes is motivated by considerations of status. The
suffix *-domo* is pejorative, for instance in the Marxist expression
shihonka-domo for capitalists. *Sensei-gata* is honorific, meaning
'respected teachers'. The other two suffixes are neutral, perhaps a
little casual or rude. For words of Chinese origin, pluralizing is done
by prefixing *sho-*. For instance, *sho-zan* means 'mountains'; however,
again it is not simple plural, since it has the sense of every or a
considerable number of mountains. Professor Kimura has remarked
that the first and third devices are resorted to with growing frequency
to render the simple plurals in European texts. All three devices are
used to pluralize pronouns. The deictic term *ware* is no longer used
in the first-person singular and is currently used as a very vulgar and
pejorative second-person pronoun. The plurals *ware-ware* and *ware-ra*

are in use in literary contexts to express manliness, 'hard style speech'. *Watashi-tachi* is reasonably polite and commonly used, with *watashi-ra* slightly more polite and *watashi-domo* at the humble pole. The last is used in formal expressions of humility and by shopkeepers when addressing customers. *Boku-ra* and *boku-tachi* 'sound like student words', as Kimura puts it, though they are in common use even among the elderly. They can also be used in contemporary Japanese speech to refer to a we-group which includes women. It is not clear to me whether these devices can be used to include the addressee. Some difficulty must surely arise in using the humble *watashi-domo* when the group referred to includes the addressee. Perhaps the growing popularity of *boku-tachi* resolves the obvious difficulties.

Between the impoverishment of English and richness of Japanese lies a vast range of possibilities of intermediate degrees of social encoding. Tamil, a language of South India, is an instructive intermediate example. I owe the following account of Tamil pronouns to Vimula Mani. The system is of interest because of both its elaboration of the TT/VV semantics, and its refinement of the first-person plural. There are four 'we' forms, sensitive to whether the addressee is or is not a member of an intimacy or solidary group. *Nam* is used among intimates, while *nangal* is used when the addressees of the immediate collective do not belong to the solidary group. Similarly the first-person dual is marked for the same distinction. Thus *namiruvar* is the unmarked dual, when the pair are members of a solidary, while the marked form *nangaliruvar* is used when the one of the pair does not belong to the solidary of the speaker. Again in second-person address three grades of social relationship are expressible. *Ni* is impolite, *ningal* is intimate and friendly, while *nangal* is polite. Interestingly Tamil has a pair of affixes which can be used to create pejorative personal exclamations, corresponding to one of the uses of the English 'you', as for instance in 'Take that, you swine!' *Chi-* is derogatory as in *chi-nay* (= you dog!), while the suffix *e* is derisive as in *kurange*! (= you monkey!).

Throughout the languages I have discussed, these kinds of distinctions are operative in some degree. But just as in Indo-European the indexical system for place and moment, though not carried by pronouns and not picking out speaker as such, nevertheless in most non-Indo-European languages is person based. The Japanese language operates in a person space independent of the demonstratives by which indexical reference to physical locations in space and time are achieved. In English the pronoun system and the demonstratives, directionals like 'left' and 'right' and other devices for expressing spatiotemporal indexicality, are independent of one another, just as they are in Japanese.

According to social constructionism the role of pronouns in conversation is to locate acts of speaking at locations in a social world. Social worlds are structured by the 'fields' we have called moral orders. We would expect, all else being equal, that these structures should be encoded in some degree in deictic systems, such as the pronouns. But people are not only moral agents but also things in the physical world. So we might expect the deictic system to ramify into various devices for locating speech acts in physical time and space. And this is just what the demonstratives enable speakers to do. Again the question of how much of the structure of the relevant world is encoded in the grammar of these devices is the matter of interest.

In English spatiotemporal indexicals are an independent system from the person indexicals amongst which are the pronouns. Not only is it an independent system, but it is markedly impoverished relative to the range of devices available in other languages. Kami (old Javanese) illustrates a system in which people space and physical space constitute one manifold, but I shall not lay out the details of its fascinating grammar here. As A.L. Becker (1974: 241) puts it, in contrasting European languages with Javanese, 'person is an obligatory inflection in deictic usage. ... It is primarily person, the marked shifts of point of view ... that gives coherence to Kami texts, somewhat as tense and the sequence of tenses ... give cohesion to English texts. ... Notions like plurality, temporality, sequence and tense are, in a sense, secondary metaphorical developments of the interplay of person, location and definiteness.' All space-time is person space-time. It is impossible to find any corresponding European model, for instance for inflecting pronouns for 'tense'.

Advantages and disadvantages

Taking all this grammatical material together, the message is clear. The intuitions of how the social basis of accounting is created that we deploy as English speakers are a poor guide for a more general social psychology of accounts. Because of the social impoverishment of English grammar as a code, most of the work of creating and marking social relationships perforce is brought off by more or less explicit devices, such as facial expressions, intonation and the use of titles and other marked forms of address. Yet if we are aiming at a comprehensive social psychology of account giving and receiving we can hardly ignore the grammar of those languages in which social relations are very richly precoded. Research into their structure and conditions of use becomes a central target of concern.

I have advanced the analysis of grammar without, so far, doing more than occasionally hint at problems that may beset the unwary researcher. What are these problems? The thesis of the grammatical *determination* of thought, inaccurately ascribed to Sapir and Whorf, is surely false. Grammar constrains but does not predetermine all the uses to which language can be put. Speech act theory makes as much use of social as of linguistic categories. Case studies, such as that of Japanese, can lure one into forgetting that language is a system in use. Limits in lexical resources can be turned by the power of context, and often are. Furthermore, studies of grammar present snapshots of a static language/society relation and so are radically incomplete. Complementary studies of current conventions of use, and of their location in the historical development of conversational implicatures, are needed to fill out the dynamics of accounting. For instance it is just not true that the grammatical similarity between masculine and generic forms in English works to conceal the role of women in society. Recourse to grammar by feminists may be a proper part of the rhetoric of reform, but it is not a contribution to sociolinguistics, though the use of grammatical observations as rhetoric is a proper subject for investigation. Context and usage almost always disambiguate formal similarities.

But, in so far as any act of accounting is the presentation not only of reasons but of oneself, the representation of relative status, power and solidarity *vis-à-vis* one's audience *of that moment* must be a central matter of concern to the speaker. And, as such, it must remain at the focus of any programme developed to research into the social practices of accounting and the conditions that make them possible.

PART IV

RHETORIC AND IDEOLOGY

12

Discourse analysis and the identification of interpretative repertoires

Margaret Wetherell and Jonathan Potter

In this chapter we intend to illustrate the approach to lay explanations taken by discourse analysts. We will attempt, in particular, to demonstrate the value of interpretative repertoires as a basic analytic unit. Firstly, however, let us situate this methodological approach within broad developments in both social psychology and modern theories of discourse.

Theoretical background

Many social psychologies – even 'new' ones – have a rather old-fashioned view of language. They assume that language acts as a neutral, transparent medium between the social actor and the world, so that normally discourse can be taken at face value as a simple description of a mental state or an event. People's utterances might occasionally be distorted by the desire for social desirability but these cases of distorted discourse are unusual. More often, accounts are taken to be simple, unintrusive, neutral reflectors of real processes located elsewhere.

The implausibility of this standard assumption in traditional social psychology and in its alternatives can be seen when we look at the burgeoning work in sociology, philosophy and literary theory on language function. Analysts in these fields have demonstrated the *essential* and *inescapable* 'action orientation' of discourse (Heritage, 1984). Discourse has become seen as a *social practice* in itself, as opposed to a neutral transmitter, with its own characteristic features and practical consequences.

There is no space here to trace the threads of our own preferred theoretical framework – discourse analysis – in the intellectual traditions of speech act theory, ethnomethodology, conversation analysis, semiology and post-structuralism. The contributions by Billig, (chapter 14), Parker (chapter 13), Heritage (chapter 9) and Cody and McLaughlin (chapter 8) are complementary to our own, and contain a great deal it would be wasteful to duplicate here. Let us start from the position that utterances are acts, and that language is functional all the time – not simply on atypical, special occasions. The meaning of an utterance is not a straightforward matter of external reference but depends on the local and broader discursive systems in which the utterance is embedded.

Clearly, we are not suggesting that disparate and contradictory perspectives on discourse such as speech act theory and post-structuralism can simply be blended together to form a new analytic perspective. These are separate traditions with their own disputes and difficulties. But they indicate some issues traditional social psychologists neglect when they continue to take participants' talk as simple referential statements indicating a more or less trouble-free path to actions, attitudes and events. And from this basis we can begin to think about the form a discourse approach to social psychology might take.

Discourse analysis

Discourse analysis can best be understood by introducing the interconnected concepts of function, construction, variation and the analytic unit: the interpretative repertoire. We will start with the notion of function.

Both speech act theory and ethnomethodology stress the action orientation of language use. People do things with their discourse; they make accusations, ask questions, justify their conduct and so on. At the same time, post-structuralist work suggests that we need to modulate and supplement a study of the performative dimension of language use with work on wider *unintended* consequences; when people deploy a particular form of discourse, it has repercussions of its own which may not have been formulated or even understood by the speaker or writer.

The discourse analyst incorporates both of these aspects under the general term *function*. We can think of a continuum from more 'interpersonal' functions such as explaining, justifying, excusing, blaming and so on, which define the local discursive context, to the wider purposes discourse might serve – where, for instance, a social analyst might wish to describe an account, very broadly, as having a particular kind of ideological effect in the sense of legitimating the power of one group in a society.

In some cases functions are very easy to identify. Some utterances, for example, emerge clearly as explicitly meant speech acts. The utterance, for instance, 'I name this ship the Titanic' is an obvious example. In the appropriate circumstances (Austin, 1962) it will be perfectly clear to the assembled dignitaries and spectators that this utterance has the function of ship naming. Similarly other specific language functions such as requests, excuses and accusations may frequently be quite unambiguous.

Functions of this kind are not always clear-cut, however. Much of the time participants have good reasons for keeping the exact nature of their utterances inexplicit. For example, Drew (1984) has demonstrated how speakers often make requests indirectly, allowing the recipient of the request to reject them without making this rejection obvious.

It can be equally difficult to specify the broader consequences of discourse. Choice of terminology can have subtle effects which may be overlooked by speakers. For instance, it is commonplace to describe the current practice of moving the handicapped and the mentally ill out of institutions and into smaller hostels as 'community care'. One of the functions of this particular description is to draw on the positive evaluations tied to 'community' discourse and to develop a characterization focused around the organic and agency metaphors which distinguish 'community' talk (Potter and Collie, 1987; Potter and Reicher, 1987). Critics of the policy may find it necessary to deconstruct or negate the 'community' emphasis to effectively argue against it. But neither users nor receivers of this discourse need be intentionally aware of these consequences when formulating their description: it seems right. In many cases talk which is simply packaged as describing the situation, 'as the speaker sees it', can be analysed in terms of discursive functions and effects which go beyond mere description.

For these reasons discourse analysis cannot be, in a straightforward way, an analysis of function, because functions are not in general directly available for study. One of the difficulties in any analysis of language function and the actions contained in utterances is that we are immediately involved in interpretation. Essentially, discourse analysis involves developing *hypotheses* about the purposes and consequences of language. As we have seen, discourse does not usually come ready labelled with the functions neatly displayed on show, so that one kind of form is always an accusation, or always marks out a rationalization, or always suggests consequences which we could describe as ideological in their effect.

The elucidation of function is one of the *endpoints* of discourse analysis. That is, functions are the *findings* rather than the raw data. How, then, are functions to be revealed from a study of discourse? There is no single answer to this question; however, one important response is that functions are revealed through a study of variation.

The fact that discourse is oriented to different functions means that it will be highly variable: what people say and write will be different according to what they are doing. An event, a social group, a policy or a personality may be described in many different ways as function changes from excusing, for example, to blaming or from formulating a positive evaluation to constructing a negative one. Speakers give shifting, inconsistent and varied pictures of their social worlds.

In many ways this is a highly counter-intuitive claim. Psychologists are accustomed to regard the individual as a coherent, consistent unit – the starting point of their investigations. Only one description is possible of a state of mind, and once that description is achieved the quest is complete. *Variability* within and between the accounts that people give is not part of this image.

Variability is best demonstrated with data, and when we move on to a concrete research example we will return to our argument. For the moment our point is that variation has a crucial analytic role. As variation is a consequence of function it can be used as an analytic clue to what function is being performed in a particular stretch of discourse. That is, by identifying variation, which is a comparatively straightforward analytic task, we can work towards an understanding of function. We can predict that certain kinds of function will lead to certain kinds of variation and we can look for those variations (Gilbert and Mulkay, 1984; Mulkay and Gilbert, 1982; Potter and Mulkay, 1985).

Again, we should emphasize that variability need not be a consequence of deliberate or intentional processes. Much of the time people in their lay explanations will not be strategically planning, or self-consciously adjusting their discourse in a machiavellian fashion, but just 'doing what comes naturally' or saying what 'seems right' for the situation.

The fact that discourse is oriented, consciously or not, to particular functions, which in turn throw up a mass of linguistic variation, tells us that discourse is being used *constructively*. The realist model, outlined earlier, assumes that discourse is organized in a way which reflects the nature of the entities it describes. For discourse analysis, however, language is put together, constructed, for purposes and to achieve particular consequences. So variation is both an index of function and an index of the different ways in which accounts can be manufactured.

The term construction is appropriate for three reasons. Firstly, it cues the analyst to the point that discourse is manufactured out of pre-existing linguistic resources with properties of their own, much as a bridge is put together using girders, concrete and cable, some of which are flexible, some hard and so on. Secondly, it reminds us that *active selection* is going on: out of the many available linguistic resources, some will be used and some not. Thirdly, the notion of construction emphasizes, once more, that discourse has an action orientation: it has practical consequences. Much of our social lives depends on dealing with events and people which are experienced *only* in terms of specific linguistic versions. In a profound sense, then, discourse can be said to 'construct' our lived reality (Potter, Stringer and Wetherell, 1984).

Several specific analytic practices have emerged from our discussion so far. Firstly, and fairly obviously, we are suggesting that close attention is paid to the detail of language use, working from transcripts or documents rather than from (in the social psychological tradition) some numerical transformation of these things or (in micro-sociology) the remembered gist of interaction. Secondly, this approach suggests that discourse itself becomes the primary research focus. It is not a subsidiary path to the true nature of events, beliefs and cognitive processes. Thirdly, we propose that discourse analysis depends on the study of variation, working from the way discourse is constructed to some conclusions about the functions discourse might be serving.

Moving on from these points we come to our final analytic tool: the *interpretative repertoire*. We suggested earlier that discourse is variable in the sense that any one speaker will construct events and persons in different ways according to function. This is not to imply that there is no regularity at all in discourse – simply that regularity cannot be pinned at the level of the individual speaker. There is regularity in the variation. Inconsistencies and differences in discourse are differences between relatively internally consistent, bounded language units which we have called, following Gilbert and Mulkay (1984), interpretative repertoires (Potter and Mulkay, 1982; Potter and Reicher, 1987; Potter and Wetherell, 1987; Wetherell, 1986; Yearley, 1985).

Once again, repertoires are best described in relation to a particular empirical example. However, some points should be noted here in abstract. In dealing with lay explanations the analyst often wishes to describe the explanatory resources to which speakers have access and to make interpretations about patterns in the content of the material. The interpretative repertoire is a summary unit at this level. Repertoires can be seen as the building blocks speakers use for constructing versions of actions, cognitive processes and other phenomena. Any particular repertoire is constituted out of a restricted range of terms used in a specific stylistic and grammatical fashion. Commonly these terms are derived from one or more key metaphors and the presence of a repertoire will often be signalled by certain tropes or figures of speech.

The 'community' talk mentioned earlier is, in fact, a classic example of a repertoire in this sense. It is a set of terms used in explanations which depend crucially on certain metaphors and tropes. The 'community' repertoire is a resource which the analyst can identify as a recurring pattern in the content of certain materials. Our empirical example examines repertoires in a quite different domain – the construction of models for 'race' relations.

Empirical example: the construction of 'race' relations

Background
The study which we will focus on is taken from an extended project on racism in New Zealand. This project was concerned with how the majority group of white European New Zealanders understand issues like inequalities of employment opportunities and how they make sense of their relationship with the indigenous Maori people.

It is not necessary, fortunately, to be familiar with the theoretical background to this work or with the New Zealand context to appreciate our study as an example of discourse analysis at work. Suffice it to say here that our project developed as a way of looking at racial prejudice that went beyond social cognition, attitude socialization and 'personality' (Wetherell and Potter, 1986a, 1986b; Wetherell and Potter, forthcoming; cf. Billig, 1987b; Reeves, 1983; Van Dijk, 1984). We were interested in how ordinary, mainstream white New Zealanders would describe their past, present and future relations with the minority Maori group, and our concern was with the ideological consequences of their discourse. We wanted to look at how our sample's practical reasoning about race might justify and work to maintain asymmetrical power relations between the majority and minority groups, rationalizing and naturalizing a certain kind of status quo (Giddens, 1979; Thompson, 1984). Needless to say, when discourse analysis is used with these kinds of goals it must be combined with a careful analysis of the particular intergroup situation in question. Discursive patterns must be located within an account of their wider context.

We conducted interviews with 40 women and 41 males, of varying political affiliation, relatively evenly spread between National (right-wing) and Labour (more left-wing) voters, and covering most age ranges from 18 years upwards. Those interviewed could be described as middle class, by education in the case of the young people, by socioeconomic circumstance in the case of the non-working women and men, or by their professional or managerial occupation for the remainder. This is a relatively large sample by discourse analytic standards, chosen because we were particularly interested in the generality of our conclusions across a wide group.

Interviews were designed to elicit extended sequences of talk on a number of topics. They focused especially on perceived causes of the disadvantaged position of the Maori people, recent multicultural social policies, proposed reasons for racism and tension, and special provision or positive discrimination for ethnic groups. All interviews were tape recorded and fully transcribed. The general procedural details of interviewing and transcription are discussed at length in Potter and Wetherell (1987).

Variation
Let us first use some of our data to illustrate variation in discourse before presenting our method and findings with regard to interpretative repertoires. We argued that variation in individuals' accounts was an essential feature of natural language use, and an important route to understanding function. In terms of this project, a contrast could be made between the expectation of attitude theory, that people's statements will reflect an underlying attitude which is either consistently prejudiced or 'tolerant', and the discourse analysis claim that people use language, including attitude-type statements, functionally and thus variably as the discursive context changes.

The extracts below have been grouped under two categories: A and B. The first extract under A is an anecdote about the speaker's bible class where an incident is described and the point drawn that children internalize racist attitudes from their parents. In the second extract under A the same speaker gives her view on racist jokes, commensurate with her point of view about racist remarks in general. Finally, under A, this speaker indicates the aspects of Maori culture she admires. Overall this speaker can be heard to feel strongly about racism and positive about Maori culture. If so inclined, we might characterize her as a liberal non-prejudiced person.

Extract A
(1) I do this bible class at the moment, not highly religious, I just think children ought to know about religion ... and last night we were just discussing one of the commandments, love your neighbour, and I had this child who said 'What would happen if you got a whole load of Maoris living next door to you?' and I said to him 'That's a very racist remark and I don't like it', and he shut up in about five seconds and went quite red in the face, and I realized afterwards that obviously it wasn't his fault he was, turned out to be thinking like that, it came directly from his parents.

(2) [*Racist jokes*] I don't like them I don't find them amusing.

(3) [*What can we learn from Maori culture?*] The extended family situation's brilliant, they've got this lovely idea that a child born

out of wedlock would have to be the best sort of child because it was obviously born in love ... I think their way with children is wonderful. ... They've got a lot to show us I think.

The three extracts under B present a different picture. The speaker here seems more willing to attribute negative characteristics to groups and unwilling to accommodate Maori culture. In the first extract, it is suggested that Australians are handling their intergroup relations in an unfortunate way – letting other groups get on top of them because of their inherent laziness. The second extract puts forward the view that because white British settlers conquered the Maoris who, in their turn, had conquered the Maorioris, Europeans have licence to define their own terms in New Zealand. And, then, the speaker suggests in the third extract that Maoris must accommodate to European society, although it is recognized that being the indigenous group they can't be repatriated in any sense unlike other Polynesian groups who are immigrants to New Zealand.

Extract B
(4)   The Greeks live in one part of Sydney, all the such and such, and they're all growing up and speaking their own language and doing everything, they're going to have all these groups, and the Australians are basically a lazy people, and that other cultures are getting on top of them, there's going to be big problems there one day.

(5)   The ridiculous thing is that, if you really want to be nasty about it, and go back, um, the Europeans really did take over New Zealand shore, and I mean that Maoris killed off the Maorioris beforehand, I mean it wasn't exactly their land to start with, I mean it's a bit ridiculous. I think we bend over backwards a bit too much.

(6)   And this is the part that I think is wrong with (.) a bit wrong with the Maoris as well there, the problems they have, they're not willing, I mean it's a European society here and they've got to learn to mix and get in and work, otherwise it's, I mean you can't tell them to go back to where they came from.

In fact, both A and B extracts come from an interview with the same speaker, whom we will call Benton. The pattern one finds in these extracts was common in our interviews in the sense that, as we have argued, people construct different versions depending on the functional context. Over an entire interview it is exceedingly difficult to summarize their views. Indeed, from the perspective of attitude theory, how would one describe Benton's underlying attitude? Is this a prejudiced person? A 'tolerant' person? A person likely to be in favour of multiculturalism and/or anti-racism, and against attributing negative qualities to people on the grounds of race or nationality? Or is this a person who supports the maintenance of white cultural hegemony?

We see Benton, then, drawing on different, often inconsistent resources, as they seem appropriate. She is not an isolated example. The same complexity is apparent in the next extract, taken from another speaker whom we will call Anna James.

(7) I think it [multicultural social policy] is a good thing, cos I said before, I think people need to know their roots and their culture and that sort of thing. But I think we've got to be really careful that we don't go overboard in that at this stage. There've been a lo ... a few injustices against the Maoris over the years, that's going to happen with any sort of racial minority in a society, um but I think at this stage we've got to be careful not to go overboard um, I think we've got to be careful not to force the white children to learn Maori if they don't want to, it's not the white children's heritage. Now, okay, you give the opportunities, I mean they have the Maori playschool, Maori language playschools, and I think that's really good for Maori kids. But I don't want my kid to learn Maori, I don't want my kid to learn about grass skirts and ... I want my kid to learn about the history of the British Isles and the history of Europe which is incredibly important to the formation of their ideas about, you know, society. Okay, um, I think we should understand how Maori (.) uh, culture works, I mean I know very little about it, I know the basics, and I would like to see my kids do a daytrip to a marae, and see how they ... but I really think we've got to be incredibly careful about pushing it down people's throats, particularly the white people's throats.

This extract can be seen to be organized around a particular kind of functional feature – namely a disclaimer. A *disclaimer* is a verbal device designed to ward off potentially obnoxious attributions (Hewitt and Stokes, 1975). Thus if someone prefaces their remarks with 'I'm no sexist but ... ', the listener can be relatively confident that obnoxious remarks about women will follow but the speaker is wishing to head off, or disclaim, the possible implication that they are sexist.

Disclaimers create a form of variation which presents particular problems for the realist model of discourse and the assumption that the individual actor can be assumed to be a coherent consistent starting point for analysis. In the case of this extract Anna James first establishes that she is not one of those people opposed to Maori culture, but then goes on to give arguments explaining why her child should not be exposed to multicultural education. Her views on multicultural social policy are clearly qualified. Now, of course, people's views are frequently qualified in this way. Something is a good thing provided certain conditions are met, and then it becomes unclear whether it is a good thing or not. But how could this complex view be summarized and put into a response category? Simplistically, does this person's utterance support multicultural education policies or not? She is clearly not indifferent to the issue, or without a view, and thus in the middle of some response scale.

These extracts, therefore, indicate the problem of variability. They demonstrate very clearly some of the difficulties involved in working with natural language. How are we going to proceed with our analysis of these data? As we noted earlier, discourse analysis attempts to study variations in content to work towards an understanding of function. By studying the resources from which an account is constructed, we can also investigate what it might achieve. We noted earlier that differences in content reflect differences between interpretative repertoires. If we look, therefore, for regularities at this level, in language, and abandon the individual as our principal unit of analysis, then progress might be made in understanding the complex inconsistencies in the discourse centred around 'race' relations.

Interpretative repertoires
The first goal in a study of this kind is to perform some preliminary coding and thus sift out a manageable subset of data from hundreds of pages of transcript. We selected out from the interviews all passages of talk relating to our topic of models of 'race' relations. This included all material relating to the respective places of Maori and European culture in New Zealand – issues such as integration versus separate development or assimilation, the teaching of Maori language, reactions to attempts at a renaissance in Maori culture and so on. The topics developed in the interview questions were set by the structure of contemporary debates and the general agendas of the main political parties.

As an aside, it is important to stress here that the analysis which follows is in no way intended as a complete presentation of our conclusions for this part of our data. The aim is simply to use some material as an example, to illustrate our method, and not to give a definite picture of the repertoires articulated or of the ideological implications of white New Zealanders' analysis of the path they suggest relations with the Maori people should follow.

Our coding policy at this stage of discourse analysis is usually an inclusive one, accepting all borderline and anomalous cases, and the end product is a file of photocopies of the original transcript. It is at this point that analysis proper begins, with careful repeated readings of the materials in a search for patterns and recurring organizations. This process is not a matter of following rules and recipes; it often involves following up hunches and the development of tentative interpretative schemes which may need to be abandoned and revised over and over again. Discourse analysis is a time consuming and laborious business, with the search for regular pattern giving way to the formation of hypotheses about that pattern of repertoire use.

From this process a number of different repertoires were identified for our general topic – too many to be discussed here. However, three particular dominant repertoires can be picked out: we have labelled these culture fostering, pragmatic realism, and togetherness (Wetherell and Potter, 1986b). It is worth spending a bit of time clarifying the overall pattern of use of these repertoires and the grounds for identifying them as different, before going on to the details of their content.

Culture fostering was used by over 90 per cent of the respondents, while pragmatic realism and togetherness were drawn on by about half the respondents. So the most common pattern of accounting was culture fostering combined with either pragmatic realism or togetherness, although an appreciable number of respondents – perhaps 10 per cent – combined all three. The immediate point, then, is that there is no sense in which we could have divided our respondents into three classes, each distinguished by a different pattern of belief. Each respondent selectively combined different repertoires. Indeed, it may be that if we had asked a few more questions *all* respondents would have drawn on *all* three repertoires. The combination of repertoires produces the kind of complex and varied versions we noted in the extracts considered earlier.

What grounds have we for defining three different interpretative repertoires here? In this analysis we used three central kinds of evidence for this. Firstly, as we will show, there are inconsistencies – noticeable to *both* analysts and participants – between the different forms of account. Secondly, these forms of account are generally separated into different passages of talk so that inconsistencies do not become a problem for participants to deal with. Thirdly, on these occasions when the different repertoires *are* deployed together, participants display in their talk an orientation to the potential inconsistencies, or the variation is organized for different functions – one repertoire presented for disclaiming, for example.

Let us now look in a bit more detail at the makeup of these repertoires. *Culture fostering* presents arguments for the development of Maori culture. It appears to advocate multiculturalist social policy and the importance of Maori culture for New Zealand society. There are two major facets to it. On the one hand, it presents the view that Maori culture should be encouraged, fostered, protected and conserved because it uniquely and distinctively identifies New Zealand, and is a worthwhile culture in itself. For example:

(8) I'm certainly in favour of a bit of Maoritanga it is something uniquely New Zealand. I guess I'm very conservation minded and in the same way as I don't like seeing a species go out of existence I don't like seeing a culture and a language and everything else fade out. (Shell)

On the other hand, culture fostering presents the view that it is important for the Maori people to have a sense of identity and history or roots, in the way it is considered important for every person to have a sense of identity or place. For example:

(9) I think the sort of Maori renaissance, the Maoritanga, is important because like I was explaining about being at that party on Saturday night, I suddenly didn't know where I was, I had lost my identity. ... I think it is necessary for people to get it [*Maori identity*] back because it's something deep rooted inside you. (Reed)

Culture fostering here is seen as positively compensating for what is viewed as a deficit or a weakness *within* Maoris. Formerly Maoris tended to be seen as deficient in relation to European culture, in need of European enculturation and civilizing influence. In modern 'liberal' New Zealand such an obviously white supremacist view is less acceptable, but this form of accounting retains the notion of deficit; specifically Maoris are seen as deficient *as* Maoris, and therefore now in need of Maori enculturation (Nash, 1983).

What function in the broader sense might this deficit notion achieve for those who use it? Firstly, it seems to make sense of another commonplace understanding that Maoris have a deprived social position and are discontented, through using the idea of rootlessness and loss of identity. In this lay sociology, people without roots – those who have 'lost' their identity in some way – do not perform well and are likely to agitate. Secondly, in using the notion of cultural deficit speakers can effectively place Maori problems elsewhere, removed from their own responsibilities and actions. In this way speakers can convey that they themselves are in no way to blame for these problems.

One of the consequences of this form of talk is that multiculturalist social policy is advocated without requiring reciprocal change in the majority European group. The development of Maori culture becomes a matter for Maoris only, assisted by Europeans who merely clear a space, as it were, for this development, as a mother might clear a space for a child to play, knowing that play is good for the mental health of the child. Respondents virtually never characterized the inclusion of Maori culture in a way which involved active effort or change on their own part; effort and change was depicted as a Maori problem and duty. We hypothesize that this is a repertoire used to positive liberal effect but which locates the problem outside the responsibility of the white majority group.

The second repertoire used in discussions of 'race' relations strategies is *pragmatic realism*. Pragmatic realism, used by roughly half the sample at some point in the interview, and thus including many of those who also draw on the culture fostering repertoire, stresses the promotion of those things which are useful, modern and relevant today. It combines with this an emphasis and appreciation of the practical constraints on action. For example:

> (10) I actually object to um them bringing um massive Maori culture curricula into schools etcetera ... because I do feel that this doesn't equip them for the modern world at all. Because what's the use of being able to speak Maori if you can only speak it to a limited number of people in a limited area and it has no use at all in the actual, you know, in the real world as it were, if you'll pardon the expression. (Bradman)

The modern world referred to in accounts of this kind is predominantly defined in Western terms. In the next extract, the same point of view is applied to learning Maori language:

> (11) You know this is a side line, you can't go back. I mean you can go back but you are not going to live in this day and age. I'd far sooner see them all learning Japanese so they can say 'Ah so' when all the visitors come. (Sedge)

When using this repertoire, it becomes incomprehensible to 'turn the clock backwards'. The idea is that on sheer pragmatic grounds there is little to be gained from Maoritanga, for Maori cultural practices are 'unrealistic' or 'impractical'.

This is a very different, even contradictory, repertoire from that of culture fostering. Its principal idea is that much of Maori culture is antiquated and should be quickly abandoned. This apparent contradiction, as we noted, does not stop the interviewees drawing repeatedly on both repertoires.

As part of this kind of talk, speakers often suggest that introducing Maori language is impractical because most Maoris no longer speak Maori. There is a depressing irony about the members of a group who have done their best in the past to suppress an indigenous culture, arguing at this stage that the success of their suppression is good grounds for continuing to suppress it. Pragmatic realism is a particularly flexible repertoire. We suggest that its effect is to enable speakers to present constraints which are beyond their control, and which they can thus regret, but at the same time to construct themselves as people who are at least realistic and practical.

The third repertoire, which we have called *togetherness*, is the most interesting in many ways. It articulates a familiar position and is the notion that there should be no divisions or barriers between people: we should all be one together. People should be treated as people, not in terms of their colour or cultural background.

> (12) I wish that we could stop thinking about Maori and European and think about New Zealanders (Int: Mmhm.) and to hell with what colour people are. (Dixon)

Or:

> (13) I think it's important that we recognize that we are in fact all New Zealanders and we should be tending to become more one rather than separately developing. We're tending to ... pull that part of our culture to almost a sense of importance that I don't think it really has. We are one people, despite history. (Barr)

On the face of it this seems a highly positive and caring approach, and indeed in psychological terms it is probably well intentioned. However, the implications of applying it *in this context* (as over half the respondents did) are not so positive. European culture is the dominant culture in New Zealand; it thus sets the normative framework for what it means to be one people together. Put another way, for these people 'New Zealanders' are often depicted as basically white Europeans and the divisions between people or barriers objected to are those created by the legitimate claims of the Maori people. The upshot of this form of talk is that Maoris should stop encouraging rifts and conflict and accommodate to dominant European values; however, this consequence is hidden behind the innocuous moral formula of togetherness.

Overall, then, respondents' talk around this general topic is made up from a combination of repertoires (and we have only discussed three of these) which produce a complex and potentially inconsistent or, at least, variable response. We have concentrated in this analysis on briefly speculating about the broader ideological consequences of these repertoires, although the functions they achieve at the level of the localized discursive context could also be considered through the study of variability.

In general these speakers could not easily be described as oppressive or racist; indeed, on a superficial hearing they may come over as well-meaning and sympathetic. However, we would want to make a strong distinction between the *psychological motivations* for using these discursive forms and their *social psychological consequences*.

Well-intentioned talk can have reactionary consequences, as we have tried to demonstrate. For this reason also, we reject psychologically reductive theories of racism (Potter and Wetherell, 1987; Wetherell and Potter, 1986a, 1986b; forthcoming).

Each repertoire is relatively innocuous in abstract and possesses its own morally virtuous self-presentation, yet the potentially disruptive force of Maori protest and anti-racism is safely contained. Put at its simplest, the critic can be silenced by culture fostering, undermined by pragmatic realism and in addition accused of creating barriers between people. It is only when looking at the organization of explanations in the discourse as a whole that the fragmented and inconsistent nature of the talk becomes apparent. We would suggest that this flexibility in articulation is crucially important to ideological effectiveness (Wetherell, Stiven and Potter, 1987).

Advantages and disadvantages

There are two areas of potential disadvantages with discourse analytic work of this kind. Firstly, there is the sheer effort involved. The time taken up by conducting a set of interviews and then fully transcribing them is considerable, and few people find transcription pleasurable – although there is nothing better for encouraging close attention to what people are saying. Analysis is a craft skill which takes time to develop and is slow to conduct. It is quite possible to follow up an analytic scheme for some days only to find that it is simply impossible to validate with the materials available.

Secondly, work of this kind is not suited to the production of the kind of broad empirical laws which are commonly the goal of social psychological research. Unlike some social cognition researchers and personality theorists, we do not claim to have found a universal psychological process underlying racism. On the contrary, our findings are specific to a particular class of New Zealanders at a particular point in New Zealand history, and we would not necessarily expect white British majority group members, say, to account for racial inequalities using the same interpretative repertoires. Nevertheless, we see this not so much as an inadequacy of the approach but as a consequence of the fact that explanations are always fitted to specific occasions and constructed out of the available interpretative resources.

A further disadvantage arises from the novelty of discourse analysis. This is not yet a tried and tested approach elaborated and honed in many empirical settings. Clearly further theoretical work is required. The notion of function, for example, needs further elucidation. This kind of elaboration, however, is best carried out in relation to particular empirical tasks and with data rather than in abstract. Undoubtedly discourse analysis will revise its operating base as its application grows.

Offset against these disadvantages we see certain crucial advantages of the discourse analytic approach. Firstly, the approach is intended to do justice to the subtlety and complexity of lay explanations as they are deployed in natural contexts. We have not had to constrain the participants' response options to obtain usable data; indeed, we could have carried out a similar analysis to the one above on purely naturalistic records of everyday conversations or newspaper articles (Potter and Reicher, 1987). And we are not treating lay explanations as a degraded form of some underlying schema or cognitive process; in discourse analysis the language used is a constitutive part of the explanation, not a medium that the explanation is translated into.

Secondly, although discourse analysis is sensitive to linguistic nuances and the kind of contextually sensitive features of talk which are extremely difficult to recover using traditional content analysis, it is a systematic approach whose findings are open to evaluation. Elsewhere we have discussed in detail the techniques through which the conclusions of discourse analysis can be validated (Potter and Wetherell, 1987); one of the most important of these is the report of the research itself. Studies of this kind include a representative set of extracts along with detailed interpretations which link the analytic points to specific features of extracts in such a way that the reader is able to assess the success of interpretations and, if necessary, offer alternatives. The overall goal is to openly present the entire reasoning process from data to conclusions.

Finally, we would argue that the results of analysis of this type are both interesting and potentially useful because they focus on both the specific linguistic content and the organization of lay explanations. When dealing with racist explanations, this means that we come to understand the various interpretative repertoires through which racist explanations are constructed and warranted, and can start to understand the techniques through which these explanations can be undermined and transformed.

13
Deconstructing accounts
Ian Parker

In this chapter I want to show how techniques developed in literary theory can be applied to everyday explanation. However, as you will see when we come to the empirical example, the deconstruction of a piece of text involves a radical overturning of traditional social scientific distinctions between what is an everyday, spontaneous account and what is an extraordinary, manufactured item of script. The approach I will focus on, that of deconstruction, extends the critiques of positivism and individualism in traditional social psychology, reformulates our notions of what constitutes lay explanation and re-emphasizes the part power plays in social life.

Theoretical background

The emergence of a deconstructive approach to social psychology should be understood in the context of attempts to provoke a paradigm shift in the discipline over a decade ago. At the time, critics of traditional laboratory-experimental social psychology hoped to reconstruct the discipline out of the ruins of the crisis-ridden 'old paradigm' (Armistead, 1974; Harré and Secord, 1972).

The 'crisis' in social psychology developed primarily out of a claim that most published research was trivial, presented a mechanistic model of the human being, and failed to engage meaningfully with real issues and experiences. We have to be aware, though, that other (as yet unresolved) problems played a role. Most important was the question of power: power as a pervasive quality of social interaction (highlighted in the classic obedience and conformity experiments), power as a profound influence on laboratory results (demonstrated in the work on experimenter effects and demand characteristics), and power inherent in the situation of a privileged researcher *vis-à-vis* his (and sometimes her) subjects. The phenomenon of power is a difficult one to conceptualize without appreciating the ideological status of social psychology in our culture. In turn, to understand the work of ideology we have to appreciate the power of language, which is where 'new paradigm' social psychology really made its mark.

New social psychology

Language, the proponents of the new paradigm argued, was the key to understanding social life. Psychology mistakenly viewed itself as a natural science, and, on top of that, it had a mistaken view of how the natural sciences obtained knowledge of their objects. Instead, psychology (and especially social psychology) should recognize that the pre-eminent role of language, of meaning, in social action necessitates a turn to the human sciences, and that a more adequate ('realist') model of inquiry could be adopted. There are, of course, two lines of attack here. The first stresses the difference between natural science and human science and tries to shift psychology from one to the other. The second stresses the value of methods actually employed in the natural sciences and tries to bring psychology up to date. There is a creative tension between the two positions advanced in the new paradigm. At the risk of caricaturing them and glossing over their points of convergence, it is useful to identify hermeneutic and structuralist strands.

The *hermeneutic* strand focuses on the ability of the social actor to produce meaning, to construct new definitions of a situation and to communicate intentions and the import of action to others. Social life is constituted by the accounts which we must give one to the other to maintain the peculiarly human quality of the world. Inquiry into the life world of social actors requires an empathetic involvement in, and elaboration of, the 'hermeneutic circle' of meaning. In this view, then, the formal properties of interaction are no more than interpretations, constructions of an interested observer, and have no other existence (Shotter, 1975, 1983, 1984).

The *structuralist* strand, in contrast, makes a determined effort to uncover the patterns of interaction, the structures which inform the activities of social actors. Accounts are gathered, 'negotiated', with those being studied because the accounts and actions have the same source. Accounts are used, then, to reconstruct a social world of which each individual actor has an imperfect, fragmentary knowledge. In this way, the researcher takes note of the explanations of action given by people and arrives at a deeper understanding, following the methods of 'realist' science, of the formal properties of the chosen social world (Harré, 1979, 1983b; Marsh, Rosser and Harré, 1974).

The debate between the two sides of the new paradigm echoes long-standing and unresolved conflicts in social psychology between agency and structure (Harré, 1983a; Shotter, 1980). What both tendencies in the new paradigm have neglected, however, is the way interpretation, conflict and resistance in social life cry out for an analysis of meaning in terms of *power*. We are able to put these issues to the forefront of our research if we adopt a deconstructive approach to texts, and move beyond the dichotomy between structuralism and hermeneutics. Deconstruction uncovers the way language, and the analysis of the texts we weave with language, works.

Deconstruction

While the arguments over the nature of the paradigm shift which fuelled the crisis inside social psychology were burning, intense debates were also raging in the other human sciences. These debates, which filtered through into some of the formulations of our own new paradigm critics, revolved around the value of structuralism and post-structuralism as ways of understanding language. In literary theory, where the conflict between the different positions was most intense, the transition from structuralism to post-structuralism also saw the emergence of a deconstructive approach to texts (Eagleton, 1983). There is some value in attending to these debates because we can then use them to extend the work of the new paradigm writers in social psychology, arrive at a more productive understanding of the nature of texts, and gain a better understanding of the relationship between explanations and power. In order to appreciate the value of deconstruction in social psychology, we have first to deconstruct structuralist and hermeneutic approaches.

Language, according to structuralism, should be understood as a system – a system in which each item, or word, gains its meaning only by way of its difference from the other items (Saussure, 1974). Intentions we express are immediately caught up in the web, system, structure of language and escape our grasp. The structuralist approach to language, then, sets up an opposition between the 'system' of the language as a whole (a structure which would be uncovered by an investigator) and the 'use' of that language by individuals (the day-to-day occasions when the words are transmitted). The first is studied and the second studiously ignored by a structuralist.

The value of structuralism, for literary theorists, was that it directed attention to the underlying pattern of a piece of writing. Whereas the old interpretative tradition had attempted to trace the meanings in the text to the intentions of the author, the structuralist approach was able to produce a rigorous explanation of the way the text worked. At an extreme, such an approach was supposed to involve the conceptual 'death of the author' (Barthes, 1977). While the conclusions they drew about the irrelevance of individual intention and agency were not, of course, shared by social psychologists interested in structuralism in the new paradigm, the model of language they adopted was taken up.

However, if you pursue that argument you will eventually arrive at the breakdown of strictly structuralist notions and their collapse into post-structuralism. It is, in short, possible to deconstruct the opposition between the structure of language and its use. Each person constructs an imperfect, fragmentary, idiosyncratic version of the structure which affects the relation between the words each time she or he communicates to another person. In addition, each act of interpretation requires the reproduction of the system of language and, crucially, the production of new metaphors which disrupt the system (Derrida, 1981).

The lesson I as a social psychologist take from these developments is that any text I would want to examine is open to further interpretation. The meanings in a text shift from one moment to the next, and according to its wider context. A reading of the text, then, is provisional, and is profoundly affected by my own and your prior understanding and expectations (themselves aspects of experience which are impossible to definitively fix as if they were confounding variables). The most that can be done is to persuade you that my interpretation identifies what is going on.

The obvious escape route from the relativism into which these debates seem to be dragging us has already, of course, been closed off. We cannot ask the authors what they 'really meant'. But what of the authors of social texts such as speeches, conversations and explanations? Here, the development of deconstruction in literary theory is particularly useful. It places into question the status of intention in the production of language.

An obvious, and appealing, way of marking the difference between literary theory and social psychology is to say that there is a crucial distinction to be drawn between writing and speech. Writing is constructed in such a way as to meet the expectations of a number of readers, and it can be interpreted in many ways as time flows on and as it becomes progressively detached from the experience and memory of the author. We believe that speech is different; it expresses thought, and as part of the accountability of conduct it is immediate and more spontaneous. The experience of speaking is one which leads us to imagine that speech flows more directly from what we really want to mean.

Speech, though, is constructed so as to be a communication to others. The language used as the medium of communication both facilitates and moulds what we say. We cannot invent anew terms to express our intentions. On the contrary, we find ourselves using words which have been repeated many times before. Old words in new contexts obtain their meaning from their identity with the way they were the last time they were used, and their difference from the way they were used before. Neither the language nor the context can be controlled by, or traced to, the intention of an individual. Is not speech, in fact, a variety of writing? This is the conclusion we might arrive at when we deconstruct the opposition between writing and speech. In turn, this warrants our use of the term 'text' to denote both written and spoken forms of language production (Derrida, 1978).

As far as social psychology is concerned, the focus on texts as our objects of inquiry should enable us to produce interpretations which are intrinsically social. Our deconstruction of an item of text is a way of arriving at interpretations which are locked into the surrounding cultural context. I take this as an opportunity to raise general issues about the way texts re-place us in positions of power. Each specific deconstruction is illustrative of, and gives more leverage to, a deconstruction of social relations.

I must confess that I am loath to formalize the deconstruction of theoretical positions into an abstract method which can be applied to 'non-theoretical' texts. Strictly speaking, deconstruction is not a method in the sense of being a set of techniques (Derrida, 1981). However, it is possible to summarize three steps or stages to a deconstruction (Wood, 1979).

The first step is to identify conceptual oppositions, or polarities, in the text, and the way one pole is privileged over the other. In the case of structuralism the key dichotomy was between structure and use. In the case of hermeneutics I pointed to the opposition between speech and writing. In the course of this chapter, I want to draw attention to further conceptual oppositions: between what is spontaneous and what is scripted; between what is real and what is fictive; and between what is to be counted as everyday and what as theoretical explanation. In the empirical example, I will draw attention to further oppositions which will serve as devices to highlight processes at work in the text: between metanarrative and narrative; between reflection and subjectivity; and between recasting and casting.

The second step is to demonstrate that the privileged pole of the opposition is dependent on, could not operate without, the other. We bring the hitherto subordinate concept to the fore. In the case of structuralism, then, the use of language profoundly affects the structure, thus making capture of the structure of a language impossible. In the case of hermeneutics, writing is brought forward as a model of speech, making invalid the traditional linking of speech and intention. The consequences of a deconstruction involve, I hope to show as we proceed, a re-emphasis in social psychology on scripted, fictitious and theoretical items of text over what we currently understand as being spontaneous, real or everyday forms of explanation. We will see, when we come to the empirical example, the importance of narrative, subjectivity and casting in the production of a text by social actors.

The third step involves a reinterpretation of the opposition, and the production of new concepts. In the cases of structuralism and hermeneutics, we arrived (implicitly) at the notions of text and deconstruction. The third step, however, requires an intervention into the production of the text (Derrida, 1981). For social psychologists, this calls for the production of new practices (and new problems for those wanting to stick to the text, as we shall see).

A deconstruction of a piece of text carries with it assumptions about the nature of meaning, and it produces new meanings out of the texts it contacts. It changes what it studies. In addition, the way I read a text is informed by the moral/political structure of the interpretation (the scene, which in this case is an academic paper), and the experiences I bring to it (which result from my participation in the production of other academic and non-academic texts). These factors give power to an interpretation, and may boil down to relations of power between those who are permitted to construct 'real theories' and those who are deemed to produce 'everyday explanation'.

Empirical example

For our text we have an item of script in which the social actors contest the nature of the distinction between reality and fiction, and the power of theory over everyday life. We will see one character attempt to construct a metanarrative and implicitly reflect and recast the other within it. We will also address the issue of implicit explanation.

The nature of text
The idea of 'text' which lies at the heart of deconstruction, and which emerges from the wreckage of structuralist and hermeneutic styles of new paradigm social psychology, has a number of useful

and exciting qualities. Any text – be it a speech, a monologue or a treatise – consists of a number of warring themes. The conflicts between the poles of any conceptual oppositions that we might uncover need not necessarily be identified with conflicts between persons. In fact we would expect that where a number of characters congregate to debate differences, each person would slip from one position to the next, exploiting ambiguities and loopholes in the other's argument. However, the stuff of everyday explanation is in the interchange of opinion. Most of the talk that people engage in is in the presence of others. We will, then, examine a text which is wrought through dialogue. Here, the different positions adopted will be easier to define and explore.

A notion we may draw from the new paradigm is that the utterances of social actors have an overwhelmingly expressive function (Harré, 1979; Shotter, 1984). When social life is viewed as self-presentation through ingeniously constructed rhetorics, or it slips into well-worn rituals, we are right to use the notion of a 'script' to highlight what is happening. Once we have deconstructed the distinction between speech and writing, however, we can go further than this. We then have a licence to turn to scripts themselves. Written scripts need be no less spontaneous than real speech. The text in this example once had the status of a script.   The objection might be made that such a text is not 'real'; it is fiction. Some fictions, however, are more real than others. The explanations we give to others – the texts we pass on – are sometimes mistaken, sometimes half-truths, occasionally deliberate lies. Some items of fiction are lived by large numbers of people in a culture, and the meanings are discussed and contested. They have effects as real as ostensibly unscripted non-fictitious explanations. They operate as an ideology.

Furthermore, a problem with much research in social psychology is that it illuminates a social world we do not implicitly know. Readers of such reports can only either take what the research says on trust or retreat into a cynical suspicion of all accounts. A deconstruction should be open to revision. An interpretation should be reopened as times and contexts change. Readers should have some space at the margins of even an academic text.

Sample text
We do know the social worlds of soaps. Sociologists have turned in recent years to analyse the way audiences receive these worlds and incorporate the narratives into their own worlds. In the case of American television series, the preoccupations and antics of the characters become templates for the understanding of the

non-soap world, metaphors for the lives of politicians, and frames to organize explanations. The advantage the soap has over discrete narratives is that actors develop a history and are attributed with personality traits and intentions.

Although the most popular television soaps have the advantage of having a large audience in many countries, their status as texts presents problems for a deconstructive analysis. There are the meanings of clothes, scenes and locations which could be treated by a semiological analysis. There are also the non-verbal cues which supplement, organize and occasionally contradict the spoken message. For these reasons I have taken a piece of text from an (English) radio soap.

'The Archers', which has been running on Radio 4 since 1950, has developed a minor cult following in the past few years. Radio 4 is the 'serious' channel of the BBC. From being a fairly traditional serial, 'The Archers' has roused controversy with the introduction of social issues. Letters to Radio 4 news programmes and *The Guardian* (a liberal middle-class newspaper) discuss the fate of characters and the corruption of the series by the unpleasant practices and vices which feed the storylines of the American soaps. Books about the characters, faked local newspapers and maps of Ambridge (the fictitious village in middle England where the action is set) are starting to appear.

The text was transcribed from a 2 minute 20 second scene broadcast on 22 October, 23 October and again on 26 October 1986. I have screened out the paraverbal paraphernalia. This, of course, excludes the new and different meanings put into the 'original' written script by the actors. This is a limitation because of the non-correspondence between the transcript and the original. However, the script-writer may have spoken the original text into a dictaphone with quite different intonation, and a complicated notation for emphases and pauses would not solve the problem; it would merely displace it.

The scene was not selected at random. I chose it because it illustrates some current concerns in the series which connect with those of its target audience. It also raises issues about social relations, in particular gender relations, in the non-soap world. Finally, it highlights a problem to do with interpretation – the interpretation we are permitted to construct of the 'real meaning' of a person's actions, and the interpretations social actors give of one another's acts. The distinction between a theoretical form of explanation and a lay form of explanation is one which is bound up with power. The distinction gives leverage to some social actors in positions who are permitted to have access to knowledge. For those in other social positions, lack of knowledge can have the effect of reducing them to silence.

An immediate problem is that the temptation to intervene and flesh out the context is almost too much to bear. As with all data collection, the researcher can undermine the supposed objectivity of the process by supplementing the data with personal knowledge ('It was like this, I was there'!). Perhaps I need only allude to the structural class relations that cast Clarrie as the wife of the son of a poor tenant farmer, and Pat as a member of the Archer family which runs the estate. Those who are outside the community of listeners will not know that Clarrie's own father works as a labourer for the Archer family. Would it be helpful to suggest that Pat's interest in organic farming also helps maintain her own marginal position within Ambridge culture? To give such information outright would destroy the integrity of the text, but perhaps to let little extra clues slide in unnoticed would be more in keeping with the spirit of deconstruction.

Pat Archer has picked up Clarrie Grundy, and she is giving her a lift to do her shopping. The scene opens with the noise of the car.

Pat: Er, look, I can drop you in the middle of the town but the trouble is I'm going almost straight home. How long do you think you'll be?

Clarrie: Oh not to worry Pat thanks. I'm dead lucky to get a lift one way. I can take the bus back easy.

Pat: What, with all your shopping?

Clarrie: Well, Dad said to start walking and he'd see if he could come and pick me up. Oh poor Dad. He was in a terrible state last night. His friend Dixie's dead.

Pat: This is his friend in Canada?

Clarrie: Yeah that's right. He ain't seen him in over thirty years.

Pat: Oh well, maybe he can go to Holland for his holiday instead.

Clarrie: Oh he were getting so excited about going to Canada too. Oh its such a shame.

Pat: Ah, is the supermarket alright for you?

Clarrie: Oh yeah, lovely thanks.

Pat: My friend Jilly lives behind the supermarket, and I'm just dropping by to pick up the scripts for the panto.

Clarrie: What panto?

Pat: The Ambridge Christmas panto. It's instead of a review this year.

Clarrie: Ooh that's nice! Which one is it?

Pat: Cinderella.

Clarrie: Oh! my favourite!

Pat: The script's written by some friends of mine. The writers' group call it a work in progress.

Clarrie: Do they?

Pat: That's not to say it isn't finished. There's a beginning, a middle, and an end. Well, er, a sort of end anyway.

Clarrie: I thought Cinderella always had the same ending. She lives happily ever after with Prince Charming don't she?

Pat: Well not in the Ambridge Christmas review she doesn't. Not exactly. We're doing a modern reworking of the story.

Clarrie: Oh, that's nice.

Pat: What we're out to challenge is the standard interpretation of the story. What the writers group calls the tyranny of the finished text.

Clarrie: Oh yeah.

Pat: I mean. Why should the ugly sisters be ugly? Why can't they just be sisters? If they were brothers, they wouldn't be the ugly brothers would they?

Clarrie: Oh I do like pantos though. They're somewhere to take the kids after Christmas. Oh, there were one in Felpersham a couple of years back.

Pat: I'm going to have to do something about Prince Charming too. I didn't do away with him completely. In real life there's no such person as Prince Charming.

Clarrie: Well who's Cinders going to fall in love with then?

Pat: She doesn't have to fall in love with anyone. She's her own person. She can find fulfilment in her work.

Clarrie: Clearing up for the ugly sisters!

Pat: No. I had something a little more elevated in mind. Erm Clarrie, can you come to auditions in the village hall next week?

Explanation

What series of explanations is Pat giving to Clarrie, and how may we understand the role and status of those explanations? As the text proceeds Pat explains why she cannot wait for Clarrie to finish her shopping and run her home. She explains what the rewriting of the panto entails, and why. Note that her first series of explanations is concerned with warranting an action which has a primarily practical aspect (dropping Clarrie), while the second set is concerned with warranting the production of a symbolic representation – an expression (writing a script).

There are two interconnected points about the nature of the relationship here between Pat and Clarrie. The first is to do with the transition from the practical resources. She is driving her car in which Clarrie is the passenger, and so she is able to determine Clarrie's behaviour. This practical leverage, however, operates through the expressive meanings through which Clarrie can understand the relationship. Thus Clarrie projects her disadvantages (heavy shopping and a bus journey) back on to Pat (concern about Clarrie: 'not to worry Pat thanks') in a display of gratitude for the lift. Pat sticks with the practical topics (where Clarrie's Dad could go for his holiday), ignoring the emotional focus of Clarrie's description of her Dad's troubles and her own concern for them. Instead, Pat waits, and then determines the transition to a later discussion of the panto. Pat handles the bridging sequence from the one realm to the other by explaining why the supermarket is convenient as a point to drop Clarrie off, what the script is about, and finally why the script is a 'modern reworking of the story'. Pat, then, carries over the control she has over practical resources into the expressive sphere.

The second point is to do with the relative status of the practical and the expressive orders. (It would be possible to deconstruct the opposition. We could argue that ostensibly expressive activities are really practical in that they determine relationships and, therefore, what is deemed to be practical.) For the purposes of the present analysis, we make no assumptions about the supposed relationship between the two spheres, preferring instead merely to use the distinction as a device to understand what is going on.

In the text, Pat is implicitly using the distinction to identify and reproduce her relationship with Clarrie. Pat is able to introduce the question of the script for the panto. Pat constructs an explanation of the contents of the script, and lures Clarrie into playing a part that (expressive) representation of (practical) life in Ambridge. We should understand the nature of this luring in both its real and metaphorical sense. In a real sense, as Pat's invitation to Clarrie (to 'come to auditions in the village hall') makes clear, the upshot of the conversation is that Clarrie should actually play a part in the panto. Prior to that, however, Pat draws Clarrie into a discussion of drudgery, subordination and fulfilment in which *Cinderella* becomes the metaphorical frame through which they both might understand the real world. Pat, then, controls the expressive sphere through which she hopes to change practical relations.

But what is Clarrie explaining to Pat? In this text Clarrie's explanations are responses to Pat's topics (practical questions of where to drop Clarrie, and expressive constructions around the contents of the panto). Clarrie explains how she might cope with the shopping (Dad would 'see if he could come and pick me up'), and why Dad is in a terrible state ('His friend Dixie's dead' and he was 'so excited about going to Canada too'). There is also a level of implicit explanation where Clarrie attempts to express her view that the 'modern reworking' of *Cinderella* is not actually a real panto ('Oh I do like pantos though'), and that 'fulfilment in her work' would not be an escape from drudgery ('Clearing up for the ugly sisters!'). Note that, for Clarrie, explanation is a function of her acquiescence in Pat's explanations. She has little power. With these issues raised, we can turn to the elaboration of the deconstructive polarities which operate as a kind of conceptual cartilage for the text.

Deconstruction
Step one. Here there are two characters upon whom the conceptual polarities can be mapped. You might like to think of the opposing poles as being the dominant points in a definition of the situation in which the antonyms are suppressed and to which Clarrie submits. I can identify three oppositions: metanarrative/narrative, recasting/casting and reflection/subjectivity. Each pair raises issues about what social actors may understand about the relationship between what they take to be practical concerns and what they imagine to be the expressive gloss through which they represent those practices to others.

The recasting Pat engages in is one which attempts to break Clarrie out of her everyday role. As the conversation proceeds Clarrie gets drawn into a symbolic representation of her life which is the script of *Cinderella*. The story parallels her own predicaments, but now Pat is raising the possibility that the story does not always have 'the same ending' (it is 'a work in progress'). The casting which stands in opposition to this is Clarrie's everyday role as dutiful daughter (with 'poor Dad') and harassed mother (where the panto is 'somewhere to take the kids after Christmas'). Clarrie refers to these aspects of the way she is cast in her life in Ambridge, but Pat resorts to inviting her to an audition which will radically recast her.

Clarrie's life, then, is being mirrored. An image is being wrought which is reflecting the character Clarrie plays in Ambridge. 'Look' says Pat to Clarrie at the opening of a text in which Clarrie is progressively reduced to silence. Her assertions about her own experiences (of 'fulfilment' equated with 'clearing up') – her own subjectivity – are discounted as Pat breaks beyond her social world ('the tyranny of the finished text') to write another for her.

Step two. Take the third polarity–reflection/subjectivity – first. How might Clarrie's view of her life be restored? More to the point, what attention might be drawn to the subjective investment Pat has in the mirror she holds up to Clarrie to recognize herself anew? Pat's control of resources, both practical and expressive, is at issue here, and her power. Note the way that Pat's own subjectivity, her own involvement and responsibilities, are sidestepped by her when she defers to the writers' group statement about 'the tyranny of the finished text'. Does not the mirror she holds reflect herself, and does not the relationship between herself and Clarrie (Pat as holder of the mirror and Clarrie as the reflected subject) reproduce the relationship between the writers' group and herself (the writers' group as interpreters of the text and Pat as the relay of that interpretation)? The mirror, then, is also an expression of subjectivity.

By the same token, Pat is engaged in an activity where the recasting of Clarrie simultaneously enacts the casting of herself in the role of producer, director and purveyor of knowledge. Could we provoke recognition of this supposed recasting as a mere reproduction of the way Pat and Clarrie are cast as actors in Ambridge (with all the power that attends the unequal distribution of knowledge)? And again, the metanarrative to which Pat appeals functions as such only because it is a narrative invested with power – power Pat enjoys as a result of her knowledge of theory.

The next step. The third step of a deconstruction involves moral/political choices. These are choices which can only be pursued by the social actors themselves. There are issues about Pat's employment of theory to shatter Clarrie's everyday explanations, and how her use of that theory frustrates her desire that Clarrie should take control of her own life. These issues, of course, are to do with the relationship between power and knowledge. To offer prescriptions to our subjects recast as naive lay folk who might be enlightened by theory and liberated from the tyranny of the finished text would surely tangle us in the same contradictions.

Advantages and disadvantages

I will have to set my discussion of the advantages and disadvantages of deconstruction in the context of two separate, though related, discourses. One is the discourse of 'analyses of everyday explanation'. The other is the discourse of politics.

As with the structuralist strands of new paradigm social psychology, deconstruction locates conceptual categories which organize the text. Rather than posit these as being underneath what is said in the deep structure of interaction or in cognitive templates located in the heads of individual speakers, deconstruction finds these conceptual categories in the surface of the text itself. It recognizes that the categories are important because of the way they are used. Oppositions are the contradictions utilized by speakers in their rhetoric to interpret and determine the actions of others. We saw this in the way Pat interpreted Clarrie's explanations within her own metanarrative as she tried to reflect Clarrie's life and recast her in a rewriting of *Cinderella*. More than this, a deconstruction also shows how the oppositions are contradictions which capture all subjects in a text and undermine the intentions of the authors of statements. We saw this in the way the power Pat wielded undermined her attempt to empower Clarrie.

As with the hermeneutic strands of new paradigm social psychology, deconstruction attends to the fluidity and indeterminacy of meaning in a text. Instead of attributing this indeterminacy to the free exercise and expression of individual human intention, however, deconstruction locates the shifts of meaning in the text itself. Again, this focuses attention on the powers distributed to social actors in different positions. Power and language are intimately linked. It supports social actors' attempts to change power relations and to engage in the overthrow of dominant ideas. So we saw how it is possible to reinterpret Pat's mirroring of Clarrie's life and her attempt to recast her accounts in a metanarrative. Pat's rhetoric depends on the very issues of subjectivity, casting and narrative which she sought to exclude.

Deconstruction goes even further when it puts into question notions of everyday explanation. Theory itself is derived from ordinary explanation and is conveyed in a medium which uses the language of the surrounding culture. Then the theories seep back into everyday usage. Even complex debates find expression in the apparatus of everyday explanation and practically deconstruct the distinction between the two realms.

While the overthrow and transcendence of conceptual oppositions in the third step of a deconstruction is possible in philosophical and literary texts, a deconstruction applied to social texts raises questions of practical political involvement of the researcher in power relations. The first two steps uncover these relations, but the next step can only be taken outside the text. Without this step, which involves the construction of non-oppressive social relations, the hierarchies will simply be written and rewritten in the same old way. Listeners to 'The Archers' will know that Pat's panto was abandoned, and the inhabitants of Ambridge returned to the Christmas review.

A lesson which proponents of the new paradigm in social psychology tried to teach those gripped by the old paradigm was that a researcher had to go beyond data to ask people what they were doing. The process of gathering accounts is part of research and is the foundation of the idea that results are provisional and open to revision. Whilst the fruits of a deconstruction are always ready for the next interpreter to get his teeth into, we are limited by the boundaries of the text. The sequences of signs which are offered to the reader are still there to be manipulated and pulled apart.

Social psychology in the new paradigm took what people said seriously, acting on the slogan 'treat people as if they were human beings.' Deconstruction, on the other hand, carries with it the danger of reducing persons to ciphers of the text. The relationship between knowledge and power, the violence which attends the prioritization of some concepts over others, also deeply affects the relationship between a researcher and subjects. The theories in and around deconstruction also find their way into everyday explanation. The conflicts between Pat and Clarrie illustrate the problems of power which attend it. So when Pat is given a book by Lacan for her birthday this thrills the *cognoscenti* and drives back the inhabitants of the realms of everyday explanation (people like Clarrie) further beyond the pale of theory.

The reader should be aware of the privilege that the position confers. The tyranny of the finished text can also operate when theoretically aware researchers approach and interpret the accounts given by the lay public. Perhaps this problem would be mitigated if proponents of deconstruction could advance a moral/political position. Both strands of the new paradigm in social psychology do propose a politics which flows from the value attached to a person's right to account for themselves and their actions. Unfortunately, in the case of deconstruction this is not possible without supplementing the approach. By its very nature it is hostile to any attempt to construct conceptual or political priorities. Further, I would want to resist the implication that Clarrie's resistance to Pat is somehow progressive. The reflection of social actors' lives and the recasting of their acts within wider political narratives is, I think, a 'good thing'.

I avoided confronting the issue of where the theory leads, and the power of theory in general, by choosing a text in which the speakers were no more than constructions. We may learn lessons about social relationships from such texts, but the pity is that a deconstruction would not necessarily lead to a progressive type of action research if it was applied to real explanations given by real people. I recommend that readers wishing to adopt deconstruction as a method take as their texts other fictions: discussions extracted from the pages of novels, or the products of role-play studies, or social psychology textbooks.

Note

Thanks to Carolyn Kagan for her comments on an earlier draft of this chapter.

14
Methodology and scholarship in understanding ideological explanation

Michael Billig

This chapter will not outline the whys and wherefores of a particular methodology as such. In fact, it will challenge the use of methodology, and the importance which social scientists give to methodological matters. When social scientists advocate the use of a methodology, whether for understanding explanations or for anything else, they are prescribing a set of procedures which the analyst is to follow. Social scientific investigation is frequently presented as being based upon the following of methodological rules. However, this chapter will recommend an alternative approach: that of traditional scholarship. The approach of the traditional scholar can be considered anti-methodological, in that hunches and specialist knowledge are more important than formally defined procedures. This anti-methodological stance will be illustrated by considering the issue of ideology and, in particular, the conspiracy theory of politics. The views of one politician will be examined in detail. It will be suggested that more understanding is to be gained by using the traditional, ill-defined skills of scholarship than by following a rigorous, up-to-date methodology.

Theoretical background

There are a number of ways in which traditional scholarship can be distinguished from what modern investigators mean by methodology. A *methodology* involves presenting rules of procedure about matters such as the collection of data and their analysis. The rules are impersonal, in that they are meant to apply equally to all researchers. It is assumed that any two researchers who approach the same problem should arrive at identical results, as long as neither infringes the methodological rules. Thereby, it is hoped that individual bias is excluded from the research process. In this way, methodology attempts to standardize the practice of the social sciences and to eliminate quirkiness. To the modern methodologist, traditional scholarship seems a haphazard and biased affair. The traditional scholar does not seem obsessed with laying bare the methodological procedures, which can be followed by anyone with sufficient training.

Individual quirkiness is very much part of traditional *scholarship*. It was taken for granted by the traditional scholar that one should read as widely as possible, and in as many languages as possible. Through wide reading, breadth and depth of knowledge would be gained, as well as the ability to make connections between seemingly disparate phenomena. The learned scholar would be able to interpret individual texts with an acuity not available to those of restricted reading. Traditional scholars are not particularly bothered with the origins of their insights, in the sense that they do not attempt the impossible task of laying bare all the intellectual experiences which lead up to the ability to make a scholarly judgement. Nor do they presume that other scholars will read the same texts in just the same way as they have. In fact, scholars spend a great deal of energy in criticizing the readings of their fellow scholars.

The major theme of this chapter is that the traditional skills of scholarship have much to offer the study of ideology. It is certainly not the case that students of ideology have adhered to a particular methodology. In fact, they have not even adhered to a simple definition of ideology itself: different theorists offer contrasting definitions (Abercrombie, 1980; Billig, 1982; Larrain, 1979; 1983). According to McLellan (1986:1), 'Ideology is the most elusive concept in the whole of social science'. Despite all the disputes about definition, there is agreement that an ideology refers to a pattern of ideas, values, interpretations and so on rather than to a single attitude. For example, Mannheim (1960: 49–50) expressed this view when he wrote that 'We refer to the ideology of an age or of a concrete historico-social group, e.g. of a class, when we are concerned with the characteristics and composition of the total structure of the mind of this epoch or of this group.' Thus, the analyst of ideology is interested in the whole pattern of a group's beliefs, not just its constituent parts, and in addition the analyst seeks to place this pattern in its social and historical context.

The last point can be illustrated by considering the issue of explanation. It is quite clear that people are prepared to offer explanations for major social events. For instance, attribution theorists have shown that people will explain phenomena such as unemployment or poverty in terms of personal or situational attributions, either blaming the victims themselves for their own condition or attributing the blame to society (Feagin, 1972; Feather, 1974; Furnham, 1982, 1983; Furnham and Lewis, 1986; Lewis et al., 1987). To probe the ideological significance of these attributions one needs to go further than documenting their existence. One needs to discover how the explanation of one sort of social event fits into a wider pattern of explaining social events. To do this, one needs to look at the way that different ideologies might be characterized by different styles, and traditions, of explaining social events.

It is possible to study ideology by attempting to situate ordinary discourse within its wider ideological context. The pattern of an individual's thinking should therefore be interpreted in terms of broader historical and social patterns. For example, the chapters written by Adorno in *The Authoritarian Personality* (Adorno et al., 1950) show a great awareness of the way that bigoted respondents could be linked to the intellectual and ideological history of racial bigotry. Similarly, Billig et al. (forthcoming) trace the heritage of Voltaire and the Enlightenment in the comments of young racist respondents (see also Billig, 1988). A further social psychological analysis of ideology is provided by Billig (1986), who links the thinking of young members of the Conservative Party with the ideology of international finance capital and the assumptions of everyday life in capitalist society. Such studies attempt to uncover the social psychological dynamics of some of the central ideological themes in contemporary society. However, the topic of ideology can be approached from an opposing direction, by examining those ideologies which remain just beyond the mainstream of everyday thinking.

The conspiracy theory of politics represents such an ideology, existing just beyond the mainstream of everyday thought. Moreover, it represents an ideological pattern especially relevant to the social psychology of explanation, for the ideology is characterized by its particular style of explaining social events. In essence the ideology of conspiracy seeks to explain all major political events in the world in terms of an evil conspiracy, or series of conspiracies. The conspiracy theorist tells a story of hidden machinations by small groups who are plotting to subvert the natural order of the world. According to Lipset and Raab (1970), the conspiracy theorist offers a monomanic explanation for social events, in that all major happenings are explained in precisely the same way: no matter what happens, the conspiracy theorist sees the malign hand of hidden conspirators. In this sense conspiracy theory represents an extreme form of personal explanation, in that nothing happens by chance, since all is to be explained in terms of deliberate plotting (see Billig, 1978: 313ff. for discussion of the conspiracy mentality and the psychological theory of attributions; see also Kruglanski, 1987; Moscovici, 1987 and Zukier, 1987). Over and above the conspiracy theorist's use of a particular type of explanation, there is the matter of explanatory style. The conspiracy theorist employs apocalyptic terms, asserting that the masses have been duped: unless people awake soon to the conspiratorial reality, all will be lost. The conspiracy theorist is like a prophet, who has glimpsed a higher reality and is berating the masses for their unseeing complacency in the face of imminent danger.

Historically this tradition of political ideology has been linked to the collapse of the old aristocratic order at the turn of the eighteenth century (Cohn, 1967; Groh, 1987; Roberts, 1974). Supporters of the old order, unable to grasp that the mass of the population no longer retained traditional feudal loyalties, suspected that freemasons had poisoned the minds of the populace. This general mentality of conspiracy has been identified as the mentality of the dispossessed, who hope that, once the evil machinations of the conspirators have been rendered harmless by revelation, all wrongs will be righted (Bell, 1962). The same ideological structure can be found amongst American nativist groups (Lipset and Raab, 1970), German Nazis (Cohn, 1967; Poliakov, 1974) and contemporary fascist groups (Billig, 1978; Seidel, 1986; Taylor, 1982; Thurlow, 1987), who, above all, fear that the conspirators are seeking to destroy the independence of nations and to take control of the world. The arch-conspirators are variously freemasons, communists, international capitalists, Jews or, better still, small groups who mysteriously share all these attributes.

In one sense, it might be thought that the conspiracy mentality represents a style in which ideologies can be expressed rather than an ideology itself. For example, the style could be found on the left wing of politics. Left-wingers might articulate their socialist ideology in such a way as to suggest that the hidden hand of capitalist plotters is seen in every failure of the masses to turn in revolutionary upsurge to the teachings of Marx and Lenin. Certainly it would not be difficult to find parallels between the ideological systems of explanation proposed by some far left- and right-wing groups (see Feuer, 1970). However, formal similarities are not proof of an ideological unity. It is easier to argue that the conspiracy theorists of the far right and the far left draw upon differing ideological traditions than that they share a common intellectual heritage. Even where there is a resemblance in content, as for example when anti-semitic themes are used, distinctions can still be made between the ideological heritages of right and left (Billig, 1987a). Therefore, the issue of exploring ideological heritage is crucial to an ideological analysis of a pattern of beliefs such as conspiracy theory.

In his study of British contemporary fascism, Billig (1978) showed that quantitative methodologies are insufficient for investigating the ideological heritage of conspiracy theory. He showed that a content analysis of UK National Front propaganda only revealed the surface characteristics of that group's ideology. To probe further the deeper meanings and traditions of the ideology it was necessary to explore the wider traditions of conspiracy theory. It was necessary to show how National Front ideologists had absorbed notions from an unbroken ideological tradition, which includes overtly Nazi theorists, non-Nazi groups such as the John Birch Society and eighteenth-century writers such as Auguste de Barruel and John Robison. The identification of this common political culture was not achieved by methodological means as much as by the practices of traditional scholarship. Texts had to be sought out and read and half-hinted allusions had to be noticed and then interpreted. The ideologies of different extremist groups had to be compared, to see whether they were drawing upon common ideological heritages. Only by so doing is it possible to discover when an ideologist is alluding to a writer or a set of ideas firmly situated within the conspiracy tradition.

The tradition of conspiracy theory is in the main to be found on the periphery of political life, although, as the history of the Nazis revealed, there can be no guarantee that it must remain marginal. At present one would not expect conspiracy theory to have a central place in conservative thinking at least as an explanation of world governmental behaviour. The political successes of contemporary conservatism should ensure that there are few failures and dispossessions which need to be explained away in terms of an overpowering conspiracy. However, there have often been links and overlaps between conservative and conspiracy thinking (see Griffiths, 1983; Webber, 1986). In investigating the political terrain where the racist right of conservatism shades into fascist extremism, one should look to see whether conservatives are adopting the ideological style and content of extremism. In particular, it is necessary to examine conservatism for signs of the conspiracy mentality.

If such an investigation is to be undertaken, it is not enough merely to see if one or other conservative politician uses conspiracy as a political explanation for a particular event. More is required if an individual conservative is to be located within the ideological traditions of conspiracy theory. The individual must show evidence of possessing an ideological structure which ties together the untidiness of the social world into a tale of deception and conspiracy. In addition there should be evidence of a linkage with the ideological tradition itself. The following sections will consider these problems in relation to the beliefs of a particular UK Conservative Party politician, Enoch Powell. They will pose the question of whether Powell's beliefs should be located within the ideological traditions of the conspiracy theory.

Empirical example: J. Enoch Powell

The political discourse to be analysed in this chapter is taken from reports of the speeches of a single politician, J. Enoch Powell. Before proceeding to an ideological analysis of Powell's discourse we need to know something of the life of this most singular of contemporary British politicians.

Until the last General Election Ulster Unionist Member of Parliament for South Down, Enoch Powell has had a notable and highly controversial career. He was born in 1912, and studied classics with great distinction at Cambridge University. At the age of 26 he became Professor of Greek at the University of Sydney. At this time he was publishing translations of Thucydides and Herodotus, as well as slim volumes of his own poetry. After two years as an Australian professor, he abandoned academic life to join the army as a private. He has explained this decision as follows: 'I was determined that I would do something to stop the disintegration of the Empire which seemed imminent' (quoted in Berkeley, 1977: 14).

After the war Powell decided upon a career in politics. He entered Parliament in 1950 as the Conservative member for Wolverhampton South East, in his native West Midlands. His intellectual capacities, as well as his talents for composing and delivering speeches, marked Powell out for high office. He became Minister of Health in Harold Macmillan's cabinet, yet he resigned when Macmillan was replaced as Prime Minister by Sir Alec Douglas-Home. He did not remain on the backbenches long, and became a senior member of Edward Heath's shadow cabinet. Ideologically Powell and Heath represented different wings of conservatism. Whilst Heath was the pragmatist, who believed in state intervention in the economy, Powell was elaborating his own political philosophy based upon the principles of a *laissez-faire* monetarism, long before the label 'monetarist' became popular.

However, it was not differences of economic policy which caused the decisive rupture between Heath and Powell. On 20 April 1968 Powell delivered a speech which was to have significant effects on the course of race relations in Britain and was to change dramatically his own political career. Powell spoke about his fears for the future of a Britain, which contained a sizeable 'New Commonwealth' or non-white population. It was not so much the anti-immigrant themes which made the speech notorious, as the choice of language. Powell, the intellectual Greek scholar, repeated stories of 'negroes' pushing excreta through letter-boxes, of 'wide-grinning piccaninnies' harassing old white ladies, and so on. The speech foretold of racial conflict, as Powell said that he was 'filled with foreboding'. The insults of the gutter were mixed with the learning of the high table: 'Like the Roman, I seem to see "the River Tiber foaming with much blood"' (text in Powell, 1969: 213ff.; for analyses see Foot, 1969; Barker, 1981).

The impact of the speech was immediate. Heath sacked Powell from the shadow cabinet, calling the speech 'racialist in content' (Schoen, 1977: 34). Immediately Powell had become a national figure of substance: letters of support for him poured in, dockers marched for him in East London, and the right-wing popular press depicted him as the man who had voiced the fears of ordinary (white) people. Studlar (1974) has shown how dramatic was Powell's simultaneous public rise and political fall. In early April 1968 Gallup surveys had shown that 1 per cent of the electorate believed that Powell should become Conservative leader were Heath to resign. One month later, the figure had risen to 24 per cent. Powell's popularity came from all income groups and was focused entirely on the issue of race (Schoen, 1977; Studlar, 1974). Although sacked by Heath from the shadow cabinet, Powell seems paradoxically to have helped Heath win the 1970 General Election. Studlar (1978) and Miller (1980) have suggested that Powell established the Conservative Party in the minds of the electorate as the party of strict immigration control. Moreover, Heath himself adopted some of Powell's policy recommendations on immigration control, but without the lurid, river-foaming rhetoric (Layton-Henry, 1984).

Had Powell bided his time and awaited a change of leadership, he might have eventually resumed his ministerial career. Certainly his *laissez-faire* economics would have been no handicap in the Conservative Party of Margaret Thatcher, for, as Gamble (1986: 49) suggests, 'all the arguments adopted by Thatcher and the leadership group she slowly assembled around her had been anticipated by Enoch Powell in the 1960s.' However, Powell continued to tread the maverick path. He attacked Heath's commitment to the Common Market, on the grounds that the EEC threatened the national integrity of Britain. His opposition to the Common Market was total. He declared that he was unable to stand as a candidate for a party whose stance he so profoundly disagreed with. Powell resigned his Wolverhampton seat and declined to stand in the February 1974 General Election. In addition, he committed the heresy of all Conservative heresies; he advised the electorate to vote Labour (the effects of Powell's appeal are analysed by Steed, 1975: 331–2).

Powell did not remain outside the House of Commons for long. The October 1974 General Election saw him take a step remarkable for a senior English politician: he was standing as an Ulster Unionist candidate for a Northern Ireland constituency. Powell was returned as the member for South Down, strongly committed to the policy of integrating Ulster totally with the rest of the United Kingdom. He retained his Northern Irish seat until the 1987 General Election but as a Unionist MP he had no reasonable hopes of entering government again. Despite his contacts with senior Conservatives to the right of the party (for example, in the Conservative Philosophy Group) Powell has remained an anomalous figure. He is a national politician but is confined to the one area above all others in Britain which thinks in local terms. Powell's Irish constituency was largely indifferent to the issue which created his national prominence. And although he might be thought the apostle of Thatcher's *laissez-faire* conservatism, he is in permanent exile from the Conservative Party. Yet he continues to disconcert his former colleagues with his unmistakable style of rhetoric, urgently predicting doom and chaos.

Selection and presentation of text
The question under consideration is whether the views of this unorthodox Conservative, Enoch Powell, can in any way be located within the conspiracy tradition of ideology. A sound methodological procedure for attempting to produce an answer would be to opt for a quantitative 'content analysis' (for an excellent discussion of the relations between quantitative and qualitative research see Bryman, 1984). The speeches of Enoch Powell could be systematically sampled – perhaps every fifth or tenth of his published orations could be selected. Word counts could be made, with or without computer assistance. Perhaps the word 'conspiracy' could be chosen for special attention. The analysis might then show how many times, per 10 000 other words, Enoch Powell uses the key term 'conspiracy'. Powell's ratio could then be compared statistically to the ratios of other speakers, whose texts had been chosen with as much methodological care.

All this might be quite interesting, but, as Beardsworth (1980) has shown in an important critique, the techniques of such content analysis are essentially limited. This sort of methodology can count words, but it cannot interpret them. Under some circumstances mere counting can lead to misleading conclusions. For example, someone who is continually scoffing at the ideas of conspiracy theories might have just as high a usage of the word 'conspiracy' as the most obsessed believer. Furthermore, the question about Powell is not whether he talks about conspiracies, but whether any such talk should be located within the conspiracy ideological tradition. As will be shown, mere talk about conspiracy, even belief in a conspiracy, is not of itself sufficient evidence for such a location. Over and above statistical identification, such beliefs need to be interpreted by the ideological analyst. Interpretation cannot be achieved by handing over the whole business of scholarship to a programme of computation.

It is one feature of traditional scholarship that attention is not confined exclusively to a single text. Perhaps the scholar might be perplexed by the meaning of a particular text, but that will often signal the start of a search which will embrace other texts and wider reading. Part of the scholar's skill is not to follow a preset programme, laid down in advance by a methodologist, but to gather up clues which can nudge the search one way or another. Scholars have to feel their way around their library and archival sources, backing hunches as they proceed. The chosen example will illustrate this process, by selecting a text which is not to be analysed in itself but which sets in motion a search for new information and new interpretations.

The text is a newspaper report of one of Powell's speeches, and therefore is one that is available to experts and laypeople alike. However, once an ideological question is raised, the analyst must go beyond the specific text. In fact the analyst has to go beyond this specific speech, or the report of the speech, and to look directly at other reports and in particular at other speeches. As the search for ideological significance proceeds, more information is required, and the analyst must widen the investigation to include conspiracy material from non-Conservative sources. In one way the original text is a starting point for a search, rather than being the object of a methodological examination in itself. In another way, the text is not the starting point: the analyst will already have built up a knowledge of the topic before starting the search required for understanding the particular text. In fact, without this background knowledge, the analyst might not even decide that the text was one which was worth detailed analysis. However, the background knowledge does not guarantee the outcome of the search.

On 19 January 1986 the British Sunday papers carried stories that Enoch Powell had suggested that the United States was responsible for the murder of a senior Conservative politician seven years earlier. *The Observer* carried the story on its front page with the headline: 'US had Neave killed – Powell'. The text summarized the main themes of Powell's speech:

> Mr Enoch Powell yesterday accused the United States, the Foreign Office and British military intelligence of a conspiracy to create a united Ireland inside the NATO alliance in an extraordinary speech to the Federation of Conservative Students in Birmingham.
>
> Mr Powell, the Unionist MP for South Down, suggested that Washington had 20 years ago 'secured from Britain an undertaking to organise the transfer of Northern Ireland out of the United Kingdom into an all-Ireland state.'
>
> He said the first step in the conspiracy was 'to eliminate the stumbling block of the Northern Ireland Unionist Government. ... MI6 and their friends proved equal to the job, and in 1969 active committal of the army in Ulster subordinated Stormont to Whitehall.'
>
> He suggested that none of the Prime Ministers of the period – Edward Heath, Harold Wilson and James Callaghan – knew what was happening as the conspiracy unfolded.
>
> Mr Powell went on to suggest that the Americans were responsible for the murder of Mrs Thatcher's close friend and shadow Northern Ireland spokesman, Mr Airey Neave, in 1979.
>
> Evidence, or what was thought to be evidence, that the new leader, Mrs Thatcher, and her aide, Airey Neave, had no intention of playing ball alarmed them.
>
> The road block was cleared by eliminating Airey Neave on the verge of his taking office; and from then onwards events were moved ahead again along the time tabled path.'
>
> Mr Powell described Mrs Thatcher as 'an unhappy traveller' who was taken 'along the road signposted' towards the next stage – signing the Anglo-Irish Agreement.
>
> Mr Powell said he was convinced Mrs Thatcher thought it was in Britain's vital interests that Ulster should be sacrificed for the good of all.

One need not translate the newspaper report into a computer input to realize that the word 'conspiracy' appears three times. It is not merely a matter of the word being repeated; Powell was obviously telling a dire story of devious conspiracy and murder. If the tale of hidden conspiracy was being told to a Conservative audience, does this imply that Powell was engaged in something more general? Was he undermining a whole series of conventional explanations, in order to spread a wider tale of conspiracy? The single report cannot answer this question. Instead, one must turn to other speeches and other reports and, in so doing, examine various possible interpretations.

Interpreting the themes of conspiracy

From a rhetorical perspective, one of the first tasks in analysing a piece of discourse is to discover the argumentative meaning (Billig, 1987; Billig in press a; Billig in press b). This involves establishing who, or what, is being criticized in a piece of argumentative discourse. In an obvious sense, one might say that Powell is attacking the Americans for their conspiratorial deeds. However, Powell is not addressing his remarks to the Americans, for they seem beyond the argumentative pale. His remarks constitute arguments against those who trust the American government. He is overtly criticizing Thatcher for not seeing the truth about the Americans. In consequence, Powell is following traditional conspiracy theorists in directing his arguments against conventional, non-conspiratorial explanations of political events.

Powell's speech was not an isolated outburst, but is of a piece with others. If the analyst wishes to probe the ideological significance of the one speech, attention should not be confined exclusively to that single text. Instead, the single text must be located within a wider pattern. The following week, after the Birmingham speech, Powell was expanding upon his theme. He suggested that the British Prime Minister had been 'obliged' to enter into 'a pre-existing compact concerned with the strategic purposes of the United States' (*The Guardian*, 27 October 1986). It was not only Airey Neave whom the Americans had silenced, but also Lord Mountbatten. Since 1969 there had been 'avowed compliance with the dictates of American strategy'. The following month, there was more of the conspiratorial same. In Ballyculter, Powell declared that 'British policy must be subservient to that of the United States', who wanted a United Ireland within NATO: 'the hunt for a traitor who would deliver goes feverishly on' (*The Guardian*, 1 December 1986). Like many conspiracy theorists, Powell evokes the image of public opinion being fooled but about to grasp the truth. According to Powell, 'The sleeping dog of British opinion ... presently will get up, yawn, stretch and set about wondering whether after all, and why, it is so essential for the United Kingdom to comply with every fantasy of the United States that it must perjure itself and betray its own people in the process.' Using a metaphor familiar in the writings of conspiracy theorists, Powell declared that 'the British score is written out for the second fiddle, and anyone looking over the shoulder of the violinist can observe how obediently the score has been played.'

Nor are all these new themes, for past texts and speeches show Powell's opposition to a United Ireland. He had previously accused Mrs Thatcher of 'treachery' over the issue (*The Times*, 8 July 1985), and similarly he had claimed that the British and

American governments aided terrorists in Northern Ireland (*The Times*, 12 August 1985). The claim that there existed an American plot to establish a United Ireland was an old theme (*The Times*, 27 September 1980; *The Times*, 7 December 1981). Nor were the American conspiracies confined to Ireland. For example, Powell had spoken about the EEC suffering the admission of Spain and Portugal in conformity with American strategic interests (*The Times*, 19 October 1985). In all these speeches it is possible to detect, in greater or lesser form, the themes of conspiracy and treachery, as powerful manipulators dupe smaller nations into abandoning their national independence.

The ideological significance of these conspiracy themes still needs to be assessed. It might be asserted that the themes possess more significance in terms of the psychology of Mr Powell than anything else. For instance, a case might be made that the disappointments in Mr Powell's own political career have led him to suspect the machinations of more successful politicians. This would imply that the images of conspiracy stem from individual motiviations and are likely to be found only in his later speeches. Even if the themes only occur since Powell's translation to the suspicious world of Ulster politics, it is still possible to find ideological significance: away from the politics of England, he may have acquired a conspiracy mentality not uncommon within the circles of Loyalist politics.

However, there is no need to entertain the hypothesis that Powell's conspiracy themes date from his period in Northern Irish politics if earlier texts also contain the theme of conspiracy. His speeches against non-white immigrations were not confined to innuendoes about 'grinning piccaninnies' and dire warnings about the future: dark conspiratorial deeds were afoot to fool and then destroy the (white) nation. He claimed that the government and public were being deliberately misled about the numbers of non-whites living in Britain (for example *The Times*, 16 February 1971). There was an 'enemy within', which was more sinister than the Nazis or the communists (*The Times*, 15 June 1973). So dreadful was the conspiracy to conceal the facts of non-white residency in Britain that 'One begins to wonder if the Foreign Office was the only Department of State into which enemies of this country were infiltrated' (11 June 1973; quoted in Schoen, 1977: 53).

The theme of conspiracy is not confined to the topics of race or Northern Ireland, but over the years it has been a constant theme in Powell's political rhetoric. When he opposed British entry into the Common Market, he did not see himself as merely opposing a political decision, but he was standing against conspiratorial forces. He declared that there was a conspiracy to force the public into accepting British entry. He warned that there was 'a conspiracy of "the best people" in parliament and the media', and that the ordinary people 'have settled down to a dazed or irritated acceptance that they are living in an age when the majority is always wrong' (speech at Rugby, reported in *The Times*, 29 November 1971).

Some of Powell's most outspoken comments about conspiracy have concerned economic issues, and in particular they are to be found in his speeches against the economic policies of Harold Wilson's first Labour government. Here the defence of *laissez-faire* economics was seen in terms of a battle against an insidious conspiracy to impose an economic policy which would destroy the nation's freedom. The tone was as apocalyptic as any conspiracy theorist's (Lispet and Raab, 1970). Powell declared 'The situation is perilous': the public had been so 'blinded' that 'you might almost suppose there was a gigantic conspiracy' (14 October 1966, quoted in Powell, 1969: 191–2). Not long later the 'almost' conspiracy had become a certain conspiracy: 'The whole prices and incomes policy' was 'a sustained and successful conspiracy against the common sense of the public' (speech in Gedling, 24 May 1968). He added that 'Unfortunately it is not without precedent for a small group of interested people to succeed in hoodwinking the vast majority of their fellow-citizens and thus bringing them under their control' (Powell, 1969: 106).

Classic conspiracy theorists are not content to view one particular governmental action as a conspiracy, but see all politics in terms of a conspiracy. As has been shown, Powell sees hidden conspiratorial designs lying behind various major issues, especially those on which he is at variance with the Conservative leadership. Powell expressed the general conspiratorial interpretation of politics when he declared in 1968 that 'We live in an age of conspiracies' and that 'The politics of the last few years have been little more than a series of conspiracies conducted by the politicians and the Press against the common sense of the public' (Powell, 1969: 109). The conspiracy is a 'mightier instrument of mass repression than machine guns' (p. 110); it aims so to mesmerize people that they 'deliver themselves passively to the guidance and domination of their betters' (p. 109). Classic conspiracy theorists claim that absence of direct proof of a conspiracy is a further sign of the cunning of the conspirators (Billig, 1978). Similarly, Powell alleged that 'The success [of the conspiracy] has been so complete that we fail not only to be astonished at it, but even to perceive it' (p. 110).

In Powell's demonology, each conspiratorial operation is a step in a wider conspiratorial pattern. He claims that people were being made 'vulnerable to the next stage of the operation, which is to subject them to control, to a dictatorship' (p. 112). Powell, like classic conspiracy theorists, poses as the visionary who has seen through the evil machinations and warns of the doom which will surely occur unless he is heeded. In a speech delivered on 13 June 1970, he declared 'Britain is at the moment under attack', just as it was in the two world wars. In fact, continued Powell, 'The danger is greater today, because the enemy is invisible or disguised so that his preparations go on hardly observed. ... I assert then, that this country is today under attack by forces which aim at the actual destruction of our nation' (quoted in Berkeley, 1977: 115–16). The conspiracy is not just directed against Britain, but it is worldwide in its aims for dominance: 'All around the world in various forms the same formula for rending societies apart is being prepared and applied by ignorance or design and there are those who are determined to see to it that Britain shall no longer be able to escape' (quoted in Berkeley, 1977: 88).

These themes suggest the conspiratorial dimension in Powell's political mentality: ordinary explanations of politics are rejected in favour of interpretations revealing hidden conspiracies. The nature of the conspirators is not fully specified, but they seem to fulfil American, rather than Soviet, aims (see, for instance, Powell's criticism of Thatcher's belief that the Soviet Union seeks world domination in *The Times*, 8 October 1983). Although it has been possible to construct the outlines of a conspiracy mentality by piecing together themes from Powell's speeches and writings, there has been no direct link to the conspiracy tradition itself. It is possible that this unusual politician had constructed his own conspiratorial themes, in ignorance of the libraries of conspiratorial publications. To locate Powell fully within this ideological tradition, it would be necessary to show evidence of a direct link.

Some sort of evidence is contained within an extraordinary speech delivered in Bridgnorth on 28 August 1969 and reported in *The Times*. It is a significant speech because it is his first upon Northern Irish matters. Ostensibly, the speech comments upon the report that a French and a German student had been gaoled at Londonderry for throwing petrol bombs. Yet Powell reads wider designs into the report of the single incident. The event was part of a pattern which is subverting nationality and which 'has all but destroyed governments and states in Asia, in Europe and in America'. This wider pattern could explain all manner of phenomena in contemporary life, including racial tensions in Britain and the payment of local property taxes or rates: 'The pattern is recognizable enough and it belongs in an international, a worldwide context.' The moral of all this was that 'We must simply have more control over the admission, the movement and the activities of aliens in this country.'

These themes of national destruction and international plotting seem familiar enough, but what marked this speech out was a remark at the beginning. Having mentioned the newspaper report of the two gaoled students, Powell declared that 'We shall do well to ponder the news item deeply: for, as Douglas Reed used to say in the 1930s: "This means you."' No individual is cited in the speech other than Douglas Reed. Nor is any information given about Reed. To most of the audience and to most of the readers of the written text the name of Douglas Reed would be unfamiliar. But it would be recognizable to those with a knowledge of the traditions of British anti-semitism and the conspiracy ideology. In this way, knowledge of the subject area can lead to insights which fall outside the range of methodological expertise.

Douglas Reed had been a prewar correspondent of *The Times* in Germany. He left Germany in 1935, an opponent of Hitler but not of National Socialism. He was a strong advocate of the Strasser brothers' form of National Socialism. When he died in 1976, *The Times* obituary declared that 'Reed had his own hobby-horses, some of which were indeed not so very unlike Nazi hobby horses.' The writer specified the allusion by mentioning Reed's 'virulent anti-semitism'. It was not merely that Reed was an anti-semite, but that he allied his anti-semitism to conspiratorial fantasies. Reed, in books such as *Far and Wide* and *The Controversy of Zion*, outlined his notions about Jewish plans to take power of the world by subverting independent nations. As Thurlow (1984) points out in his study of British fascism, Reed was one of the first anti-semitic writers to deny the reality of Hitler's persecution of the Jews.

Today Reed's work is unread by mainstream political thinkers, but continues to be much venerated by anti-semitic and fascist groups on the extreme right. Reed is an especial favourite of the UK National Front, which is currently following a Strasserite line. His books, alleging Jewish conspiracies for world domination, are distributed in fascist circles and frequently quoted in anti-semitic publications. For example, *Candour* (July/August 1986) quoted conspiratorial notions from Reed's *Far and Wide* in 'an effort to persuade readers that there is a very cogent argument in support of the Conspiracy Theory' (p. 62). The National Front's magazine, *Nationalism Today*, recently ran a series featuring quotations from writers who 'laid the foundations' of its ideology: issue 19 featured Reed and his ideas about Jews, conspiracies and Jewish conspiracies. It is unsurprising that the sayings of Douglas Reed should appear in National Front publications. It is more noteworthy, to say the least, when they are quoted by Enoch Powell.

Advantages and disadvantages

The procedures followed in this brief examination of Powell have scarcely been methodological in the accepted sense. The starting point was a single text, which needed to be interpreted in terms of other texts before the ideological patterns could emerge. A methodologist might prescribe a system of sampling other texts, but the scholar knows that as much as possible should be read, lest something important be missed. Nor can the results of reading be reduced to a quantitative matrix. A single quotation might have more ideological significance than an oft-repeated one. George (1959), describing the analysis of Nazi propaganda during the war, stressed the importance of uniquely occurring messages. Similarly, in the analysis of Powell, the ideological significance of the quotation from Reed is not diminished by its unusualness; if anything, it is increased by it.

Moreover, the scholar knows that the task of scholarship cannot be reduced to getting through a list of set reading. It is not, for example, merely a matter of ploughing through the collected works of Enoch Powell, in the belief that all necessary reading then will have been completed. Wider reading is also required. At all times in the foregoing analysis there was an implicit comparison with conspiracy material and, indeed, with the orthodox, non-conspiratorial versions of conservatism. Thus, the analysis depended upon familiarity with wider material. Of course it should not be presumed that, because the preceding analysis sought to use the skills of traditional scholarship, it is satisfactorily scholarly. In fact, it is a very limited sketch. A fuller analysis would have required more details, and scholars must hope to deepen their expertise, not merely as a result of having engaged in study, but as part of the process of studying.

The main drawback of such traditional scholarship is that it places a burden of responsibility upon the scholar. The procedures of methodology make the individual expert anonymous, in the hope of reducing the vagaries of individual bias. Yet this abolition of bias also involves abolishing judgement. The traditional scholar cannot avoid the task of judging whether a piece of evidence is important or not. Moreover, the scholar cannot avoid responsibility for making judgements which can be criticized by other scholars with different views about the essential features of the issue in question. Thus, judgements about the patternings of ideology are potentially controversial. Scholars, with different complexions to their expertise, will argue matters, putting different interpretations on each others' evidence. This is particularly true when one is asserting what are the essential features of an ideological patterning. It cannot be expected that the foregoing analysis is the last word on the subject of Enoch Powell and the shape of his ideology. At best it raises further questions, even as it suggests possibilities for answers.

Moreover, it must be recognized that the analyses of traditional scholarship, or the judgements of traditional scholars, are potentially controversial. In this sense, scholarship is located firmly within the domain of argumentative rhetoric (Billig, 1987; Shotter, 1987). The traditional scholar, amongst many other responsibilities, also has the responsibility not to shirk the possibility of receiving and administering criticism. There are no neutral methodological procedures to hide behind. The analyses of others, even of colleagues, must be criticized if the scholar finds their judgement to be lacking. Moreover, each scholar exposes himself or herself to the danger of criticism, especially to that most damaging accusation of being unscholarly. In consequence, the so-called cosy world of scholarship is, or should be, a controversial place of criticism.

References

Abercrombie, N. (1980) *Class, Structure, and Knowledge*. Oxford: Basil Blackwell.

Abramson, L., M.E.P. Seligman and J. Teasdale (1978) 'Learned Helplessness in Humans: Critique and Reformulation', *Journal of Abnormal Psychology*, 87: 49–74.

Adorno, T.W., E. Frenkel-Brunswik, D.J. Levinson and R.N. Sanford (1950) *The Authoritarian Personality*. New York: Harper and Row.

Alvey Knowledge Based Systems Club, Explanation Special Interest Group (1987) Proceedings of the Second Workshop, University of Surrey, England, January.

Anderson, N.H. (1968) 'Likeableness Ratings of 555 Personality Trait Words', *Journal of Personality and Social Psychology*, 9: 272–9.

Antaki, C. (ed.) (1981) *The Psychology of Ordinary Explanations of Social Behaviour*. London: Academic Press.

Antaki, C. (1985) 'Ordinary Explanation in Conversation: Causal Structures and their Defence', *European Journal of Social Psychology*, 15: 213–30.

Antaki, C. and C.R. Brewin (1982) *Attributions and Psychological Change: Applications of Attributional Theories to Clinical and Educational Practice*. London: Academic Press.

Antaki, C. and A. Lewis (eds) (1986) *Mental Mirrors: Metacognition in Social Knowledge and Communication*, London: Sage.

Antaki, C. and S. Naji, 'Events Explained in Conversational "Because" Statements', *British Journal of Social Psychology*, 26: 119–26.

Appelt, D.E. (1985) *Planning English Sentences*. Cambridge: Cambridge University Press.

Armistead, N. (ed.) (1974) *Reconstructing Social Psychology*. Harmondsworth: Penguin.

Atkinson, J.M. and J.C. Heritage (eds) (1984) *Structures of Social Action: Studies in Conversation Analysis*. Cambridge: Cambridge University Press.

Austin, J.L. (1962) *How to Do Things with Words*. Oxford: Clarendon Press.

Bachnik, J. (1982) 'Deixis and Self/Other Discourse in Japanese', *Sociolinguistic Working Papers*, No. 99: 1–34.

Backman, C.W. (1985) 'Identity, Self Presentation, and the Resolution of Moral Dilemmas: Towards a Social and Psychological Theory of Moral Behavior', pp. 251–89 in B.R. Schlenker (ed.), *The Self and Social Life*. New York: McGraw-Hill.

Barker, M. (1981) *The New Racism*. London: Junction Books.

Barthes, R. (1977) Image-Music-Text. London: Fontana/Collins.

Beardsworth, A. (1980) 'Analyzing Press Content: some Technical and Methodological Issues', *Sociological Review Monograph*, 29: 371–95.

Beck, A.T. (1967) *Depression*. Philadelphia: University of Pennsylvania Press.

Becker, A.L. (1974) 'Person in Kawi', *Oceanic Linguistics*. 13: 229–55.

Bell, D. (1962) 'The Dispossessed', in D. Bell (ed.), *The Radical Right*. New York: Anchor Books.

Berkeley, H. (1977) *The Odyssey of Enoch*. London: Hamish Hamilton.

Bettelheim, B. (1976) *The Uses of Enchantment*. New York: Knopf.

Bettman, J.R. and B.A. Weitz (1983) 'Attributions in the Boardroom: Causal Reasoning in Corporate Annual Reports', *Administrative Science Quarterly*, 28: 165–83.

Billig, M. (1978) *Fascists: a Social Psychological View of the National Front*. London: Academic Press.

Billig, M. (1982) *Ideology and Social Psychology*. Oxford: Basil Blackwell.

Billig, M. (1986) 'Very Ordinary Life and the Young Conservatives', in H. Beloff (ed.), *Getting into Life*. London: Methuen

Billig, M. (1987) *Arguing and Thinking: a Rhetorical Approach to Social Psychology*. Cambridge: Cambridge University Press.

Billig, M. (1987a) 'Anti-semitic Themes and the British Far Left: some Social Psychological Observations on Indirect Aspects of the Conspiracy Tradition', in C.F. Graumann and S. Moscovici (eds), *Changing Conceptions of Conspiracy*. New York: Springer.

Billig, M. (1988) 'The Notion of 'Prejudice': some Rhetorical and Ideological Aspects', *Text*, 8: 91–110.

Billig, M. (in press a) 'Historical and Rhetorical Aspects of Attitudes: the Case of the British Monarchy', *Philosophical Psychology*.

Billig, M. (in press b) 'Common-places of the British Royal Family: a Rhetorical Analysis of Plain and Argumentative Sense', *Text*.

Billig, M., S. Condor, D. Edwards, M. Gane, D. Middleton and A.R. Radley (forthcoming) *Ideological Dilemmas in Everday Thinking*. London: Sage.

Bluck, S., E.J. Ballard, G. Baker-Brown, B. de Vries and P. Suedfeld (1985) *The UBC Scoring Manual for Integrative Complexity*. Unpublished manuscript, Department of Psychology, University of British Columbia, Vancouver.

Bowerman, W.R. (1981) 'Applications of a Social Psychological Theory of Motivation to the Language of Defensiveness and Self-Justification', pp.00–00 in M.M.T. Henderson (ed.), *1980 Mid-America Linguistics Conference Papers*, Lawrence, KA: University of Kansas.

Brende, J.S. and E.R. Parson (1985) *Vietnam Veterans: the Road to Recovery*. New York: Plenum.

Brewin, C.R. and C. Antaki (1987) 'An Analysis of Ordinary Explanations in Clinical Attribution Research', *Journal of Social and Clinical Psychology*. 5: 79–98.

Brown, P. and S. Levinson (1978) 'Universals in Language Usage Politeness Phenomena', in E. Goody (ed.), *Questions and Politeness Strategies in Social Interaction*. Cambridge: Cambridge University Press.

Brown, R.W. and A. Gillman (1970) 'Pronouns of Power and Solidarity', chapter 1 in R. Brown (ed.), *Psycholinguistics*. New York: Free Press.

Brunson, B.I. and K.A. Matthews (1981) 'Type A Coronary-prone Behaviour Pattern and Reactions to Uncontrollable Stress: an Analysis of Performance Strategies, Affect, and Attributions during Failure', *Journal of Personality and Social Psychology*, 40: 906–18.

Bryman, A. (1984) 'The Debate about Quantitative and Qualitative Research', *British Journal of Sociology*, 35: 75–92.

Burleson, B., S. Wilson, M. Waltman, E. Goering, T. Ely and B. Whaley (November, 1986) 'Item Desirability Effects in Compliance-gaining Research: Seven Empirical Studies Showing why the Checklist Methodology Produces Garbage', paper presented to the Speech Communication Association, Chicago, November.

Campbell, J. (1956) *The Hero with a Thousand Faces* (1949). New York: Meridian.

Carlson, L. (1983) *Dialogue Games*. Dordrecht: Reider.

218   *References*

Carroll, J.T. and J.W. Payne (1977) 'Judgments about Crime and the Criminals:
a Model and a Method for Investigating Parole Decisions', in B.D. Sales (ed.),
Perspectives in Law and Psychology (Vol. 1). New York: Plenum.
Cody, M.J. (1982) 'A Typology of Disengagement Strategies and an Examination of
the Role Intimacy, Reactions to Inequity and Relational Problems Play in Strategy
Selection', *Communication Monographs*, 49: 148–70.
Cody, M.J., D. Canary and S.W. Smith (in press) 'Compliance-gaining Goals', in J.
Daly and J. Wiemann (eds.), *Communicating Strategically*. Hillsdale, NJ: Erlbaum.
Cody, M.J. and M.L. McLaughlin (1985) 'Models for the Sequential Construction
of Accounting Episodes: Situational and Interactional Constraints on Message
Selection and Evaluation', pp. 50–69 in R.L. Street Jr and J.N. Cappella (eds.),
Sequence and Pattern in Communicative Behaviour. London: Edward Arnold.
Cohen, P.R. and C.R. Perrault (1979) 'Elements of a Plan-based Theory of Speech
Acts', *Cognitive Science*, 3: 177–212.
Cohler, B.J. (1979) 'Personal Narrative and Life-course', unpublished manuscript,
University of Chicago.
Cohn, N. (1967) *Warrant for Genocide*. London: Chatto/Heinemann.
Coleman, R.V. (1976) 'Court Control and Grievance Accounts: Dynamics of Traffic
Court Interaction', *Urban Life*, 5: 165–87.
Crano, W. and H.M. Schroder (1967) 'Complexity of Attitude Structure and Process
of Conflict Resolution', *Journal of Personality and Social Psychology*, 5: 110–4.
Cronbach, L.J. and P. Meehl (1955) 'Construct Validity in Psychological Tests',
Psychological Bulletin, 52: 281–302.
Davidson, J. (1984) 'Subsequent Versions of Invitations, Offers, Requests and
Proposals Dealing with Potential or Actual Rejection', in J.M. Atkinson and
J.C. Heritage (eds.), *Structures of Social Action: Studies in Conversation Analysis*.
Cambridge: Cambridge University Press.
de Waele, J.P. and R. Harré (ed.) (1979), *Personality*. Oxford: Basil Blackwell.
Derrida, J. (1978) *Writing and Difference*. London: Routledge and Kegan Paul.
Derrida, J. (1981) *Positions*. London: Athlone Press.
Dewey, J. (1975) *Lectures on Psychological and Political Ethics* (1898). New York:
Hafner Press.
Diener, C.T. and C.S. Dweck (1978) 'An Analysis of Learned Helplessness:
Continuous Changes in Performance, Strategy, and Achievement Cognitions
Following Failure', *Journal of Personality and Social Psychology*, 36: 451–62.
Doyle, J. (1978) 'Truth Maintenance Systems for Problem Solving', report AI-TR-419,
AI Laboratory, Massachusetts Institute of Technology.
Drew, P. (1984) 'Speakers Reportings in Invitation Sequences', in J.M. Atkinson and
J.C. Heritage (eds), *Structures of Social Action: Studies in Conversation Analysis*.
Cambridge: Cambridge University Press.
Driver, M.J. (1965) 'A Structural Analysis of Aggression, Stress and Personality in
an Inter-nation Simulation', paper 97, Institute for Research in the Behavioral,
Economic, and Management Sciences, Purdue University.
Duncan, S. and D.W. Fiske, (1977) *Face to Face Interaction: Research, Methods
and Theory*. Hillsdale, NJ: Erlbaum.
Eagleton, J. (1983) *Literary Theory: an Introduction*. Oxford: Basil Blackwell.
Edmonson, W. (1981) *Spoken Discourse: a Model for Analysis*. London: Longman.
Elig, T.W. and I.H. Frieze (1979) 'Measuring Causal Attributions for Success and
Failure', *Journal of Personality and Social Psychology*, 37: 621–34.
Ericcson, K.A. and H.A. Simon (1984) *Protocol Analysis*. Cambridge, MA: MIT Press.

Feagin, J.R. (1972) 'Poverty: We Still Believe that God Helps Those that Help Themselves'. *Psychology Today*, 6: 101–29.

Feather, N.T. (1974) 'Explanations of Poverty in Australian and American Samples: the Person, Society or Fate?', *Australian Journal of Psychology*, 26: 199–216.

Feuer, L.S. (1970) *Ideology and the Ideologists*. New York: Blackwell.

Figley, C.R. (1984) 'Catastrophes: An Overview of Family Reactions', pp. 222–48 in C.R. Figley and H.I. McCubbin (eds), *Stress and the Family: Coping with Catastrophe*. New York: Brunner-Mazel.

Fincham, F.D. (1985) 'Attributions in Close Relationships', pp. 203–34 in J.H. Harvey and G. Weary (eds), *Attributions: Basic Issues and Applications*. New York: Academic Press.

Fiske, S.T., D.A. Kenny and S.E. Taylor (1982) 'Structural Models for the Mediation of Salience Effects on Attribution', *Journal of Experimental Social Psychology*, 18: 105–27

Fiske, S.T. and S.E. Taylor (1984) *Social Cognition*. New York: Random House.

Fodor, J.A. (1975) The Language of Thought. Harvard: Harvard University Press.

Foot, P. (1969) *The Rise of Enoch Powell*. Harmondsworth: Penguin.

Forsyth, D.R. (1980) 'The Functions of Attributions', *Social Psychology Quarterly*, 43: 184–9.

Frye, N. (1957) *Anatomy of Criticism*. Princeton: Princeton University Press.

Furnham, A. (1982) 'Why are the Poor Always With Us? Explanation for Poverty in Britain', *British Journal of Social Psychology*, 21: 311–22.

Furnham, A. (1983) 'Attributions for affluence', *Personality and Individual Differences*, 4: 31–40.

Furnham, A. and Lewis, A. (1986) *The Economic Mind*. Brighton: Wheatsheaf Books.

Gamble, A. (1986) 'The Political Economy of Freedom', in R. Levitas (ed.), *The Ideology of the New Right*. Oxford: Polity Press.

Garfinkel, H. (1967) *Studies in Ethnomethodology*. Englewood Cliffs, NJ: Prentice-Hall.

George, A.L. (1959) *Propaganda Analysis*. Evanstone, IL: Row, Peterson.

Gergen, K.J. (1982) *Toward Transformation in Social Knowledge*. New York: Springer.

Gergen, K.J. and M.M. Gergen 'Narratives of the Self', in T.R. Sarbin and K.E. Schiebe (eds), *Studies in Social Identity*. New York: Praeger.

Gergen, K.J. and M.M. Gergen (1984) *Historical Social Psychology*. Hillsdale, NJ: Erlbaum.

Gergen, K.J. and M.M. Gergen (in press) 'Narratives and the Self as Relationship', in L. Berkowitz (ed.), *Advances in Experimental Social Psychology*. London: Academic Press.

Gergen, M.M. (1980) 'Antecedents and Consequences of Self-attributional Preferences in Later Life', doctoral dissertation, Temple University.

Gergen, M.M. (in press) 'Towards a Feminist Metatheory and Methodology in the Social Sciences', in M.M. Gergen (ed.), *Feminist Thought and the Structure of Knowledge*. New York: New York University Press.

Giddens, A. (1979) *Central Problems in Social Theory*. London: Macmillan.

Gilbert, G.N. and P. Abell, (eds), (1983) *Accounts and Action*. Aldershot: Gower.

Gilbert, N. and M. Mulkay (1984) *Opening Pandora's Box: a Sociological Analysis of Scientists' Discourse*. Cambridge: Cambridge University Press.

Gilovich, T. (1983) 'Biased Evaluation and Persistence in Gambling', *Journal of Personality and Social Psychology*, 44: 1110–26.

Goffman, E. (1955) 'On Face Work', *Psychiatry*, 18: 213–31.

Goffman, E. (1971) *Relations in Public: Microstudies of the Public Order*. New York: Basic Books.

Goffman, E. (1981) *Forms of Talk*. Oxford: Oxford University Press.

Greenstein, F.I. (1975) 'Personality and Politics', in F.I. Greenstein and N. Polsby (eds), *Handbook of Political Science* (vol. 2). Reading, MA: Addison-Wesley.

Grice, H.P. (1957) 'Meaning', *Philosophical Review*, 66: 377–88.

Grice, H.P. (1981) 'Presupposition and Conversational Implicature', in P. Cole (ed.), *Radical Pragmatics*. New York: Academic Press.

Griffiths, R. (1983) *Fellow Travellers of the Right*. Oxford: Oxford University Press.

Groh, D. (1987). 'The Temptation to Conspiracy Theory', in C.F. Graumann and S. Moscovici (eds), *Changing Conceptions of Conspiracy*. New York: Springer Verlag.

Habermas, J. (1975) *The Theory of Communicative Action, Vol. 1: Reason and Rationalisation in Society*. Boston: Beacon Press.

Harré, R. (1979) *Social Being: A Theory for Social Psychology*, Oxford: Basil Blackwell.

Harré, R. (1981) 'Expressive Aspects of Descriptions of Others', in C. Antaki (ed.), *The Psychology of Ordinary Explanation of Social Behaviour*. London: Academic Press.

Harré, R. (1983a) 'Commentary from an Ethogenic Standpoint', *Journal for the Theory of Social Behaviour*, 13: 69–73.

Harré, R. (1983b) 'Ethogenics', in R. Harré and R. Lamb (eds), *The Encyclopaedic Dictionary of Psychology*. Oxford: Basil Blackwell.

Harré, R. and P.F. Secord (1972) *The Explanation of Social Behaviour*. Oxford: Basil Blackwell.

Harvey, J.H., G. Agostinelli and C. Claiborn (1987) 'Attributional Mediators of Adaptation in Vietnam Veterans', unpublished raw data. Iowa City: University of Iowa.

Harvey, J.H., R. Flanary and M. Morgan (1986) 'Vivid Memories of Vivid Loves Gone By', *Journal of Social and Personal Relationships*, 3: 359–73.

Harvey, J.H. and K.S. Galvin (1984) 'Clinical Implications of Attribution Theory and Research', *Clinical Psychology Review*, 4: 15–33.

Harvey, J.H. and G. Weary (1984) 'Current Issues in Attribution Theory and Research', *Annual Review of Psychology*, 35: 427–59.

Harvey, J.H., A.L. Weber, K.S. Galvin, H. Hustzi and N. Garnick (1986) 'Attribution and the Termination of Close Relationships: a Special Focus on the Account', pp.189–201 in R. Gilmour and S. Duck (eds), *The Emerging Field of Personal Relationships*. Hillsdale, NJ: Erlbaum.

Harvey, J.H., A.L. Weber, K.L. Yarkin and B. Stewart (1982) 'An Attributional Approach to Relationship Breakdown and Dissolution', pp. 107–26 in S. Duck (ed.), *Dissolving Personal Relationships* London: Academic Press.

Harvey, J.H., G.L. Wells and M.D. Alvarez, (1978) 'Attribution in the Context of Conflict and Separation in Close Relationships', in J.H. Harvey, W.J. Ickes and R.F. Kidd (eds), *New Directions in Attribution Research* (vol. 2). Hillsdale, NJ: Erlbaum

Harvey, J.H., K.L. Yarkin, J.M. Lightner and J.P. Town (1980) 'Unsolicited Interpretation and Recall of Interpersonal Events', *Journal of Personality and Social Psychology*, 38: 551–68.

Hastie, R. (1984) 'Causes and Effects of Causal Attribution', *Journal of Personality and Social Psychology*, 46: 44–56.

Heider, F. (1958) *The Psychology of Interpersonal Relations*. New York: Wiley.

Heider, F. (1976) 'A Conversation with Fritz Heider', pp. 3–18 in J.H. Harvey, W.J. Ickes and R.F. Kidd (eds), *New Directions in Attribution Research* (vol. 1). Hillsdale, NJ: Erlbaum.

Henriques, J, W. Hollway, C. Urwin, C. Venn and V. Walkerdine (1986) *Changing The Subject*. London: Methuen.

Heritage, J.C. (1984) *Garfinkel and Ethnomethodology*. Cambridge: Polity Press.

Heritage, J.C. (1985) 'Recent Developments in Conversation Analysis', *Sociolinguistics*, 15: 1–19.

Heritage, J.C. (forthcoming) 'Current Developments in Conversation Analysis', in P. Bull and D. Roger (eds), *Interdisciplinary Approaches to Interpersonal Communication.*. Bristol, Avon: Multilingual Matters.

Hewitt, J.P. and R. Stokes (1975) 'Disclaimers', *American Sociological Review*, 92: 110–57.

Hill, C.T., Z. Rubin and L.A. Peplau (1976) 'Breakups Before Marriage: the End of 103 Affairs', *Journal of Social Issues*. 32: 147–68.

Horowitz, M.J. (1976) *Stress Response Syndrome*. New York: Aronson.

Janis, I.L. and L. Mann (1977) *Decision Making*. New York: Free Press.

Janis, I.L. and J. Rodin (1979) 'Attribution, Control and Decision Making: Social Psychology and Health Care', pp. 487–521 in G. Stone, F. Cohen, N.E. Adler and associates, *Health Psychology: A Handbook*. San Francisco: Jossey-Bass.

Jones, E.E. and K. Davis (1965) 'From Acts to Dispositions: The Attribution Process in Social Perception", in L. Berkowitz (ed.), *Advances in Experimental Social Psychology* (vol. 2). New York: Academic Press.

Jones, E.E. and D. McGillis (1976) 'Correspondent Inferences and the Attribution Cube: a Comparative Reappraisal', pp. 389–420 in J.H. Harvey, W.J. Ickes and R.F. Kidd (eds), *New Directions in Attribution Research* (vol. 1). Hillsdale, NJ: Erlbaum.

Jones, E.E. and R.E. Nisbett, (1971) *The Actor and the Observer: Divergent Perceptions of the Cause of Behavior*. Morristown, NJ: Silver Burdett/General Learning Press.

Kelley, H.H. (1973) 'The Processes of Causal Attribution', *American Psychologist*, 28: 107–28.

Kelley, H.H. (1983) 'Perceived Causal Structures', in J. Jaspars, M. Hewstone and F. Fincham (eds), *Attribution Theory and Research: Conceptual, Developmental and Social Distinctions*. London: Academic Press.

Kohli, M. (1981) 'Biography: Account, Text, Method', in D. Bertaux (ed.), *Biography and Society*, London: Sage.

Kruglanski, A.W. (1980) 'Lay Epistemologic Process and Contents: Another Look at Attribution Theory', *Psychological Review*, 87: 70–87.

Kruglanski, A. (1987) 'Blame-placing Schemata and Attributional Research', in C.F. Graumann and S. Moscovici (eds) *Changing Conceptions of Conspiracy*. New York: Springer Verlag.

Labov, W. and D. Fanshel (1977) *Therapeutic Discourse: Psychotherapy as Conversation*. New York: Academic Press.

Larkin, J., J. McDermott, D.P. Simon and H. Simon (1980) 'Expert and Novice Performance in Solving Physics Problems', *Science*, 208: 1335–42.

Larrain, J. (1979) *The Concept of Ideology* London: Hutchinson.

Larrain, J. (1983) *Marxism and Ideology*. London: Macmillan.

Lau, R.R. (1984) 'Dynamics of the Attribution Process', *Journal of Personality and Social Psychology*, 46: 1017–28.

Lau, R.R. and D. Russell (1980) 'Attributions in the Sports Pages', *Journal of Personality and Social Psychology*, 39: 29–38.

Layton-Henry, Z. (1984) *The Politics of Race in Britain*. London: George Allen and Unwin.

Lehnert, W.G. (1978) *The Process of Question Answering*. Hillsdale, NJ: Erlbaum.

Levi, A. and P.E. Tetlock (1980) 'A Cognitive Analysis of the Japanese Decision to Go to War', *Journal of Conflict Resolution*, 24: 195–212.

Levinson, S. (1979) 'The Essential Inadequacies of Speech Act Models', in H. Perret, M. Sbissa and J. Verscheuren (eds), *Possibilities and Limitations of Pragmatics*. Amsterdam: Benjamin.

Levinson, S. (1983) *Pragmatics*. Cambridge: Cambridge University Press.

Lewis, A., Snell, M. and Furnham, A. (1987) 'Lay Explanations for the Causes of Unemployment in Britain: Economic, Individualistic, Societal or Fatalistic?', *Political Psychology*, 8: 427–39.

Lippman, S. (1986) '"Nothing but the Facts, Ma'am": The Impact of Testimony Construction and Narrative Style on Jury Decisions', unpublished senior thesis, Swarthmore College.

Lipset, S.M. and E. Raab (1970) *The Politics of Unreason*. London: Heinemann.

Lord Raglan (1956) *The Hero: a Study in Tradition, Myth, and Drama* (1936). New York: Vintage.

MacIntyre, A. (1981) *After Virtue*. South Bend, IN: University of Notre Dame Press.

Mannheim, K. (1960) *Ideology and Utopia*. London: Routledge and Kegan Paul.

Marsh, P., E. Rosser and R. Harré (1974) *The Rules of Disorder*. London: Routledge and Kegan Paul.

McClosky, H. (1967) 'Personality and Attitude Correlates of Foreign Policy Orientation', in J.M. Rosenau (ed.), *Domestic Sources of Foreign Policy*. New York: Free Press.

McDermott, D. and J. Doyle (1980) 'Non-monotonic Logic', *Artificial Intelligence*, 13: 41–72.

McGinn, C. (1983) *The Subjective View*. Oxford: Clarendon Press.

McLaughlin, M.L., M.J. Cody, and H.D. O'Hair (1983) 'The Management of Failure Events: some Contextual Determinants of Accounting Behavior', *Human Communication Research*, 9: 208–24.

McLaughlin, M.L., M.J. Cody and N.E. Rosenstein (1983) 'Account Sequences in Conversations Between Strangers', *Communication Monographs*, 50: 102–25.

McLellan, D. (1986) *Ideology*. Milton Keynes: Open University Press.

Mead, G.H. (1973) *Philosophy of the Act*. Chicago: Chicago University Press.

Miller, F.D., E.R. Smith and J. Uleman (1981) 'Measurement and Interpretation of Situational and Dispositional Attributions', *Journal of Experimental Social Psychology*, 17: 80–95.

Miller, W.L. (1980) 'What was the Profit in Following the Crowd? The Effectiveness of Party Strategies on Immigration and Devolution', *British Journal of Political Science* 15–38.

Mills, C.W. (1940) 'Situated Actions and Vocabularies of Motive', *American Sociological Review*, 5: 904–13.

Moore, B.S., D.R. Sherrod, T.J. Liv and B. Underwood (1979) 'The Dispositional Shift in Attribution over Time', *Journal of Experimental Social Psychology*, 15: 553–69.

Morris, G.H. (1985) 'The Remedial Episode as a Negotiation of Rules', pp.70–84 in R.L. Street Jr and J.N. Cappella (eds), *Sequence and Pattern in Communicative Behaviour*. London: Edward Arnold.

Mulkay, M. and N. Gilbert (1982) 'Accounting for Error: How Scientists Construct their World when they Account for Correct and Incorrect Belief', *Sociology*, 16: 165–83.

Moscovici, S. (1987) 'The Conspiracy Mentality', in C.F. Graumann and S. Moscovici (eds) *Changing Conceptions of Conspiracy*. New York: Springer Verlag.

Nash, R. (1982) 'Measuring Up and Falling into Line: the Discourse of Maori Education', paper presented to the NZARE Conference, December.

Neugarten, B.L. and G.O. Hagstad (1976) 'Age and the Life Course', in R.H. Binstock and E. Shanas (eds), *Handbook of Aging and the Social Sciences*. New York: Van Nostrand Reinhold.

Newell, A. (1980) 'One Final Word', pp. 175–89 in D.T. Tuma and F. Reif (eds), *Problem Solving and Education: Issues in Teaching and Research*. Hillsdale, NJ: Erlbaum.

Newell, A., J.C. Shaw and H.A. Simon (1958) 'Elements of a Theory of Human Problem Solving', *Psychological Review*, 65: 151–66.

Newell, A. and H.A. Simon (1972) *Human Problem Solving*. Englewood Cliffs, NJ: Prentice-Hall.

Nisbett, R.E., D. Harvey and J. Wilson (1979) '"Epistemological" Coding of the Content of Everyday Social Conversations', unpublished manuscript, University of Michigan.

Nisbett, R.E. and L. Ross (1980) *Human Inference*. Englewood Cliffs, NJ: Prentice-Hall.

Norman, D. and S.W. Draper (1986) *User Centred System Design*. London: Erlbaum.

Novack, G. (1975) *Pragmatism versus Marxism*. New York: Pathfinder Press.

Oyamai, S. (1985) *The Ontogeny of Information*. New York: Cambridge University Press.

Pennebaker, J.W. (1985) 'Traumatic Experience and Psychosomatic Disease: Exploring the Roles of Behavioural Inhibition, Obsession, and Confiding', *Canadian Psychology*, 26: 82–95.

Peters, R.S. (1958) *The Concept of Motivation*. London: Routledge and Kegan Paul.

Peterson, C. and M.E.P. Seligman (1984) 'Causal Explanations as a Risk Factor in Depression: Theory and Evidence', *Psychological Review*, 91: 347–74.

Poliakov, L. (1974) *The Aryan Myth*. London: Chatto/Heinemann.

Pollner, M. (1974) 'Mundane Reasoning', *Philosophy of the Social Sciences*, 4: 35–54.

Pollner, M. (1975) '"The very Coinage of your Brain": the Anatomy of Reality Disjunctures', *Philosophy of the Social Sciences*, 5: 411–30.

Pollner, M. (1987) *Mundane Reason: Reality in Everyday and Sociological Discourse*. Cambridge: Cambridge University Press.

Pomerantz, A.M. (1984) 'Agreeing and Disagreeing with Assessments', pp. 54–101 in J.M. Atkinson and J.C. Heritage (eds), *Structures of Social Action: Studies in Conversation Analysis*. Cambridge: Cambridge University Press.

Porter, C.A. and P. Suedfeld (1981) 'Integrative Complexity in the Correspondence of Literary Figures: Effects of Personal and and Social Stress', *Journal of Personality and Social Psychology*, 40: 321–30.

Potter, J. and F. Collie (1987) 'Community Care as Persuasive Rhetoric: a Study of Discourse', unpublished manuscript, St Andrews University.

Potter, J. and M. Mulkay (1982) 'Making Theory Useful: Utility Accounting in Social Psychologists' Discourse', *Fundamenta Scientiae*, 34: 259–78.

Potter, J. and M. Mulkay (1985) 'Scientists' Interview Talk: Interviews as a Technique for Revealing Participants' Interpretative Practices', in M. Brenner, J. Brown and D. Canter (eds), *The Research Interview: Uses and Approaches*. New York: Academic Press.

Potter, J. and S. Reicher (1987) 'Discourse of Community and Conflicts: the Organization of Social Categories in Accounts of a "Riot"', *British Journal of Social Psychology*, 26: 25–40.

Potter, J., P. Stringer and M. Wetherell (1984), *Social Texts and Context*. London: Routledge and Kegan Paul.

Potter, J. and M. Wetherell (1987) *Discourse and Social Psychology: Beyond Attitudes and Behaviour*. London: Sage.

Powell, J.E. (1969) *Freedom and Reality*. London: Batsford.

Power, R. (1979) 'The Organisation of Purposeful Dialogues', *Linguistics*, 17: 107–52.

Propp, V. (1968) *Morphology of the Folktale* (1928) (trans. and ed. Laurence Scott). Austin: University of Texas Press.

Pruitt, D.G. and S.A. Lewis (1975) 'Development of Integrative Solutions in Bilateral Negotiation', *Journal of Personality and Social Psychology*, 31: 621–33.

Putnam, H. (1975) 'The Meaning of Meaning', in *Mind, Language and Reality*. Cambridge: Cambridge University Press.

Reason, J. (1987) 'The Chernobyl Errors', *Bulletin of the British Psychological Society*, 40: 201–6.

Reeves, W. (1983) *British Racial Discourse*. Cambridge: Cambridge University Press.

Remler, J.E. (1978) 'Some Repairs on the Notion of Repairs', papers from the ninth regional meeting of the Chicago Linguistic Society, pp. 391–402.

Rest, J.R. (1984) 'The Major Components of Morality', pp. 24–38 in W.M. Kurtines and J.L. Gewirtz (eds), *Morality, Moral Behaviour and Moral Development*. New York: Wiley.

Roberts, J.M. (1974) *The Mythology of the Secret Societies*. St. Albans: Paladin.

Rosaldo, R. (1986) 'Ilongot Hunting as Story and Experience', in V. Turner and E. Bruner (eds), *The Anthropology of Experience*. Urbana: University of Illinois Press.

Ross, L. (1977) 'The Intuitive Psychologist and his Shortcomings: Distortions in the Attribution Process', in L. Berkowitz (ed.), *Advances in Experimental Social Psychology* (vol. 10). New York: Academic Press.

Rule, B.G. and G.L. Bisanz (1987) 'Goals and Strategies of Persuasion: a Cognitive Schema', in M. Zanna, P. Herman and J. Olson (eds), *Social Influence: the Fifth Ontario Symposium in Personality and Social Psychology*. Hillsdale, NJ: Erlbaum.

Rule, B.G., G.L. Bisanz and M. Kohn (1985) 'Anatomy of a Persuasion Schema: Targets, Goals and Strategies', *Journal of Personality and Social Psychology*, 48: 1127–40.

Sacks, H., E. Schegloff and G. Jefferson (1974) ' A Simple Systematics for the Organisation of Turn-taking in Conversation', *Language*, 50: 696–735.

Sarbin, T.R. (ed.) (1986) *Narrative Psychology: the Storied Nature of Human Conduct*. New York: Praeger.

Saussure, F. de (1974) *Course in General Linguistics*. London: Fontana.

Schegloff, E.A. (1968) 'Sequencing in Conversation Openings', *American Anthropologist*, 70: 1075–95.

Schegloff, E.A. (1972) 'Notes on a Conversational Practice: Formulating Place', pp. 75–119 in D. Sudnow (ed.), *Studies in Social Interaction*. New York: Free Press.

Schegloff, E.A. (1988) 'Goffman and the Analysis of Conversation', in P. Drew and A. Wootton (eds), *Erving Goffman: an Interdisciplinary Appreciation*. Oxford: Polity Press.

Schegloff, E.A. and H. Sacks (1973) 'Opening Up Closings', *Semiotica*, 7: 289–327.

Schenkein, J. (ed.) (1985) *Studies in the Organisation of Conversational Interaction*. New York: Academic Press.

Schoen, D. (1977) *Enoch Powell and the Powellites*. London: Macmillan.

Schonbach, P. (1980) 'A Category System for Account Phases', *European Journal of Social Psychology*. 10: 195–200.

Schonbach, P. (1985) 'A Taxonomy for Account Phases: Revised, Explained, and Applied', unpublished manuscript, Ruhr-Universität Bochum.

Schonbach, P. (1986) 'A Theory of Conflict Escalation in Account Episodes', unpublished manuscript, Ruhr-Universität Bochum.

Schroder, H.M., M.J. Driver and S. Streufert (1967) *Human Information Processing*. New York: Holt Rinehart and Winston.

Scott, M. and S. Lyman (1968) 'Accounts', *American Sociological Review*, 33: 46–62.

Searle, J. (1969) *Speech Acts*. Cambridge: Cambridge University Press.

Searle, J. (1975) 'Indirect speech acts', pp. 59–78 in P. Cole and J.L. Morgan (eds), *Syntax and Semantics: Speech Acts* (vol. 3). New York: Academic Press.

Searle, J., F. Kiefer and M. Bierwish (eds) (1980) *Speech Act Theory and Pragmatics*. Dordrecht: Reidel.

Seibold, D.R., N.K. Baym, C.R. Berteotti, S.C. Bergener, S.A. McCornack, L.P. McQuillan and M. Rivers (1986) 'Gar'bage or Gar bag' – It's All in Where you Place the Accent. A Response to Burleson et al.'s "Item Desirability Effects in Compliance-gaining Research: Seven Empirical Studies Showing why the Checklist Methodology Produces Garbage"', paper presented to the Speech Communication Association, Chicago, November.

Seidel, G. (1986) *The Holocaust Denial*. Leeds: Beyond the Pale.

Shoeneman, T.J. and D.E. Rubanowitz (1983) 'Attributions in the Advice Columns: Actors and Observers, Causes and Reasons', paper presented at the meeting of the American Psychological Association, Anaheim, CA, August.

Shotter, J. (1975) *Images of Man in Psychological Research*. London: Methuen.

Shotter, J. (1980) 'Action, Joint Action and Intentionality', in M. Brenner (ed.), *The Structure of Action*. Oxford: Basil Blackwell.

Shotter, J. (1983) 'Hermeneutic Interpretative Theory', in R. Harré and R. Lamb (eds), *The Encyclopaedic Dictionary of Psychology*. Oxford: Basil Blackwell.

Shotter, J. (1984) *Social Accountability and Selfhood*. Oxford: Basil Blackwell.

Shotter, J. (1987) 'Rhetoric as a Model for Psychology', paper given to the British Psychological Society conference on the future of the psychological sciences, Harrogate.

Silverstein, M. (1985) 'Who shall Regiment Language?' unpublished manuscript.

Snyder, C.R. and R.L. Higgins (1986) 'Excuses: their Effects and their Role in the Negotiation of Reality', paper presented to the second attribution-personality theory conference, Los Angeles, September.

Snyder, M. (1979) 'Self-monitoring: The Self in Social Action', in L. Berkowitz (ed.), *Advances in Experimental Social Psychology*. New York: Academic Press.

Spence, D.P. (1982) *Narrative Truth and Historical Truth*. New York: Norton.

Staw, B.M. (1980) 'Rationality and Justification in Organizational Life', in B.M. Staw and L. Cummings (eds), *Research in Organizational Behavior* (vol. 2). Greenwich, CT: JAI Press.

Steed, M. (1975) 'The Results Analysed', in D. Butler and D. Kavanagh, *The British General Election of October 1974*. London: Macmillan.

Stone, W.F. (1980) 'The Myth of Leftwing Authoritarianism', *Political Psychology*, 2: 3–20.

Streufert, S. and W. Fromkin (1972) 'Complexity and Social Influence', in J.T. Tedeschi (ed.), *Social Influence Processes*. Chicago: Aldine.

Streufert, S. and S. Streufert (1978) *Behavior in the Complex Environment.* Washington, DC: Winston.

Streufert, S., and R.W. Swezey (1986) *Complexity, Managers, and Organizations.* New York: Academic Press.

Studlar, D.T. (1974) 'British Public Opinion, Colour Issues and Enoch Powell: a Longitudinal Analysis', *British Journal of Political Science*, 4: 371–81.

Studlar, D.T. (1978) 'Policy Voting in Britain: the Coloured Immigration Issue in 1964, 1966 and 1970 General Elections', *American Political Science Review*, 72: 46–72.

Suedfeld, P. (1978a) 'Characteristics of Decision Making as a Function of the Environment', pp. 203–14 in B. King, S. Streufert and F.E. Fiedler (eds), *Managerial Control and Organizational Democracy*. Washington, DC: Winston.

Suedfeld, P. (1978b) 'Die Messung integrativer Komplexitat in Archivmaterialen (The Measurement of Integrative Complexity in Archival Materials)', pp. 179–92 in H. Mandl and G.L. Huber (eds), *Kognitive Komplexitat*. Gottingen: Hogrefe.

Suedfeld, P. (1981) 'Indices of World Tension in *The Bulletin of Atomic Scientists'*, *Political Psychology*, 2: 114–23.

Suedfeld, P. (1985) 'APA Presidential Addresses: The Relation of Integrative Complexity to Historical, Professional, and Personal Factors', *Journal of Personality and Social Psychology*, 49: 1643–51.

Suedfeld, P. (1985b) 'Stressful Levels of Environmental Stimulation', pp. 83–104 in I.G. Sarason and C.D. Spielberger (eds), *Stress and Anxiety. Vol. 10: A Sourcebook of Theory and Research*. Washington, DC: Hemisphere.

Suedfeld, P. and L.E. Piedrahita (1984) 'Intimations of Mortality: Integrative Simplification as a Precursor of Death', *Journal of Personality and Social Psychology*, 47: 848–52.

Suedfeld, P. and A.D. Rank (1976) 'Revolutionary Leaders: Long-term Success as a Function of Changes in Conceptual Complexity', *Journal of Personality and Social Psychology*, 34: 169–78.

Suedfeld, P. and P.E. Tetlock (1977) 'Integrative Complexity of Communications in International Crises', *Journal of Conflict Resolution*, 21: 169–84.

Suedfeld, P., P.E. Tetlock and C. Ramirez (1977) 'War, Peace, and Integrative Complexity: United Nations Speeches on the Middle East Problem', *Journal of Conflict Resolution*, 21: 427-42.

Taylor, S. (1982) *The National Front in English Politics*. London: Macmillan.

Taylor, S.E., R.R. Lichtman and J.V. Wood (1984) 'Attributions, Beliefs about Control, and Adjustment to Breast Cancer', *Journal of Personality and Social Psychology*, 46: 1192–211.

Tedeschi, J.T. and N. Norman (1985) 'Social Power, Self-presentation, and the Self', in B.R. Schlenker (ed.), *The Self and Social Life*. New York: McGraw-Hill.

Tetlock. P.E. (1979) 'Identifying Victims of Groupthink from Public Statements of Decision Makers', *Journal of Personality and Social Psychology*, 37: 1314–24.

Tetlock, P.E. (1981a) 'Personality and Isolationism: Content Analysis of Senatorial Speeches', *Journal of Personality and Social Psychology*, 41: 737–43.

Tetlock, P.E. (1981b) 'Pre- to Post-election Shifts in Presidential Rhetoric: Impression Management or Cognitive Adjustment?' *Journal of Personality and Social Psychology*, 41: 207–12.

Tetlock, P.E. (1983a) 'Policy Makers' Images of International Conflict', *Journal of Social Issues*, 39: 67–86.

Tetlock, P.E. (1983b) 'Psychological Research on Foreign Policy: a Methodological Overview', pp. 45–79 in L. Wheeler (ed.), *Review of Personality and Social Psychology* (vol. 4). Beverly Hills: Sage.

Tetlock, P.E. (1984) 'Cognitive Style and Political Belief System in the British House of Commons', *Journal of Personality and Social Psychology*, 46: 365–75.

Tetlock, P.E. (1985) 'Integrative Complexity of American and Soviet Foreign Policy Statements: a Time-series Analysis', *Journal of Personality and Social Psychology*, 49: 1565–85.

Tetlock, P.E. (1986) 'A Value Pluralism Model of Ideological Reasoning', *Journal of Personality and Social Psychology*, 50: 865–75.

Tetlock, P.E., J. Bernzweig and J.L. Gallant (1985) 'Supreme Court Decision Making: Cognitive Style as a Predictor of Ideological Consistency of Voting', *Journal of Personality and Social Psychology*, 48: 1227–39.

Tetlock, P.E., F. Crosby and T. Crosby (1981) 'Psychobiography', *Micropolitics*, 2: 58–81.

Tetlock, P.E. and K. Hannum (1984) *The Berkeley Integrative Complexity Scoring Manual*. Unpublished manuscript, Department of Psychology, University of California, Berkeley.

Tetlock, P.E., K. Hannum and P. Micheletti (1984) 'Stability and Change in Senatorial Debate: Testing the Cognitive versus Rhetorical Style Hypotheses', *Journal of Personality and Social Psychology*, 46: 621–63.

Tetlock, P.E. and A.S.R. Manstead (1985) 'Impression Management versus Intrapsychic Explanations in Social Psychology: a Useful Dichotomy?' *Psychological Review*, 92: 59–77.

Thompson, J. (1984) *Studies in the Theory of Ideology*. Cambridge: Polity Press.

Thurlow, R. (1984) 'Anti-Nazi, Anti-semite', *Patterns of Prejudice*, 18: 23–34.

Thurlow, R. (1987) *Fascism in Britain*. Oxford: Blackwell.

Tololyan, K. (in press) 'Cultural Narrative and the Motivation of the Terrorist', *Journal of Strategic Studies*.

Totman, R. (1982) 'Philosophical Foundations of Attribution Therapies', in C. Antaki and C. Brewin (eds), *Attributions and Psychological Change*. London: Academic Press.

Toulmin, S.E. (1958) *The Uses of Argument*. Cambridge: Cambridge University Press.

van Dijk, T.A. (1984) *Prejudice in Discourse: an Analysis of Ethnic Prejudices in Cognition and Conversation*. Amsterdam: Benjamin.

van Fraassen, B.C. (1980) *The Scientific Image*. Oxford: Clarendon Press.

Voss, J.F., J. Blais, M.L. Means, T.R. Greene and E. Ahwesh (in press) 'Informal Reasoning and Subject Matter Knowledge in the Solving of Economics Problems by Naive and Novice Individuals', *Cognition and Instruction*.

Voss, J.F., T.R. Greene, T.A. Post and B.C. Penner (1983) 'Problem Solving Skill in the Social Sciences', pp. 165–213 in G.H. Bower (ed.), *The Psychology of Learning and Motivation: Advances in Research Theory* (vol. 17). New York: Academic Press.

Voss, J.F., S.W. Tyler and L.A. Yengo (1983) 'Individual Differences in the Solving of Social Science Problems', pp. 205–32. in R.F. Dillon and R.R. Schmeck (eds), *Individual Differences in Cognition*. New York: Academic Press.

Webber, G.C. (1986) *The Ideology of the British Right, 1918–1939*. London: Croom Helm.

Weber, A.L., J.H. Harvey and M.A. Stanley (in press) 'The Nature and Motivations of Accounts for Failed Relationships', in R. Burnett, P. McGhee and D. Clark (eds), *Accounting for Relationships*. London: Methuen.

Weiner, B. (1985) '"Spontaneous" Causal Thinking', *Psychological Bulletin*, 97: 74–84.

Weiner, B. (1986) 'Attribution, Emotion and Action', in R.M. Sorrentino and E.T. Higgins (eds), *Handbook of Motivation and Emotion*. New York: Guildford Press.

Weiss, R.S. (1975) *Marital Separation*. New York: Basic Books.

Wertsch, J.V. (ed.) (1985) *Culture, Communication and Cognition*. Cambridge: Cambridge University Press.

Wetherell, M.S. (1986) 'Linguistic Repertoires and Literary Criticism: New Directions for a Social Psychology of Gender', in S. Wilkinson (ed.), *Feminist Social Psychology*. Milton Keynes: Open University Press.

Wetherell, M. and J. Potter (1986a), 'Discourse Analysis and the Social Psychology of Racism', *Social Psychology Section Newsletter*, 15: 24–30.

Wetherell, M. and J. Potter (1986b) 'Majority Group Representations of "Race" and "Race Relations"', paper presented at the BPS Social Psychology Section annual conference, University of Sussex, September.

Wetherell, M. and J. Potter (forthcoming) *Mapping the Language of Racism*. London: Sage.

Wetherell, M., H. Stiven and J. Potter (1987) 'Unequal Egalitarianism: a Preliminary Study of Discourses Concerning Gender and Employment Opportunities', *British Journal of Social Psychology*, 26: 59–71.

White, H. (1980) 'The Value of Narrative in the Representation of Reality', *Critical Inquiry*, 7: 5–28.

Wittgenstein, L.W. (1953) *Philosophical Investigations*. Oxford: Basil Blackwell.

Wong, P.T.P. amd B. Weiner (1981) 'When People Ask "Why" Questions, and the Heuristics of Attributional Search', *Journal of Personality and Social Psychology*, 40: 650–63.

Wood, D.C. (1979) 'An Introduction to Derrida', *Radical Philosophy*, 21: 18–28.

Wootton, A.J. (1981) 'The Management of Grantings and Rejections by Parents in Request Sequences', *Semiotica*, 37: 59–89.

Yarkin, K.L. and J.H. Harvey (1982) 'The Structure of Attribution', *Journal of Social Psychology*, 117: 311–12.

Yarkin, K.L., J.H. Harvey and B.M. Bloxom (1981) 'Cognitive Sets, Attribution, and Social Interaction', *Journal of Personality and Social Psychology*, 41: 243–52.

Yearley, S. (1985) 'Vocabularies of Freedom and Resentment: a Strawsonian Perspective on the Nature of Argument in Science and Law', *Social Studies of Science*, 15: 99–126.

Young, K.G. (1987) *Taleworlds and Storyrealms*. Boston: Martinus Nijhoff.

Zukier, H. (1987) 'Conspiracy as a Crime in Solidarity', in C.F. Graumann and S. Moscovici (eds), *Changing Conceptions of Conspiracy*. New York: Springer.

Index

language of thought, 152
Latin, 158
leaders, revolutionary, studies of, 45, 50–4
Lehnert, W.G., 18
Leudar, Ivan, 145–55
Levinson, S., 147
linguistics, 9–10; *see also* language
Lipset, S.M., 201
literary theory, 184, 186
logical proofs, 120, 121–3, 125–6
Lyman, S., 113

McLaughlin, Margaret L., 113–26
McLellan, D., 200
Mani, Vimula, 165
Mannheim, K., 200
markers, *see* surface cues
Mead, G.H., 145, 146, 150–3
meaning, shared, 29, 150
memory, 34, 36
metacognitive background of explanations, 12–14
methodology, in understanding ideological explanation, 199–215; definition, 199–200
Miller, W.L., 205
mitigation, 144, 116–17
Mulkay, M., 172
myths, 95–6

Naji, S. 22, 35
narrative forms, 97–102; progressive, 99–100; regressive, 99–100; stability, 99
narrative structures, in social explanation, 94–112
Newell, A., 74, 77
Norman, D., 115, 145
normative aspects of conversation analysis, 128, 129
Norwegian language, 163

observation, 123–4
'open souls doctrine', 73
openness, 147–8
operators, of problem-solving and reasoning structures, 83
oral explanations: identifying attributions in 32–42; in traffic court, 113–26; *see also* verbal behaviour
Oxford English Dictionary, 17

Paragraph Completion Test, 43–5

paraphrases, 17–18
Parker, Ian, 184–98
Payne, J.W., 35
perlocutionary effect, 26
personality: psychometric approach, 110; social constructionist approach, 102–12
polarities in deconstruction, 188–9, 195–6
politics: conspiracy theory of, 201–14; discourse of, 196–8
post-structuralism, 187
Potter, Jonathan, 168–83
Powell, J. Enoch, 204–14
power, meaning in terms of, 184–5, 186, 189, 196–8
Power, R., 26
pragmatic realism, 178, 180–1
pragmatics, 145, 146
problem-solving, and reasoning in ill-structured domains, 74–93
pronouns, role of, 156–67
propaganda, 2–3
Propp, Vladimir, 94
protocol analysis, 74–93
psychohistorians, 54–5
psycholinguistics, 157
Putnam, H., 20

Quakers, 160
qualifiers, 77
question threat, 124
questions: about causation, analysis of, 18–19; cognitivist, 8–9; pedagogic and 'sincere', 27; relevance answers, 18, 140

Raab, E., 201
race relations; in Britain, 204–5; construction of, 173–82
Raglan, Lord, 95
Ramirez, C., 55–6
Rank, A.D., 45, 50–2, 56
reason maintenance, 20, 22
reasoning: in ill-structured domains, 74–93; and social action, 127
reasons, offered in explanations, 20–6
reduction of explanations into simple causal categories, 61–2
Reed, Douglas, 213
refusals, 114, 119
register, 161
reinterpretation, 189, 196
'repair', 151
research, explanations, 5–12
response bias, self-presentational, 41
response sheets, fixed-format, 10–11, 12